The Guru Investor

The Guru Investor

*How to Beat the Market
Using History's Best
Investment Strategies*

John P. Reese

with

Jack M. Forehand

WILEY

John Wiley & Sons, Inc.

Published by John Wiley & Sons, Inc., Hoboken, New Jersey.
Published simultaneously in Canada.

For general information on our other products and services or for technical support, please contact our Customer Care Department within the United States at (800) 762-2974, outside the United States at (317) 572-3993 or fax (317) 572-4002.

Wiley also publishes its books in a variety of electronic formats. Some content that appears in print may not be available in electronic books. For more information about Wiley products, visit our web site at www.wiley.com.

Library of Congress Cataloging-in-Publication Data:
Reese, John, 1953-
    The guru investor : how to beat the market using history's best investment strategies / John P. Reese, Jack M. Forehand.
        p.   cm.
Includes bibliographical references and index.
ISBN 978-0-470-37709-3 (cloth)
    1. Investments.   2. Investment analysis—Data processing.   3. Capitalists and financiers—United States—Biography.   4. Quantitative analysts—United States—Biography.   I. Forehand, Jack M.   II. Title.   III. Title: Best investment strategies.
HG4521.R368   2009
332.6—dc22
                                                                              2008040631

Printed in the United States of America

10 9 8 7 6 5 4 3 2

To Michael, Daniel, and Heather
—John P. Reese

To Mom, Dad, and Aimee
—Jack M. Forehand

Contents

Acknowledgments

We would like to thank our partner, Justin Carbonneau, whose tremendous contributions to this book began the day we decided to write it and didn't end until the final draft was submitted. A huge thank you also goes to Chris Ciarmiello, whose writing, editing, and insightful advice made this book possible. We also want to recognize the efforts of Keith Guerraz, who was always willing to take the time to discuss and review our ideas for the book, and Philip Moldavski for his design work and consultation. In addition, we would like to thank the founding members of Validea.com, Keith Ferry, Todd Glassman, Dean Coca, and Norman Eng, for all their work in the creation of the guru-based investing system utilized in this book.

We certainly wish to acknowledge the gurus who are the basis for this book. These legendary investors and researchers are not only unique in their extraordinary investing accomplishments, but also in their willingness to share their approaches with others. Although this book can never totally capture the true genius of these men, we hope that our outline of their quantitative principles can be a benefit to investors just like their original published writings were.

We would also like to thank David Pugh, Senior Editor at John Wiley & Sons, for his encouragement and support throughout this process, and Kelly O'Connor, our go-to Development Editor whose wisdom, insights, and patience were also invaluable.

Last, but certainly not least, we would like to thank our families, Ellen, Michael, Daniel, and Heather Reese and Jack, Sandy, and Aimee Forehand, whose support and patience throughout the many years of work that went into developing this investing system were essential to its success.

Introduction

Human beings, who are almost unique in having the ability to learn from the experience of others, are also remarkable for their apparent disinclination to do so.

—AUTHOR DOUGLAS ADAMS, *LAST CHANCE TO SEE*

T he list of books written about investing is long, perhaps too long, but I'm pretty certain none of the investment books you've read has begun with the author admitting what I'm about to admit to you right now: When it comes to the stock market, my instincts are not good. In fact, they're pretty bad. You could even say I've made just about every mistake possible, and have made them with my own money.

This admission, of course, leads to an obvious question: Why would someone who admittedly has poor investing instincts be wasting your time with a book on investing? (And, just as importantly, how would he get a book deal?) The answer is complicated and requires a deeper look at the realities of investing, and at a series of cold, hard facts that your broker, financial advisor, or mutual fund manager probably don't want you to know. It was the understanding of these facts that led me, bad instincts and all, to find a way to consistently beat the market—and beat it by a wide margin.

We'll get to those facts, and how you too can take advantage of them, soon enough. But to fully appreciate them, I need to go back about a decade-and-a-half and explain to you how my investing journey began. Back then, I was a successful computer engineer and had been fortunate enough to build up my own computer networking company, which I sold to a much bigger firm for a good deal of money. It was very rewarding to see all the hard work that I had put into building my company pay off. What I didn't know at the time, however, was that I had absolutely no idea what to do with the money once I got it. There was of course one obvious choice—spend it—but I wanted to use the money I had made to secure my family's financial future.

This was the 1990s. Grunge music was king, the Beanie Baby craze was sweeping the nation, and the only type of investment that seemed worthwhile was stocks. The markets were performing well and I was constantly hearing from friends about all the money they were making—and how easy it was. So I began to invest the chunk of money I got when I sold my business. To do that, I used a variety of methods. I picked some stocks on my own, tried following the advice of several newsletters and tips from popular financial media sources, and worked with several brokers (these guys come out of the woodwork when you come into a large amount of money) to try to produce a reasonable return on my investment.

How did this whole process work for me, a successful businessman with degrees from MIT and Harvard Business School? In short, not well. It was a humbling experience, to say the least. If it had worked, I would be writing a book about how you can rely on your own instincts or broker to invest your money, but that turns out almost always not to be true.

Eventually, I became frustrated with my poor returns and the fact that I seemed to consistently lag the market averages. I knew there had to be a better way, but I didn't know how to find it. Given my background in engineering and computers (while at MIT I was a member of the Artificial Intelligence Laboratory), I approached the problem analytically. I began researching the issue, and one thing I quickly learned was that my investment experience was far from unique—even among the pros. In fact, most (actually most is being nice; the actual figure, depending on the study you look at, is around 75 to 80 percent) active money managers underperform the market over the long term.

Think about that. Of all the "experts" who appear on CNBC and other programs, offer advice online, or write recommendations in the major financial newspapers and magazines, only a very small percentage actually deliver any value to their viewers and readers. Only a few help you achieve better returns than you'd get if you just bought and held an index fund like the S&P 500, which simply tracks the broader market's movements.

So it seems professional investors have something in common with television weathermen: They are in one of the few professions in which you can make a good deal of money while still being wrong most of the time.

I make this comparison not because I want to start a quarrel with the meteorological community. Far from it. In fact, I have a good deal of respect for weathermen because they are put in the precarious position of having to predict something that is impossible to predict on a consistent basis.

But that, alas, is exactly the same position in which most professional investors find themselves—trying to make predictions on the short-term movements of the stock market. If you watch business television, you will see some of the smartest people in our country tell you where the market is going this year, and do it with the type of conviction that makes you want to believe them. The problem is that despite their intelligence and bravado, history suggests they are going to be wrong just as often as they are going to be right, if not more.

Okay, so most professional investors may not be as good as they would lead you to believe. But what about individual, nonprofessional investors? I hadn't succeeded in picking stocks on my own. Maybe I was in the minority. Maybe making money in the market is less about having the research and analytical tools that professional investors have, and more about common sense. Would I be better off just listening to the investing advice of friends or neighbors? Could my butcher hold the secrets to my stock market success?

Well, there is not a ton of data available about how individual, non-professional investors perform relative to the market (the little guys are not required to report their results to regulatory agencies like the pros are), but what little there is doesn't bode well. According to "Quantitative Analysis of Investor Behavior," a study performed by the investment research firm Dalbar Inc. in July 2003, "Individuals have historically underperformed the markets, earning just 2.6 percent versus the S&P 500 gain of 12.2 percent between 1984 and the end of 2002." The study explains that "research in the U.S. has shown that this dramatic underperformance comes as a direct result of client behavior, or more specifically, the attempt to avoid bad performance while seeking out better returns."

The bottom line: It's probably best to leave your relationship with your butcher strictly meat-based.

By this point in my research, I was quickly running out of places to look for investing help. I had been failed by my investment advisors and my own instincts, and now I was learning that the vast majority of amateurs and professionals didn't have the answer as to how to beat the market. Still, I was convinced that there must be a way, that there had to be some strategy that I could use to succeed in the market over the long term. After all, the fact that my own data suggested that the majority of active managers underperform the market had a flipside to it—there had to be a group of investors that did beat the market. I wanted to know how they did it, and how I could do it. And that's when Peter Lynch, the man considered by many to be the greatest mutual fund manager in history, walked into my life.

Alright, maybe it wasn't as much Lynch walking into my life as it was me walking into a bookstore and picking up Lynch's book, *One up on Wall Street*. For dramatic purposes, I prefer the former image. Whichever way you slice it, the event was a watershed moment in my investing career. Lynch had established one of the greatest track records ever at Fidelity Investments' Magellan Fund (he averaged a 29 percent annual return during his 13-year tenure) and his book, written in a style that laypeople could understand, explained how he did it. And the best part was that most of the techniques he outlined were not all that complex. In fact, many can be performed by a computer using the

fundamental information that companies are required to file with the
Securities and Exchange Commission when they report their results at
the end of each quarter.

Reading Lynch's book was really the first step in my evolution
from an investing pessimist, who had been burned by constant underperformance, to the market optimist I am today, who believes anyone
who shows some discipline and follows some simple and sound techniques can beat the market over the long term. .

Moreover, while Lynch's book had given me just what I was looking for—a proven, implementable stock-picking strategy I could use to
beat the market—it was also only the beginning of my search for stock
market success. I began to wonder if there were others out there like
Lynch, who had beaten the market and told how they did it.

What I quickly found was that Lynch was not, in fact, alone, and
over the last 12 years I have identified many other individuals with
outstanding long-term track records who have written books detailing the techniques they used to achieve those outstanding results.
People like Martin Zweig, James P. O'Shaughnessy, David Dreman,
Benjamin Graham, and Kenneth Fisher had also written about strategies that consistently beat the market over the long run. A little-
known college accounting professor, Joseph Piotroski, had even written
a research paper about a fairly simple quantitative strategy that would
have trounced the market from the mid-1970s to the mid-1990s. And
Warren Buffett's daughter-in-law, who worked closely with Buffett
for a period of time, had also written a book that provided wonderful
insights into the stock selection techniques used by Buffett, who many
consider to be the greatest investor of all time.

Reading these books was the easy part. The hard part was figur-
ing out how to take an incredibly large volume of data and condense
it into something that could be used to pick stocks. I hired a couple of
researchers to help me and founded Validea.com (yes, this is a shame-
less plug). The goal of Validea.com was to take the strategies outlined
in the published writings of the Wall Street legends mentioned above,
break them down into simple steps, and make them easy to use for the
individual investor.

The best way to do that, I found, was through my background in
computers. Using the criteria that each of these investing greats had

laid out in their writings, I was able to develop computer models that simulated their approach. In some cases, the gurus had referenced very specific criteria, making the process pretty straightforward. But I should be clear that in other cases, some of the gurus had left a bit of room for interpretation, so I did my best to interpret what they were saying.

After creating my models, I linked up with a financial data service, allowing me (and the users of my site) to filter thousands of stocks through my "Guru Strategies" and find out which stocks passed which guru's approaches.

Being able to get a report card showing how a stock stacked up at any given time against some of the most successful investment strategies of all time was a powerful tool. But it was a tool that I didn't yet know how best to use practically (i.e., to make money). Should I pick my favorite strategy and follow it, or should I use more than one of them at one time? Should I buy the top couple of stocks selected using the system or should I build a much larger portfolio? And perhaps the most difficult question of all, when do I know it is time to sell a stock? I was, in a sense, like someone who had just built a souped-up Porsche with a standard transmission, but didn't yet know how to drive stick.

As time went on, however, I didn't just learn how to drive my guru-based models; I learned how to use them to run laps around the market, developing a system that combines my individual guru strategies to minimize risk and maximize returns, while also letting me know when I should buy, hold, and sell individual holdings. Using this system, all 10 of the 10-stock model portfolios I track on my website based on the strategies in this book have beaten the S&P 500 since their respective inceptions, with nine more than doubling it, eight more than tripling it, and five more than quadrupling it (as of this writing).

In the coming chapters, I'll teach you about each of the gurus that inspired me, laying out their investment philosophy and achievements, detailing step-by-step the secret formulas they used to beat the market, and explaining why these legendary investors considered certain factors to be so important when analyzing individual stocks. You'll also get another benefit: access to www.guruinvestorbook.com, a website I've created specifically so that readers of this book can, free of charge, utilize some of my guru-based stock screening tools.

Just as important as giving you access to these individual guru-based models, I'll also explain how you too can combine and implement these approaches to get the most out of your stock investments. I'll share with you the system I've developed for building and managing portfolios, which includes my key rules for when to buy, when to hold, and when to sell.

Put another way, I'll give you both the keys to the car (the free use of my guru-based models) and the training you need to drive it.

Before we get started, I do want to make a disclosure. Although I have spent a portion of this introduction talking about how research shows that professional money managers consistently underperform the market, I am, in fact, a member of this group. My firm, Validea Capital Management, manages money for high-net-worth individuals using the principles that I outline in the following pages. I wrote this book, however, because I believe all investors can learn from the thinking, the writing, and the experience of Wall Street's greatest investors. The coming chapters will teach you the lessons of those greats, and give you all the tools you need to put those lessons to use.

And now, without further delay, let's take to the road.

Authors' Note: *The Validea investing system detailed in the coming chapters is one that has evolved in several ways over the years. Both John Reese and Jack Forehand have played major roles in different parts of that evolution. To differentiate between their experiences, references to "I" generally refer to John, and his work in developing the initial idea for Validea and the quantitative, guru-based models that rest at its core. References to "we" generally refer to John and Jack Forehand, and the collective thoughts and experiences they have had in implementing and refining these strategies and developing the overall investment approach and model portfolio system that has evolved at Validea over many years.*

Part One

WHY YOU NEED THIS BOOK

I t sounds simple enough: Over the past six decades, the U.S. stock market has averaged an annual return of about 11 percent per year. By simply investing in a broad market index and sticking with it for the long haul, the odds are thus overwhelming that you'll end up with returns that dwarf those of savings accounts, bonds, Treasury bills, and even gold. Do a little better than the market average, and you'll really be raking in the profits.

Yet throughout history, the vast majority of investors—both amateur and professional—have been humbled by the market, failing to come anywhere close to those 11 percent average annual gains. Why do they fail? What is it that makes it so difficult for investors to take advantage of the stock market's long-term benefits? And what can we learn from those rare few who have consistently generated outstanding returns over the long haul?

You're about to find out.

Chapter 1

Learn from
the Worst

From the errors of others, a wise man corrects his own.
—PUBLILIUS SYRUS, FIRST-CENTURY ROMAN WRITER

P eter Lynch, Benjamin Graham, David Dreman, and others have all left roadmaps showing just how the average investor can make a bundle in the stock market. Their formulas are relatively simple and don't involve the kind of complex mathematics that only a rocket scientist could understand. And, to top it all off, between the access I'll give you to my new website—www.guruinvestorbook.com—and the ease with which you can find stock information on the Internet these days, you won't have to do too much digging and research to put these formulas into action. This is going to be a piece of cake, right?

Not exactly. While people such as Lynch, Graham, and Dreman have been kind enough to lay out paths to investing success for us to follow, the stock market will throw obstacles and challenges into even the most carefully crafted roads to riches. The first stop along our journey isn't going to be a pretty one. We're going examine how and why investors before us have failed so that you'll be ready when confronted with the same pitfalls.

The Fallen

As we begin our survey of the graveyard of failed market-beaters, one thing should quickly jump out: It's a pretty crowded place. To start with, there are the professionals—the mutual fund managers. Over the past couple decades, mutual funds have become a widely used stock market tool, allowing investors to buy a broad swath of stocks with less transaction costs than they'd incur if they tried to buy each holding individually. The problem is that most mutual fund managers fail to beat the returns you'd get if you had just bought an index fund that tracks the S&P 500 (The S&P 500 index is generally what people refer to when they talk about beating "the market").

In fact, in a 2004 address to the United States Senate Committee on Banking, Housing, and Urban Affairs, John Bogle—the renowned founder of the Vanguard Group, one of the world's largest investment management companies—stated that the average equity fund returned 10.5 percent annually from 1950 through 1970, while the S&P 500 averaged a 12.1 percent return. From 1983 through 2003, as mutual funds became more popular, the gap was even worse: The average equity fund returned an average of 10.3 percent annually, while the S&P grew at a 13 percent pace.

A 2.7 percent spread between the S&P and mutual fund managers' performances may not seem like all that much. But remember, the compounded returns you get in the stock market can turn that kind of difference into a lot of money very quickly. A $10,000 investment that grows at 13 percent per year compounded annually, for example, will give you a shade over $115,000 after 20 years; at 10.3 percent per year, you'd end up with about $44,000 less than that (approximately $71,000).

Bogle's not the only one whose research highlights the poor track record of fund managers. In his book *What Works on Wall Street,* James

O'Shaughnessy, one of the gurus you'll read about later in this book, looked at what percentage of equity funds beat the S&P 500 over a series of 10-year periods, beginning with the 10-year period that ended in 1991 and ending with the 10-year period that ended in 2003. According to O'Shaughnessy, "the *best* 10 years, ending December 31, 1994, saw only 26 percent of the traditionally managed active mutual funds beating the [S&P] index." That means that just over a quarter of fund managers earned their clients market-beating returns in the best of those periods!

In addition, those that beat the S&P didn't exactly crush it. O'Shaughnessy said, for example, that less than half of the funds that beat the S&P 500 for the 10 years ending May 31, 2004 did so by more than 2 percent per year on a compound basis. What's more—and this is a key point—O'Shaughnessy noted that these statistics didn't include all the funds that failed to survive a particular 10-year period, meaning that his findings actually *overstate* the collective performance of equity funds.

Along with fund managers, another group of market under-performers mired in the stock market muck are newsletter publishers. These are investors—some professional and some amateur—who write monthly or quarterly publications (many of which are published online) that give their assessment of the economy as well as their own stock picks. They sound official and authoritative, and sometimes even have large research staffs working for them. But while they can attract thousands of readers, more often than not their advice is lacking. In fact, Mark Hulbert, whose *Hulbert Financial Digest* monitors investment newsletters and tracks the performance of their picks (Hulbert is considered the authority on investment newsletter performance and has been tracking newsletters for over 25 years), said in a 2004 *Dallas Morning News* article that about 80 percent of newsletters don't keep pace with the S&P 500 over long periods of time.

And just as their individual stock picks are often subpar, newsletter publishers also have a difficult time just picking the general direction of the market. A National Bureau for Economic Research study of 237 newsletter strategies done in the 1990s found that, between June 1980 and December 1992, there was "no evidence to suggest that investment newsletters as a group have any knowledge over and above the common level of predictability," according to the *International Herald Tribune*.

So, while their advertisements and promises may sound tempting, the data indicates that newsletter publishers and money managers have a weak record when it comes to beating the market. Their collective track record, however, is far better than that of individual investors, whose poor performance we examined in the Introduction.

Bogle has also addressed the issue of individual investors' returns, and his findings paint an equally glum picture. He told that congressional committee in 2004 that he estimated equity fund investors had averaged an annual gain of just 3 percent over the previous 20 years, during which time the S&P 500 grew 13 percent per year.

The Futility of Forecasting

Having established that most investors—professional and amateur—underperform the market, the obvious question is, why? After all, professional investors are, for the most part, intelligent people. Just about all of them have college degrees, some from very prestigious schools, and they are required to pass multiple licensing examinations before being allowed to invest clients' money. Similarly, there are a lot of very smart amateur investors out there. As I noted earlier, I have degrees from Harvard and MIT and successfully built up my own business, yet I struggled for a long time to beat the market. How can so many smart people fare so poorly?

Well, for the first—and perhaps greatest—reason, we don't have to look far: It is the fact that we are human. Our own humanity—the way we think, the way we perceive things and feel emotions—has become a major topic in the investing world in recent years. There are even branches of science—behavioral finance and neuroeconomics—that examine how psychology and physiology affect the way we deal with our money. And, in general, the findings show that we humans are investing in the stock market with the deck stacked against us.

Some great research into this topic has been done by *Money* magazine writer Jason Zweig (no relation to Martin, another of the gurus you'll soon read about), who last year authored a book on neuroeconomics titled *Your Money and Your Brain*. One of the main points Zweig stressed is that human beings are excellent at quickly recognizing patterns in their environment. Being able to do so has been a key to our species' survival, enabling our ancestors to evade capture, find shelter, and learn how to plant the right crops in the right places. Zweig further explains that today this natural inclination allows us to know what train we have to catch to be on time, or to know that a crying baby is hungry. Those are all good, and often essential, things to know.

When it comes to investing, this ability ends up being a liability. According to Zweig, "Our incorrigible search for patterns leads us to assume that order exists where it often doesn't. It's not just the *barus* of Wall Street who think they know where the stock market is going. [*Barus* were divinatory or astrological priests in ancient Mesopotamia who declared the divine will through signs and omens.] Almost everyone has an opinion about whether the Dow will go up or down from here, or whether a particular stock will continue to rise. And everyone *wants* to believe that the financial future can be foretold." But the truth, he says, is that it can't—at least not in the day-to-day, short-term way that most investors think it can.

You don't have to look too far to find that Zweig is right. Every day on Wall Street, something happens that makes people think they should invest more money in the stock market, or, conversely, makes them pull money out of the market. Earnings reports, analysts' rating changes, a report about how retail sales were last month—all of these things can send the market into a sudden surge or a precipitous decline. The reason: People view each of these items as a harbinger of what is to come, both for the economy and the stock market.

On the surface, it may sound reasonable to try to weigh each of these factors when considering which way the market will go. But when we look deeper, this line of thinking has a couple of major problems. For one thing, it discounts the incredible complexity of the stock market. There are so many factors that go into the market's day-to-day machinations; the earnings reports, analysts' ratings, and retail sales figures I mentioned above are just the tip of the iceberg. Inflation readings, consumer spending reports, economic growth figures, fuel prices, recommendations of well-known pundits, news about a company's new products, the decisions of institutions to buy and sell because they have hit an internal target or need to free up cash for redemptions—all of these and much, much more can also impact how stocks move from day to day, or even hour to hour or minute to minute. One stock can even move simply because another stock in its industry reports its quarterly earnings. Very large, prominent companies such as Wal-Mart or IBM are considered bellwethers in their industries, for example, and a good or bad earnings report from them is often interpreted—sometimes inaccurately—as a sign of how the rest of companies in their industries will perform.

What's more, when it comes to the monthly, quarterly, or annual economic and earnings reports like the ones I've mentioned, the market doesn't just move on the raw data in the reports; quite often, it moves more on how that data compares to what analysts had projected it to be. A company can post horrible earnings for a quarter, and its stock price might rise because the results actually exceeded analysts' expectations. Or conversely, it can announce earnings growth of 200 percent, but fall if analysts were expecting 225 percent growth.

Finally, let's throw one more monkey wrench into the equation: the fact that good economic news doesn't even always portend stock gains, just as bad economic news doesn't always precede stock market declines. In fact, according to the *Wall Street Journal,* the market performed better during the recessions of 1980, 1981–1982, 1990–1991, and 2001 than it did in the six months leading up to them. And in the first three of those examples, stocks actually gained ground during the recession.

Expert, Shmexpert

As you can see, with all of the convoluted factors that drive the stock market, predicting which way it will go in the short term is just about impossible. But wait—aren't we forgetting something? A certain group of people that the media refer to as "experts"? These self-assured sounding commentators that we find on TV, the Internet, or print news tell us that they know just what the latest round of earnings reports or economic figures will mean for stocks. After all, they're *experts*; don't they have to be at least pretty good at predicting economic and stock market tends?

Unfortunately, research shows that they don't. Before I created my investment research website and started my asset management firm, my company first specialized in researching how well the stock picks of most "experts" who appeared in the media actually did. What we found was that there was no consistency or predictability in the performance of these pundits. The best performers in one week, one month, one quarter, six months, or one year were almost guaranteed to be entirely different in the next period; basically, you couldn't make money by picking a top performing expert as measured over a short period of time and following him or her.

But you don't have to trust my experience to find out that "experts" are far from infallible. In a 2006 article for *Fortune*, Geoffrey Colvin examined this concept by reviewing the book *Expert Political Judgment: How Good Is It? How Can We Know?* Written by University of California at Berkeley professor Philip Tetlock, the book detailed a seven-year study in which both supposed experts and nonexperts were asked to predict an array of political and economic events. It was the largest such study ever done of expert predictions—over 82,000 in total. The study, Colvin noted, found that the best forecasters—even the "experts"—couldn't explain more than 20 percent of the total variability in outcomes. Crude algorithms, on the other hand, could explain 25 to 30 percent, while more sophisticated algorithms could explain 47 percent. "Consider what this means," Colvin wrote. "On all sorts of questions you care about—Where will the Dow be in two years? Will the federal deficit balloon as baby-boomers retire?—your judgment is as good as the experts'. Not almost as good. Every bit as good."

There's more. Colvin also noted that the study found that the experts' "awfulness" was pretty consistent regardless of their educational background, the duration of their experience, and whether or not they had access to classified materials. In fact, it found "but one consistent differentiator: fame. The more famous the experts, the worse they performed," Colvin said.

So, if that's the case, why do so-called "experts" still get so much publicity and air time? Colvin said the reason is another result of our human nature. As humans, we want to believe the world "is not just a big game of dice," he wrote, "that things happen for good reasons and wise people can figure it all out." And since people like to hear from confident-sounding experts who appear to be able to figure it all out, the media likes to give them air time—and the experts like to get that air time because it pays, Colvin noted. Tetlock himself described this relationship as a "symbiotic triangle," explaining, "It is tempting to say they need each other too much to terminate a relationship merely because it is based on an illusion."

The bottom line: Just because someone sits in front of a camera with a microphone and speaks confidently doesn't mean he or she has any sort of clairvoyant powers when it comes to the stock market. In fact, the odds are that four out of every five times, they'll be wrong!

Market Timing: The Most Dangerous Game

With all of the research that shows humans—even experts—have pretty terrible predictive abilities when it comes to economic and stock market issues, you'd think that people would refrain from trying to predict the market's short-term movements. They don't. Every day, millions of investors try to discern where the market will head tomorrow, next week, or next month. And the way this manifests itself is the doomed practice of market timing.

Market timing occurs when people move in and out of the stock market with the intent of taking advantage of anticipated short-term price movements. Market timing can be as simple as you want it— maybe you've heard from a friend that the market is about to take off, so you invest in stocks—or as complex as you want it—perhaps you've developed an elaborate model that uses various economic indicators to predict which way the market will go in the next month. Whatever way you go about it, though, it's not likely to end well, because the market is simply too complex and irrational in the short-term for anyone to correctly and reliably predict its movements.

Want proof that market timing doesn't work? There's plenty. Take, for example, the research performed by Dalbar, Inc. In its "2007 Quantitative Analysis of Investor Behavior," the firm notes that the S&P has grown an average of 11.8 percent per year from 1987 through 2006, an impressive gain. During this period, however, the average equity investor averaged a return of just 4.3 percent. The reason? As markets rise, the data shows that investors "pour cash" into mutual funds, and when a decline starts, a "selling frenzy" begins. In other words, the research shows that investors tend to do the opposite of the old stock market adage, "Buy low, sell high."

Dalbar isn't the only firm that's found that investors do a pretty awful job at trying to time the market's short-term moves. A few years ago, the investment research company Morningstar began tracking mutual fund performance in a new way. Normally, mutual fund returns are reported as though an investor remained invested in the fund throughout the full reporting period. A fund's three-year return, for example, is reported as the percentage increase or decrease an investor would have seen if he had been invested in the fund for the entire three previous years.

In a methodology paper ("Morningstar Investor Return"), Morningstar says it found that this "total return" percentage doesn't accurately portray how well investors in a particular fund really fare. The reason: While the "total return" percentage measures how a fund does over a specific period, people often don't stick with the fund for that entire period; instead, they jump in and out of it. And, according to Morningstar, the returns that the typical investor in a particular fund actually realizes (the "investor returns") tend to be lower than the fund's total return—implying that people pick the wrong times to jump in and out of the fund (or the market).

While investors themselves deserve some of the blame for this, mutual funds sometimes don't help. In its investor returns methodology paper, Morningstar states that if firms encourage short-term trading and trendy funds, or if they advertise short-term returns and promote high-risk funds, they may not be looking out for their investors' long-term interests. Their investors' actual returns will likely be lower than the fund's total return. (The fees mutual funds charge also don't help, something Bogle stresses; those costs make it so that the fund manager has to beat the market just for his client to net market-matching returns.)

Need for an Emotional Rescue

The research that Zweig, Tetlock, Dalbar, and Morningstar have conducted all bears out the notion that we as humans are not good market-timers. This then brings us to our next important question: If we don't succeed at it, why do we keep trying to time the market? We know that, given the short-term unpredictability of the stock market, it's pretty much inevitable that we'll fail if we try to time our participation in stocks, yet we always think we can do learn to do it. "Man, it was so obvious what I *should* have done last time; now that I've learned my lesson, I'll be able to time things right next time," we tell ourselves— even though it wasn't obvious what we should have done last time, and it won't be obvious when it comes to future market-timing decisions (behavioral finance terms this *hindsight bias*). And time and time again, when one of our stocks starts declining, we jump off of it and onto the latest "hot" stock, only to watch our old stock rise and our new, flashy stock fall.

Again, one of the main reasons for these habits starts inside ourselves: our emotions. As human beings, we are emotional creatures, and in many cases throughout life, that's a good thing. When we are in danger, for example, we feel fear, and our brains interpret this feeling as a signal to flee for safety's sake. In the stock market, however, emotion is one of our greatest enemies. Our instincts tell us to flee when we see danger, and danger is what we see when our investments start losing value—danger of losing our money, danger of not being able to afford to send our children to college, danger of not being able to afford to retire when we want to retire. And, just as with other dangers we perceive, our first reaction is to flee—or, in this case, sell.

Now, when it comes to being attacked by an animal or a mugger who is trying to hurt you, fleeing from harm is a good instinct to have. But in the stock market, fleeing can, in fact, lead to great harm. That's because the danger we often sense in the stock market is false danger. Perfectly good stocks fluctuate over the short-term (there's typically a 40 to 50 percent difference between a stock's high and the low for the previous 12 months), and sometimes it's due to factors that have nothing to do with their real value. (Think of the bellwether example I referenced earlier, in which one company is negatively impacted when another company in its industry posts a bad earnings report.) And as we've seen, because of the array of factors that go into its day-to-day movements, we just can't predict what the market's or an individual stock's short-term fluctuations will be with any degree of accuracy.

Nevertheless, we still act on them, and a big reason is emotion. Peter Lynch once explained this phenomenon in an interview with PBS. "As the market starts going down, you say, 'Oh, it'll be fine,'" Lynch said. Then "it starts going down [more] and people get laid off, a friend of yours loses their job or a company has 10,000 employees and they lay off two hundred. The other 9,800 people start to worry, or somebody says their house price just went down. These are little thoughts that start to creep to the front of your brain." People even start thinking about past financial disasters, Lynch said, bringing thoughts of such calamities as the Great Depression to the front of their minds, even if the current situation is nowhere near as bad.

In today's world of nonstop media hype and sensational headlines, it's very difficult to keep those thoughts from entering our minds. And the more they do, the more likely we are to make bad investment decisions. Dalbar's study of investor behavior shows that the percentage of investors who correctly predict the direction of the market is much lower during down markets than it is during rising markets. During falling markets, when people have already been losing money, the fear of losing even more can cause many to cash out, even if the downturn is just one of Wall Street's periodic short-term hiccups. (Behavioral finance refers to this as *myopic loss aversion*.) Often, investors are then slow to jump back in when the market turns around, so they miss out on the bounce-back gains.

And it's important to remember that the market does bounce back, even when your fears and worries are telling you that "this time is different, this time the market won't recover." In fact, over time, the market climbs higher than any other investment vehicle. According to research performed by Roger Ibbotson, Rex Sinquefield, and Ibbotson Associates, in the 20-year period that ended at the end of 2006, the S&P averaged an 11.8 percent annual compound return, beating long-term corporate bonds (8.6 percent), long-term government bonds (8.6 percent), and Treasury bills (4.5 percent). When you stretch the time frame out to the previous 30, 40, or 50 years, the spreads between stocks and other investments are similar, and in some cases greater.

This is the great paradox of the stock market: While unpredictable in the short term, its performance becomes quite predictable—and predictably good—when looked at over the long term.

If that seems illogical, imagine, for a moment, that the market is a helium-filled balloon that you set loose outside on a gusty day. From moment to moment, it's hard to tell where the balloon is headed. It gets pushed around from side to side by the wind—that is, earnings reports, economic data, analysts' ratings, pundits' predictions—and sometimes even gets knocked downward. From moment to moment, you'd be foolish to bet someone exactly which way the balloon will go, since there's no way predict which way the wind will blow. But it's almost a sure bet that, over a longer period of time, it will end up a lot higher than it started.

The market, just like the balloon, will almost surely rise over time—but it's not going to rise in a straight line. It will stop and start, fall back at times, and surge forward at other times. That can make for a lot of anxious moments in the short term as the winds of Wall Street blow every which way.

And you should be aware just how blustery it can get. In his book *Stocks for the Long Run,* investment author, noted professor, and commentator Jeremy Siegel states that the market has averaged an annual compound return of 11.2 percent in the post–World War II period (1946–2006). But Siegel also examines those returns for their *standard deviation*, a statistical measure essentially designed to show the range of returns in a "normal" year during a particular period. If a stock has returned an average of 10 percent annually over a particular period with a standard deviation of 5 percent, for example, that means that about two-thirds of the time its returns have been between 5 percent (the average return minus the standard deviation) and 15 percent (the average plus the standard deviation).

According to Siegel, the annual standard deviation of the market has been about 17 percent in the post–World War II period, which means that about two-thirds of the time during the 60-year time frame, returns were between −5.8 percent and 28.2 percent—a huge potential year-to-year difference. (And that's the range returns fell into about two-thirds of the time; in other years they were even further from the average.)

The fact that such major year-to-year fluctuations can—and many times do—occur in the stock market makes for a lot of anxious times in the short term, but that anxiety is simply the price you pay for the excellent long-term returns that the stock market gives you. If stocks earned 10 or 12 percent per year and were a smooth ride, why would anyone ever invest in anything else? This concept is known as the *equity risk premium.*

The bottom line: There are no free lunches in the stock market. If you want the long-term benefits of stocks, you've got to pay the price of short-term discomfort.

The Best Way Not to Miss the Boat: Don't Get Off in the First Place

Many investors, however, either don't expect or just plain can't tolerate the short-term discomfort of the stock market, and they'll do just about anything to try to avoid it. Some, on the one hand, will ignore stocks altogether, not wanting to deal with the short-term risk involved. Instead, they'll put their money into bonds, Treasury bills, or even just keep it in a CD or savings account. After all, while those options don't have nearly the upside of stocks, you can't lose money with them. Or can you?

While stocks are generally thought of as riskier investments than bonds or T-bills, David Dreman (the great "contrarian" investor you'll soon read about in Chapter 5) found flaws in that logic. The reason: inflation. If, for example, all of your money is in a savings account that is earning 2 percent interest per year but inflation is at 3 percent per year, the relative worth of your money isn't increasing by 2 percent annually; it's actually declining.

Since World War II, the threat of inflation to fixed-income investments has been very real. In his book *Contrarian Investment Strategies,* Dreman notes that when adjusted for inflation, stocks returned an average of 7.5 percent from 1946 to 1996; when also adjusted for inflation, however, bonds had an average annual return of just 0.86 percent, gold actually declined by 0.13 percent per year, and T-bills returned just 0.42 percent annually. Looked at another way, the average annual T-bill return before inflation was 4.8 percent during that period, about two-and-a-half times less than what stocks returned before inflation—not great, but not bad considering that T-bills are essentially risk-free; after inflation is factored in, however, stocks returned about *18 times* as much as T-bills per year. Based on information like that, Dreman concluded that inflation was a far greater risk to long-term investors than short-term stock market volatility.

Now, while some will try to avoid short-term market discomfort by avoiding stocks altogether, others, of course, believe they can have their cake and eat it too—that they can skirt the stock market's short-term anxiety and still reap the long-term rewards. But much more often than not, they will end up with all the short-term discomfort and none of the long-term gains.

Part of the reason is that, as we discussed earlier, most investors who try to time the market end up buying high and selling low. But there's also another important reason that is critical to understand—the nature of when and how the stock market makes its gains. In a 2007 article for *CNNMoney*, Jeanne Sahadi touched on this concept. Citing data from Ibbotson Associates, Sahadi said that if you had invested $100 in the S&P 500 in 1926, you would have had $307,700 in 2006—a pretty staggering gain. But if you had been out of the market for the best-performing 40 months of that lengthy 972-month period, you would have had just $1,823 in 2006. That means that 99 percent of the gains over that 81-year period came in just 4 percent of the months.

The principle holds over shorter periods, as well. If you invested $100 in 1987, you'd have had $931 by the end of 2006, Sahadi noted. But if you were out of the market for the 17 best trading months of that 240-month period, you'd have ended up with just $232. In this case, 84 percent of the gains came in 7 percent of the months.

The bottom line: While the market rises substantially over time, much of its increases come on a relatively small portion of trading days—and no one knows for sure when they're going to come. If you jump in and out of the market based on short-term fluctuations, you're bound to miss some of those big days—and you can't get them back.

This phenomenon brings me to the final point I'll make, one last warning in case you're still suffering from the delusion that you can time the market: In a market where the vast majority of gains come on a small number of days, you don't just have to be right more than you're wrong if you want to make money timing the market—you have to be right a whole lot more than you're wrong. That's what the research of William Sharpe shows. Sharpe (who created the widely used *Sharpe ratio*, a statistic that measures risk-adjusted returns) found that in order to make money with a market-timing approach, you need to be right in your timing decisions at least 74 percent of the time— not just 51 percent, as many assume. Consider that statistic in combination with some of the others I've presented—such as the Tetlock study that showed the most accurate human forecasters were right about 20 percent of the time—and you see that most market timers won't even come close to succeeding.

Now, the Good News . . .

Whew. I warned you that this chapter wasn't going to be pretty. We've learned that we have a lot going against us when it comes to investing in the stock market—our brains, our emotions, timing and even the mutual fund industry itself. But we've also learned that if we want to grow our money by any substantial margin over the long run, the market is the best place to be. Sounds like quite the pickle. Don't worry, however; advice from some of the greatest investors in history on how to stay in the market and avoid these pitfalls is just a few pages away.

The Guru Summary

- While the stock market is unpredictable in the short term, it becomes predictable—and predictably good—over the long term. In fact, it has proven to be far and away the best long-term investment vehicle of all-time, especially when inflation is factored in.
- Despite that fact, the vast majority of individual investors, mutual fund managers, and stock recommendation newsletters fail to beat the market over the long run, often underperforming by wide margins.
- The reason for most underperformance is that investors' emotions lead them astray, causing them to react to short-term price movements and the interpretation of those movements by experts featured in the media. This leads to selling low and buying high.
- Much of the stock market's gains come on a limited number of days—and no one knows exactly when those big days will occur; if you jump in and out of the market, you risk missing them.
- In order to make money by timing the market, you need to be right on about 75 percent of your market calls—and research shows that most investors, even so-called experts, don't come close to that success rate.

Chapter 2

The Cavalry Arrives

The investor cannot enter the arena of the stock market with any real hope of success unless he is armed with mental weapons that distinguish him in kind—not in a fancied superior degree—from the trading public.
—BENJAMIN GRAHAM, *THE INTELLIGENT INVESTOR* (1949)

G iven all of the challenges we've just discussed, you might be thinking that it seems impossible to beat the market over the long term. In fact, there are those who would tell you not to even bother trying. People who believe in the efficient market hypothesis believe that a stock's price always accurately reflects all of the known information about it, so that buying stocks at "bargain" prices—prices below their real value—simply isn't possible.

The efficient market hypothesis is, however, quite simply not true if you ask me—and the gurus I'm about to teach you about have proved it. By consistently avoiding the dangers examined in the previous chapter, these investing greats have been able to exploit very real inefficiencies in the stock market, producing returns that far outpace the market over long periods of time.

Just who are these investors, and how did they do it? Well, it's easy to imagine them as some sort of Wall Street superheroes, people who, either through a gift of birth or years upon years of experience have the ability to enter the market at just the right time and then cash out just before things go south. After all, if most people fail to make money in stocks because they try unsuccessfully to time the market, wouldn't it follow that those who have succeeded were simply on the other end of the market-timing success/failure spectrum?

That would make for a great story, the notion of these prescient, unbeatable investors. The problem is that it's just not true. Sure, some people have been fortunate enough to make a lot of money with good (perhaps "lucky" is a better word) timing in the short term. But as I began researching how the best investors of all-time made their fortunes, I quickly found that the Peter Lynches and Warren Buffetts of the world succeeded over the long term not by playing the game better than the average investor, but by playing it differently.

A Numbers Game

Playing the game *differently*? What exactly does that mean? Well, essentially it is what Ben Graham, the man known as "The Father of Value Investing," alluded to in the quote that began this chapter. In Graham's time (his investment career began around 1914), just as today, millions of investors around the world bought and sold stocks based on whether those stocks (or the market in general) were going up or down on a particular day. They were market-timers. Graham believed, however, that trying to be better than other investors at timing the market or speculating about the future of a stock was no way to succeed over the long term. Banking on the idea that you were the rare exception to the rule of market timing failure was simply too risky a gamble for the average investor. Instead, Graham believed that you needed to find a way to assess a stock's long-term value other than by looking at recent shifts in its market price.

Looking for other ways to value stocks was, in fact, just what all of the gurus I follow did—and the way they did it was by focusing on the numbers. By "the numbers," I'm not just talking about a stock's per-share price (though price was certainly one of the things that they examined when deciding whether to buy or sell); I mean a stock's fundamentals—the measures of how its underlying business is performing. A stock's price can shift from day to day or month to month because of a variety of factors that have nothing to do with the company's quality. But its fundamentals—earnings, sales, debt, cash flows, and the like—usually give you a true indication of how strong its business really is.

What the gurus understood was that companies that had strong fundamentals tended to continue to run successful businesses, and that their long-term business success correlated with long-term gains in their stock prices. They also knew that in the short term, a business' fundamentals don't always match up with its market price—in particular, they knew that the investing world can sometimes undervalue a good company. These are the companies on whose stocks the gurus tended to pounce, believing that over time, other investors would realize the value in these stocks and drive their prices upward.

What's interesting to note isn't just the fact that these gurus were able to exploit inefficiencies in the market, but that they did it in a wide variety of ways. Some, like Graham and his protégé, the great Warren Buffett, were very conservative, deep-value investors. They focused on companies that had long histories of steady earnings and low debt, trying to minimize risk as much as possible. Martin Zweig, meanwhile, focused primarily on growth, looking for stocks that were growing earnings with increasing speed and appeared poised to continue that growth. Still others used a blend of growth and value approaches, with the most obvious example being James O'Shaughnessy, who used two separate strategies: one value and one growth.

Even within the broad categories of strategies—growth, value, blended—there were significant differences in the specific variables each guru examined. While I had set out in search of *the* path to stock-picking success, I quickly found that there were actually numerous paths to choose from.

Despite the great successes that these diverse paths had led to, I also found that most investors were unaware of them. By using my background in computers, I realized, I could not only turn these strategies into easy-to-use models for my own benefit; I could also help others take advantage of these various paths to investment success. That's just what this book does, by teaching you how to find your way in the stock market using the paths laid out by 10 of history's greatest investing trailblazers.

Why Them?

In reality, there are other ways to beat the market besides the 10 strategies I show you in this book. Investors such as Bill Miller and George Soros have both also made huge sums of money in stocks over the years with their own approaches. Why, then, did I select only these 10 gurus? The reasons are pretty simple, actually.

Disclosed Strategy

First off, the guru's strategy had to be disclosed. And in almost all of the cases you'll soon read about, it was the gurus themselves who disclosed their methods. Eight did so in books they wrote. One, Joseph Piotroski, did so in a highly regarded academic paper. The lone example among my guru-based models not derived from the writings of the guru himself is my Buffett-based approach. That's because Buffett, considered by many to be the greatest investor of all-time, hasn't publicly disclosed his strategy. His former daughter-in-law, Mary Buffett—who worked closely with Warren—has written a book about Warren's strategy titled *Buffettology*. This is the best book thus far on Warren's strategy and, for that reason, forms the basis for my Buffett-inspired model.

Verifiable Track Record

Another factor I required while developing my guru-based models was that the guru have not only an excellent long-term track record of beating the market, but that his track record be verifiable. In other words, it wasn't enough to know that someone had made a lot of money in the stock market by using a particular strategy and was now worth $10 billion; I wanted to see year-by-year results of just how his strategy had fared over a long period of time.

The track records of the gurus in this book were verifiable mostly through two general sources. First, several of the gurus—Peter Lynch, David Dreman, and John Neff, to name a few—gained their fame and fortune by managing highly successful mutual funds or investment companies for long periods of time. The track records of those funds or groups during the years they were in charge are fairly easy to obtain.

While some gurus' track records were verifiable because of real-world track records, others' were verifiable through back-tested results. O'Shaughnessy and Piotroski, for example, both did extensive studies of historical stock market returns and developed quantitative formulas that, if they had been used during the periods involved in the studies, would have produced excellent returns. They were able to determine this by using computer applications that back-tested the models they developed.

Note: Year-by-year track records for each guru covered in this book are listed in Appendix B.

Quantifiable Criteria

Still, there are other well-known investors besides these ten who possess verifiable track records and have also published books that explain, to some degree, how they established those track records. Why didn't I computerize their approaches? In most cases, it was because most criteria they used to pick stocks were not quantifiable. If a successful investor had simply said that one of his major criterion was that a company has "strong management," but did not offer specific, unambiguous rules for how to determine what "strong management" entailed, that was no good to me.

Similarly, if a successful investor had simply said that "you should look for stocks with a low price-earnings (P/E) ratio," that also was no good to me, because "low" is too vague a term to decipher what that guru really looked for when investing. Depending on your point of view, low P/E ratios could mean "5 or below," "15 or below," "anything less than the median P/E of the S&P 500 industrials," "in the bottom 20 percent of the market," "between 40 percent and 60 percent of the market P/E," or "less than the annual *earnings per share* (EPS) growth rate of the company." In fact, all of these precise definitions of "low P/E" have been used by the different gurus in this book. Without that kind of specificity, you simply can't come anywhere close to reliably duplicating the style of a guru. The guru's criteria thus had to involve variables that could be obtained through a financial data-providing service, and they needed to be definitive enough that my models could use that data to decide whether or not a particular stock met a particular criterion.

You should be aware that some of the gurus I follow consider nonquantitative measures in addition to using their quantitative methodologies. Buffett, for example, famously looks for firms that have a "durable competitive advantage" over their competitors. A company such as Coca-Cola, one of Buffett's major holdings, has name recognition and its products are interwoven into people's daily lives, giving it a huge inherent advantage over its competitors. Name recognition is certainly worth something; exactly how much it's worth isn't clear, however, so that criterion is not part of my Buffett-based computer model.

In cases such as these, however, I've found that the quantitative parts of the gurus' approaches still work amazingly well on their own, as you'll see when I examine the track records of my models.

While certain criteria can't be quantified, my background in computers and artificial intelligence has, however, allowed me to develop guru-based models that aren't restricted to simple "black" and "white" or commonly utilized criteria. The models I have developed consist of thousands of lines of programming code and analyze more than 300 unique fundamental variables, and sometimes a single guru-based criterion will require a complex use of these hard-to-construct variables.

For example, one area that former mutual fund star John Neff examined was the ratio of a firm's total return (its earnings per share growth plus its yield) to its P/E ratio. Neff realized that variables such as this could vary widely depending on a stock's industry, so he looked for stocks whose total return/price-earnings ratio figures were either greater than the market average, *or* greater than their industry average. The Neff-based model is able to not only perform the calculations needed to determine a stock's total return/price-earnings ratio, but it is also able to compare that figure to the market average and the stock's industry average and then decide whether the stock meets the criterion.

In addition to helping me develop models that can perform multifaceted calculations, my knowledge and experience in artificial intelligence also enabled me to make many of my computerized guru methodologies come as close as possible to emulating real-life, human-type analysis. For a simple example, take a company's EPS growth rate. Most computer screens use an EPS growth rate for a single period (some will measure only the rate EPS have grown over the past year, while others will measure only the rate EPS have grown over the past five years, for example). We've found that those numbers can, in many cases, be highly misleading.

A common problem in the way most screening sites measure EPS growth is that many stocks have an abnormally high or low growth rate in a given year because of a one-time event. This makes it appear that the company's underlying business is growing much faster or slower than it really is. The strategies I run, however, look at a company's EPS over several different periods and from a number of angles in much the same way that a human being would. They are smart enough to use a series of yearly averages to come up with a broader picture of how the firm has been growing earnings. Said another way, my models go through a series of *intelligent* steps to find a growth rate (using a myriad of yearly combinations) that accurately reflects the firm's growth picture.

Meet the Dream Team

As you can see, a lot went into the development of my models. In the end, after considering all of the requirements thus far explained—a publicly disclosed, quantitative approach that my models could mimic with a high degree of accuracy used by an investor with an excellent, verifiable track record—my search for market-beating strategies led me to the 10 gurus covered in this book. We look deep into each of these investors' accomplishments and strategies in the coming chapters. But to whet your appetite, let's take a quick glance at each of them now:

- **Benjamin Graham**. Widely considered the father of value investing, Graham averaged a 17.4 percent gross annual return from 1945 to 1956. He looked for stocks that were significantly

undervalued relative to their intrinsic worth, which he measured
principally by their future earnings potential. Graham's defensive
investor strategy is considered by many to be the ultimate value
strategy, and has stood the test of time more than perhaps any
strategy ever created

- **John Neff**. Neff managed the highly successful Windsor Fund
  from 1964 to 1995, averaging a 13.7 percent annual return in that
  31-year period, which beat the S&P 500 by more than 3 percent
  per year. His approach focused on finding stocks with low price-
  earnings ratios and other strong fundamentals.

- **David Dreman**. Dreman is a contrarian. He focused on the least
  popular stocks—those that have been shunned because they're
  in a troubled industry, or because of investor apathy—and found
  stocks within that group that had strong underlying financials. At
  the time he published *Contrarian Investment Strategies,* his Kemper-
  Dreman High Return Fund was one of the best-performing
  mutual funds ever, having been ranked number one in more time
  periods than any of the 3,175 funds in Lipper Analytical Service's
  database.

- **Warren Buffett**: Probably the most famous and, perhaps, greatest
  investor of all-time, Buffett's Berkshire Hathaway averaged a 24 percent
  annual return over a 32-year period. Buffett is known for his patient,
  highly selective, long-term investment style.

- **Peter Lynch**. From the time he took over Fidelity Investment's
  Magellan Fund in 1977 until the time he retired in 1990, Magellan
  averaged an incredible 29.2 percent annual return—almost double
  the S&P 500 average of 15.8 percent. In the last five years of his
  tenure, the fund beat 99.5 percent of all other funds, according to
  Barron's. Lynch is known for developing the *price-earnings/growth
  ratio,* a way to measure how pricey growth stocks are.

- **Kenneth Fisher**. Fisher is the son of Phil Fisher, who is generally
  considered the father of growth stock investing. The younger Fisher
  gained fame with his book *Super Stocks,* in which he popularized
  the use of the price-sales ratio for picking stocks. From 1995
  through 2007, Fisher's Global Total Return strategy produced
  average net returns of 13.0 percent per year, beating both the

MSCI World index benchmark (9.1 percent) and the S&P 500 (11.3 percent).

- **Martin Zweig**. During the 15 years that it was monitored, Zweig's stock recommendation newsletter returned an average of 15.9 percent per year and was ranked number one based on risk-adjusted returns by Hulbert Financial Digest, a publication that tracks the records of investment newsletters. Zweig looks for growth stocks and his methodology is highly selective.

- **James O'Shaughnessy**. O'Shaughnessy's *What Works on Wall Street*—in which he detailed what he learned from examining 44 years worth of stock market data—made a couple of surprising findings, including that P/E ratios aren't the best criteria for selecting stocks. He developed two models, one targeting larger value-oriented stocks and the other targeting growth stocks. His back-tested results averaged 22 percent per year over those 44 years.

- **Joel Greenblatt**. Greenblatt, the founder and managing partner of Gotham Capital, has by far the simplest strategy of all the gurus we follow. His "magic formula," which he details in *The Little Book That Beats the Market,* consists of just two variables: return on capital and earnings yield. The strategy nonetheless produced a 30.8 percent average annual return from 1988 through 2004, more than doubling the S&P 500's 12.4 percent return during that period.

- **Joseph Piotroski**. This little-known college professor published a highly regarded research paper on high book-market ratio (i.e., unpopular) stocks while teaching at the University of Chicago in 2002. The paper outlined a brilliant strategy for distinguishing the high book-market stocks that were likely to be successful performers from those that deserved their unpopularity. His strategy would have produced a 23 percent average annual return from 1976 to 1996.

Crucial Similarities

As we can see, the gurus listed above all produced excellent returns using a variety of different methods. As interesting as it is to note the differences in their specific strategies, however, it is absolutely critical to understand the similarities in their mindsets—and how their mindsets fundamentally differed from those of other investors.

In Chapter 1, we examined how humans are emotional beings, which helps us in many aspects of life but hurts us when investing. When the market or individual stocks go down, we have the urge to sell, and when they rise, we have the urge to buy, even though there is often no real long-term significance to these short-term movements. And when we try to predict these short-term price changes we often fail, and end up buying high and selling low.

The gurus, however, all understood that short-term market fluctuations were simply part of life when you invested in stocks, and they didn't let their emotions convince them otherwise. They took a long-term outlook, never wavering from their approaches—even when the market was down or their individual stocks were down in the short term. If they believed a stock was still a good buy for the long haul, they stuck with it. Buffett, for example, so believed in his own method of valuing stocks that he once said, "As far as I am concerned, the stock market doesn't exist. It is there only as a reference to see if anybody is offering to do anything foolish."

Buffett, like the rest of the gurus, knew that no strategy could beat the market every quarter, or even every year. Indeed, all of the gurus whom we've studied have gone through down periods compared to the market, which, when you think about it, is inevitable. If there were a strategy that outperformed the market every quarter or every year, everyone would flock to it. That would then drive the prices of stocks favored by that strategy through the roof, which at some point would limit your gains and lead to the strategy's failure.

In reality, what happens is that *every* strategy goes through a down period that can last a year or more—even those you're about to read about. And when they do, many investors see the value of their portfolios declining and abandon the approach, letting their emotions get the best of them. Other investors won't even consider starting to follow a strategy following a down period. They'll scrap a proven strategy that's having a down quarter or down year in favor of the latest "hot" strategy from the last year, which usually lacks a long-term track record and is more hype than substance. When that strategy fails, they'll jump again, chasing "hot" strategies—and returns—all the way. Meanwhile, the disciplined investor who withstands the short-term discomfort and sticks to a proven long-term strategy ends up reaping the long-term gains.

And therein lies the gurus' true greatness. It's not that they've developed complicated theories that are unintelligible to laypeople, or that they have some sort of otherworldly ability to predict where the market will head. It's that they possess the discipline to withstand the assault that the market makes on our emotions from day to day, and focus on what they knew was best for the long term. As Peter Lynch once said in a PBS interview, "Stomach is the key organ here. It's not the brain."

If you have the stomach to deal with the market's idiosyncrasies, the coming chapters should be very valuable to you. We examine each of the gurus, learning about their achievements, their track records, and, most importantly, the strategies they used to build their wealth and reputations. We take you step by step through each of their approaches, showing you how you can implement each of these individual methods on your own, while also giving you priceless general advice that the gurus have given over the years about the mindset you need to succeed in the stock market. Then we show you ways to take these individual guru strategies to another level, detailing how you can combine different methods to further enhance your returns and limit your risk.

If you don't have the stomach to withstand the market's short-term discomfort for the sake of long-term rewards, let's be frank: The coming chapters probably won't help you. And, to be honest, the stock market is probably not the right place for you. But if you are willing to stick to a disciplined approach no matter how rocky it gets—that is, if you are willing to distinguish yourself from other investors in *kind,* not in *superior degree,* as Graham put it—you're now ready to start receiving the tools that will make adopting such a mindset well worth your while.

So, fasten your seatbelts. It's going to be a bumpy—but very worthwhile—ride.

The Guru Summary

- The stock market is not totally efficient; that is, at any given time, certain stocks are overvalued and others are undervalued.
- Stocks with strong fundamentals (the measures of the strength of their underlying businesses, such as earnings, sales, debt, and cash flow) tend to perform best over the long term.
- By sticking to the numbers (the fundamentals), history's greatest investors were able to develop systematic methods to identify undervalued stocks—and several have been kind enough to share their methods with the public.
- Every strategy—even the most successful in history—goes through down periods. If you abandon a proven strategy when times get tough, you'll end up selling low—and you'll miss out when the strategy bounces back.
- You don't need to be a rocket scientist to beat the market. What you do need is discipline and a willingness to stick with a proven strategy—despite what your emotions are telling you—during periodic down times.

Part Two

THE VALUE LEGENDS

Warren Buffett has defined value by explaining, "Price is what you pay; value is what you get." When it comes to the four gurus in this section, the value they've gotten out of their investments is measured by the millions (or in some cases, billions), and the esteem they've earned is incalculable. From the man credited with founding the entire value investing field (the late Benjamin Graham), to a renowned "contrarian" (David Dreman), to an unassuming market-bottom-feeder (John Neff), to value investing's greatest modern day champion (Buffett)—each of these four legends earned his fortune by investing in companies whose stocks were selling on the cheap, relative to the underlying values of their businesses. Their methods were different, but their overall philosophies similar: Buy stock in solid companies, and buy it at good prices; "hot," hyped-up, flavor-of-the-month picks were of no interest to them. If you've ever done any bargain shopping—be it for shoes, groceries, or, of course, stocks—you should be able to relate well to their approaches.

Part Two

THE VALUE LEGENDS

Chapter 3

Benjamin Graham

The Granddaddy of the Gurus

Greatness be nothing unless it be lasting.

—NAPOLEON BONAPARTE

Benjamin Graham was Warren Buffett before Warren Buffett. Just as Buffett is widely considered the greatest investor of today's generation, Graham, born more than a century ago, was viewed as the greatest of his time. His opinions were often quoted, his decisions made millions for those whose money he handled, and his reputation and fortune were built using a conservative, long-term philosophy—decades before Buffett would gain fame by embracing the same type of approach. And, like Buffett, Graham possessed a quick wit, straightforward style, and common sense approach that both professional and lay investors could understand and benefit from.

The similarities between Graham and Buffett are by no means coincidental. While thousands, if not millions, of investors now look to Buffett for investment advice and wisdom, a young Buffett himself looked for—and received—just that from Graham. In fact, Buffett attended graduate school at Columbia University in large part because Graham taught there, and he later talked Graham into taking him on as an employee at Graham's investment firm. The two developed a strong, lifelong bond, with Graham impacting Buffett both professionally and personally. "To me," Buffett wrote in his introduction to the fourth revised edition of Graham's classic, *The Intelligent Investor,* "Ben Graham was far more than an author or a teacher. More than any other man except my father, he influenced my life." Buffett has also called *The Intelligent Investor* "by far the best book on investing ever written."

But Graham's guru status goes far beyond simply having been Buffett's teacher and mentor. A native Briton who immigrated to the United States as a child, Graham first rose out of his family's own financial struggles and then out of the Great Depression to establish a remarkable track record of his own. From 1936 to 1956, the Graham-Newman Corporation (which Graham ran along with Jerome Newman) averaged annual returns of about 20 percent, during which time the S&P 500 grew 12.2 percent. That's a two-decade-long track record that few investors in history can match.

To establish that track record, Graham used a conservative, risk-averse approach. Trendy, hot stocks didn't garner his attention; he was concerned with companies' balance sheets and their fundamentals. How much debt did they carry? How did their stock price compare to the amount of per-share earnings they were generating? Did the firm have strong sales figures? This value-centric, company-focused approach may be used by a lot of investors today, but it was Graham who first popularized it, earning him the nickname of "The Father of Value Investing."

Graham is also considered the founder of the entire field of security analysis. His 1934 book *Security Analysis* (which he coauthored with David Dodd) remains something of a bible for stock analysts, a detailed "how-to" that highlights the incredible care and analysis that went into Graham's stock-picking decisions.

Still, while his own accomplishments and track record were remarkable, you can't fully appreciate Graham's brilliance and impact on the investing world until you consider the track records of his follow-ers. Mario Gabelli, John Templeton, Walter Schloss, John Neff (another of the gurus you'll soon read about), Warren Buffett—these are just a few of the investors who worked with, studied under, or learned from Graham and went on to great stock market success of their own.

In a speech he gave at Columbia in 1984 entitled "The Superinvestors of Graham-and-Doddsville," Buffett addressed this point. He explained that from 1954 to 1956, there were four "peasant level" employees working under Graham and his two partners at the Graham-Newman Corporation. Three of those "peasants" (Walter Schloss, Tom Knapp, and Buffett himself) established easily traceable track records after leav-ing the firm, Buffett said—and all of those track records were tremen-dous. The updated version of *The Intelligent Investor* includes year-by-year return records for funds managed by even more Graham disciples, and every one of them is impressive.

Thumbing his nose at those who would believe markets are supremely efficient and can be beaten only by chance, Buffett says the records of Graham's protégés are proof of how successful and enduring the invest-ment strategy used by Graham, Dodd, and Newman has been. "A concen-tration of winners that simply cannot be explained by chance can be traced to this particular intellectual village," he wrote. We'd add that the returns of Validea.com's Graham-based model, which you'll find at the end of this chapter, offer even more proof of how remarkably successful—and timeless—Graham's strategy has proven.

And so, given the lasting, dramatic effect he has had on the world of stock investing, it is only appropriate that we begin our conversation about the investment gurus with Graham's strategy and story.

The Proof Is in the Pupils

Benjamin Graham's great legacy isn't just attributable to his own excellent track record and ingenuity; it's also due to the excellent track records of his many protégés. Mario Gabelli, John Templeton, Warren Buffett, and John Neff are just a few of the investors who worked under or learned from Graham and went on to make names for themselves on Wall Street. According to Buffett, their success is a clear indication of just how impressive and enduring Graham's investment approach was. Here's a look at how some of Graham's pupils and disciples fared when they spread their own investment management wings.

Protégé	Company/Fund	Annualized Compound Gain
Walter J. Schloss	WJS Ltd. Partners	16.1% over 28¼ years
	WJS Partnership	21.3% over 28¼ years
	S&P 500 (w/dividends)	8.4% over 28¼ years
Tom Knapp & Ed Anderson	Tweedy, Browne Inc.	20% over 15¾ years
	Tweedy, Browne Inc. Ltd. Partners	16% over 15¾ years
	S&P 500 (w/dividends)	7.0% over 15¾ years
Warren Buffett (pre-Berkshire Hathaway)	Buffett Partnership, Ltd. (Overall Partnership)	29.5% over 13 years
	Buffett Partnership, Ltd. (Limited Partners)	23.8% over 13 years
	Dow Jones Industrial Average	7.4% over 13 years
Bill Ruane	Sequoia Fund, Inc.	17.2% over 13¾ years
	S&P 500 (w/dividends)	10.0% over 13¾ years
Charles Munger	Overall Partnership	19.8% over 14 years
	Limited Partners	13.7% over 14 years
	Dow Jones Industrial Average	5.0% over 14 years
Rick Guerin	Pacific Partners, Ltd. (Overall Partnership)	32.9% over 19 years
	Pacific Partners, Ltd. (Limited Partnership)	23.6% over 19 years
	S&P 500	7.8% over 19 years

Source: Benjamin Graham, Jason Zweig, and Warren E. Buffett. *The Intelligent Investor,* rev.ed. FirstCollins Business Essentials, 2006, Appendix 1.

Who Was Benjamin Graham?

While Graham was a highly accomplished scholar who possessed a brilliant mind for academics, his approach to investing appears to have come as much from his own personal experiences as it did from books and study. To fully understand how his investing philosophy came to be, then, it is helpful to understand how his life developed.

Born in London in 1894 as Benjamin Grossbaum, Graham was the son of a dealer in china dishes and figurines. When he was just a year old, the family moved to New York, and for a while lived quite well. When Graham was nine, his father died leaving his mother Dora with the task of raising Ben and his two brothers. She must have been a risk-taker because it's reported that she tried several business ventures, all of which failed; she even invested in the stock market just before the famous financial panic of 1907, which wiped out her investment. Those experiences may well have left their mark on young Benjamin, whose investment style was grounded in the belief that preserving capital was every bit as important—if not more important—than producing big gains.

The family's financial straits also may have had another impact on Graham—he worked during both high school and college to make money, demonstrating a work ethic that was a precursor to the intensity and dedication he showed when dealing with his clients' money.

A gifted student, Graham went to Columbia University on a scholarship and made quite an impression. Upon his graduation, he was asked to teach math, English, and philosophy at the school, but instead opted for a job on Wall Street because the income potential was better there than in academia.

Initially, Graham worked in 1914 in the bond department of a brokerage firm, Newburger, Henderson and Loeb. Shortly thereafter the outbreak of World War I precipitated a couple of big changes for him. For one thing, due to the suspicion of people with German-sounding names, his family dropped "Grossbaum" and adopted "Graham" as their surname. For another, the financial markets panicked, and the New York Stock Exchange closed for several months that year. Restrictions were put on the prices and the trading of some stocks, which continued into the following year. When trading resumed, Graham's employer was understaffed, giving Graham an opportunity to work at—and learn from—a variety of jobs at the firm. Among the things he learned was that many investors actually had limited knowledge of investing.

As the years passed, Graham decided to open his own investment firm, and did so with accountant Jerome Newman in 1926. But just as his entrance into the workforce was marked by bad timing with the panic of 1914, so too was his entrance into business ownership. Only three years after he and Newman started their firm, the crash of 1929 sent the stock market into a long-term trough. Janet Lowe, an author who has written extensively about Graham, notes that, despite his skills and dedication, Graham's clients lost money along with everyone else during the crash.

But while it took the Dow Jones Industrial Average 25 years to climb back to the high it hit before the crash, Graham's clients wouldn't have to wait anywhere near as long. After the crash, Graham and his partner Newman worked five years without compensation until their clients' fortunes were fully restored. In *Value Investing Made Easy,* Lowe wrote, "Though the experience was dreadful, it earned Graham widespread respect for his integrity as a money manager. . . . Once the Graham-Newman Co. recouped its portfolio of 1929–1930, Graham never again lost money for his clients." After living through his own family's financial difficulties and then seeing the effects of the stock market crash on his clients, it's no wonder Graham honed an investment strategy based on conservative, low-risk purchases that preserved his clients' capital.

While his investing record is remarkable, Graham's legacy goes beyond the great returns he achieved for his clients and his groundbreaking securities analysis research. For instance, he spent nearly 30 years as a lecturer at Columbia, where he taught a popular course on investing, and he later spent 10 years at the University of California at Los Angeles as an adjunct professor of finance. And on a personal level, Graham was known not only for his brilliant mind, but also for his great generosity. "I knew Ben as my teacher, my employer, and my friend," Buffett wrote in *Financial Analysts Journal* in late 1976, shortly after Graham died at his second home in Aix in the south of France. "In each relationship—just as with all his students, employees, and friends—there was an absolutely open-ended, no-scores-kept generosity of ideas, time, and spirit. If clarity of thinking was required, there was no better place to go. And if encouragement or counsel was needed, Ben was there."

Value Investing: Good Companies, Low Prices

So, how did Graham make back the money his clients lost in the crash of 1929? And what was it about his approach that made it not only incredibly successful, but also so enduring? Part of the answer is in the specifics of his methodology, but a big part is also in the broader way Graham viewed investing and the stock market, something that is reflected in the way he defined the two main words that make up the title of his bestselling book, *The Intelligent Investor.*

In Graham's time—and still today—hordes of "investors" buy and sell stocks with the hope of catching onto a fast-rising issue. As mentioned in the previous chapters, they have visions of getting rich in a couple years, or in some cases, a matter of months or weeks. To Graham, however, an "investor" wasn't someone who bought and traded stocks simply because he thought the market or an individual stock's price was about to go up; someone who did that was a speculator, and to Graham their hunch-playing trading was a recipe for ruin. "The people who persist in trying it," he said of such trading, "are either (a) unintelligent, or (b) willing to lose money for the fun of the game, or (c) gifted with some uncommon and incommunicable talent. In any case, they are not investors."

Graham didn't see an investment as something that could be turned into quick, easy profits, because anything that offers quick and easy profits also comes with substantial risk. Investment was instead something that took a lot of research and study, something that was as much about protecting your initial capital as it was about making profits off of it. True "investment," he wrote, considers the future "more as a hazard to be guarded against than as a source of profit through prophecy." Not surprising words, considering they came from someone who saw how wild speculation helped lead to the devastating crash of 1929.

The other main word in the title of his book—"intelligent"—also holds some clues to Graham's approach. Many people think that in order to succeed in the stock market, you have to have incredible financial acumen or tremendous mathematical ability. But when Graham used the word intelligent, he wasn't talking about intellect, and he wasn't referring to someone who is shrewd or gifted with unusual foresight or insight. Rather, he wrote, "Successful investment may become substantially a matter of techniques and criteria that are learnable, rather than the product of unique and incommunicable mental powers. . . . The intelligence here presupposed is a trait more of the character than of the brain." In other words, you don't need to be born with rocket scientist brainpower to succeed in the market; what you need—the ability to think long-term, control your emotions, and stick to a sensible, disciplined plan—are all things that just about anyone has the capacity to learn.

To Graham a big part of how investors become successful involved developing a willingness to act altogether differently from the crowd, by distinguishing themselves "in kind—not in a fancied superior degree," from the trading public, which by and large reacts emotionally to short-term price fluctuations. To beat the market, Graham believed that you couldn't just play the game better than the masses—being a better speculator than others doesn't change the fact that you're a speculator. Instead, Graham believed that you needed to play the game differently.

What does "differently" mean in this sense? Unlike most investors, Graham didn't approach stock purchases as though he were buying pieces of paper that would hopefully rise quickly in value so they could be sold for a profit. Instead, he approached stock buys as though he were buying the company itself—all its profits, all its debts, all its assets, all its revenue streams. So while technical analysts and chartists use a variety of complex measures to assess a stock's past price patterns and predict its future movements, only two simple factors are important to Graham and his followers—the real value of a company and how that relates to what you're paying for its stock.

Graham's rationale was quite simple: In the short-term, stocks are unpredictable, but in the long run, a stock's price tends to move with and reflect the real value of its business, which is indicated by its fundamentals—its price-earnings and price-book ratios, the amount of sales it does, the level of debt it has in relation to its assets, the ratio of its assets to its liabilities. The lower the price you can get on the stock of a good company—one that is financially stable and historically profitable—the better. If the company is truly strong, the rest of Wall

Street will eventually catch on and bid its stock price up toward—or beyond—the real value of its business. So, the lower the price at which you bought the stock, the greater your profits would eventually be. To Graham and his protégés, the idea of trying to time stock purchases to "catch the wave" of a stock whose price is rising was thus totally foreign. "Can you imagine buying an entire business simply because the price of the business had been marked up substantially last week and the week before?" Buffett asked in his 1984 Columbia speech. In a sense, that's just what technical analysts do.

This is an important point that distinguishes Graham from many other security analysts. Graham wasn't concerned with trading volume or the market's direction. And you can bet that if he were alive today, he wouldn't be logging on to *Yahoo! Finance* or *MSN Money* to check his portfolio's value every 20 minutes, like many investors do.

All of this isn't to say that Graham was oblivious to what was happening around a stock—the market in general, the company's industry. But he thought that in the long run, what would produce value for the investor was the stock of a solid company with good prospects that is selling below its worth. In the introduction to *The Intelligent Investor*, he wrote:

> Experience has taught us that, while there are many good growth companies worth several times net assets, the buyer of such shares will be too dependent on the vagaries and fluctuations of the stock market. By contrast, the investor in shares, say, of public utility companies at about their net-asset value can always consider himself the owner of an interest in sound and expanding businesses, acquired at a rational price— regardless of what the stock market might say to the contrary. The ultimate result of such a conservative policy is likely to work out better than exciting adventures into the glamorous and dangerous fields of anticipated growth.

Safety First

Indeed, Graham's approach was far from glamorous. In *The Intelligent Investor*, he discussed two different general types of investors—the defensive investor and the enterprising investor—but his focus on the former highlights his highly conservative approach. According to Graham, the defensive (or passive) investor's main aims were the avoidance of serious mistakes or losses, and the freedom from effort, annoyance, and the need to make lots of decisions. Enterprising (or active or aggressive) investors, on the other hand, are willing to spend more time seeking out better-than-average stocks.

Graham noted that the enterprising investor, over time, expects a reward for his skill and efforts over the defensive investor—though he had doubts that this necessarily happens. Nonetheless, for those intent on taking an "enterprising" approach, Graham loosened his strict, conservative criteria, allowing for investment in small companies and those with higher price-earnings ratios.

Most of Graham's strategy, however, seems aimed at the defensive investor. He was, after all, skeptical that most investors can beat the market and that most have an interest in spending much time studying and analyzing companies on an ongoing basis. For these reasons, we focus our analysis of Graham solely toward the defensive investor, who is conservative and fairly passive. (If you want to take a more active, risk-taking approach to your investments, we suggest you refer to other growth-focused strategies that we discuss in Chapters 9 and 10).

An important part of what makes Graham's defensive investor approach "defensive" is what Graham called the "margin of safety"— that is, the difference between a stock's price and the company's under-lying value. Remember, while a variety of factors can send a stock's price soaring or plummeting in the short term, over the long term stock price is driven by what the real value of a company is—based on its assets, its earnings, its debts, and so forth. Graham recommended buy-ing stocks with a high margin of safety, meaning that their prices were low relative to the real value of their businesses. As we discussed before, over the long run, such stocks should rise to reflect the company's true value. But just as importantly (if not more so to Graham), such under-valued stocks come with downside protection. They are already selling at a discount compared to their real value—that's the margin of safety—so even if the company encounters problems and its earning power declines a bit, the stock still might gain ground because it was so under-valued to begin with. And, if the stock declines, it's unlikely that it will drop too far since it's already selling at a relatively low price. Those are benefits you don't get if you focus on high-flying, glamorous growth stocks that have lots of high expectations built in to their prices.

This notion goes back to Graham's idea that minimizing losses is every bit as important as realizing gains in the stock market. Remember, Graham came from a family that lost much of its money, and he later saw his clients and millions of other Americans have their investments wiped out by the 1929 crash. The larger the margin of safety, the more comfortable he was, because that decreased his chances of losing money. "The buyer of bargain issues places particular emphasis on the ability of the investment to withstand adverse developments," Graham wrote in *The Intelligent Investor.* "If these [undervalued issues] are bought on a bargain basis, even a moderate decline in the earning power need not prevent the investment from showing satisfactory results. The margin of safety will then have served its proper purpose." Such an approach doesn't make for flashy stock picks, but it works.

Think of it this way: Suppose that, for $10, someone is willing to sell you a baseball card of a current player that you believe is worth about $20. That's a margin of safety of 50 percent. If the player doesn't perform quite as well as usual or as well as expected this year, maybe the book value of the card drops a bit, to, say, $17. Even though the player had a down year—perhaps he was injured, perhaps his skills declined, perhaps he had personal problems—you're still in position to sell the card at a profit because you got such a good discount on it to begin with. That's margin of safety.

How did Graham find stocks with a high margin of safety? One way was by using fundamentals that compared a stock's price to concrete financial variables such as earnings and book value. For example, he liked stocks whose price-earnings and price-book ratios were relatively low. He wrote that stocks should have a P/E of no greater than 15, and that their P/E and P/B ratios, when multiplied, shouldn't exceed 22. This meant that these companies were selling on the cheap compared to their earnings and the net asset value of their businesses.

Another way Graham targeted "safe" stocks was by looking for companies that were conservatively financed. He wanted a firm's current ratio—the ratio of its current assets to its current liabilities—to be greater than two, and he wanted its long-term debt to be no greater than the value of its assets. Companies that have a lot of debt or liabilities can find themselves in trouble if their earnings decline or don't grow as much as expected. By focusing on firms that met these criteria, Graham helped ensure that he was investing in companies that weren't overextending themselves and weren't at risk of running into financial trouble.

Note that while Graham discussed the margin of safety, and his reputation is in part built on this concept, he didn't give clear-cut rules for determining what constitutes an adequate margin of safety. He seemed to imply that he wanted to see stocks whose prices are 30 to 50 percent below their real value, but he never made this a hard-and-fast rule. The most one can say is that if you follow his specific guidelines, which we'll examine in a bit, there's an implicit margin of safety.

Graham believed that the margin of safety was closely related to another risk-reducing concept: portfolio diversification. "Even with a margin in the investor's favor, an individual security may work out badly," he wrote. "For the margin guarantees only that he [the investor] has a better chance for profit than for loss—not that loss is impossible. But as the number of such commitments is increased, the more certain does it become that the aggregate of the profits will exceed the aggregate of the losses." The bottom line: Even if you get a really good deal on a really nice basket, there's always the chance that it could break; it's safer to buy a few other baskets—even if they're not quite as nice or quite as discounted—and divide your eggs up among them.

Graham recommended holding, as a minimum, 10 value stocks, and to consider holding as many as 30.

Graham's Strategy: Step by Step

About the Benjamin Graham Strategy

The Track Record:	Graham's Graham-Newman Corp. (an investment company he ran with Jerome Newman) posted per annum returns of about 20 percent from 1936 to 1956, far outpacing the 12.2 percent average return for the market during that time.
Risk:	Graham's approach is suitable for investors seeking lower-risk stock plays. He looked for stocks that were deeply value-priced, in the belief that they

shield investors from losses because they are already trading at low prices compared to their intrinsic values. Such stocks are unlikely to drop much further (though there is, of course, never a guarantee they won't drop significantly). Graham thus appeals to thrifty, discount-oriented investors.

Time Horizon: Long term. Like his famous protégé, Warren Buffett, Graham believed that a true investor invested in good companies, not hot stocks. He thus didn't make trading decisions based on short-term price movements, provided that the firm's underlying business was still strong.

Effort: Low. There's a bit of effort involved in choosing stocks in the first place, but very little is required after that.

As we've seen, it seems that events in Graham's own life may have played a big part in shaping the investment philosophy that made him famous. Having experienced his own family go from the good life to the impoverished life and having watched his investment company devastated in the 1929 crash, it's not hard to understand why Graham focused so much on limiting risk. Since that concept was such a key part of his approach, we'll begin our step-by-step analysis of Graham's methodology with two ways that he limited risk: by looking at sector and sales.

Note: In commentary written for a 2003 revised edition of *The Intelligent Investor,* Jason Zweig states that the 20 percent return figure for the Graham-Newman Corp., which Graham himself cites in the book, "appears not to take management fees into account." Graham-Newman still fared quite well net of fees, however, averaging "at least" a 14.7 percent annual return over the period.

Sector Graham lived in an era when technology was far less developed—and a far riskier investment—than it is today. Since he focused so much on avoiding risk and preserving his original investment, he avoided tech stocks, yet embraced all other sectors as they did not seem to pose a substantial risk. Today technology has become a critical part of our society, and many tech firms have been around long enough to establish solid long-term track records. Still, while not quite as risky nowadays, the tech sector is on the riskier end of the spectrum, so tech stocks are excluded from our Graham-based model.

Sectors

1. All stocks (including public utilities) besides   Pass
   technology firms
2. Technology stocks   Fail

Company Sales Another way Graham limited risk was by focusing on large, prominent companies. He believed such firms tended to have less volatile stocks, larger assets and fewer negative surprises, and better track records than their smaller counterparts. In addition, larger stocks better lend themselves to financial analysis.

Graham acknowledged that "large" and "prominent" can be difficult to define, but suggested that thresholds of $50 million in assets or $50 million in sales should be used. The model portfolio that we have developed focuses on the latter. (Prices, of course, have changed a great deal from Graham's day, and we equate Graham's suggestion to a modern-day figure of $340 million in trailing 12-month sales.)

Company Sales

1. ≥ $340 million   Pass
2. < $340 million   Fail

Current Ratio Graham believed that when buying a share of stock, you should focus on the kind of "real" value that you'd look for when buying a stake in a private company. And if you were buying a stake in a private firm, one way you'd value your investment was by comparing the value of the company's assets to the value of its liabilities. Naturally, Graham liked it when a company's assets were more than its liabilities, and the model we base on his writings requires a firm's "current ratio"— the ratio of its current assets to its current liabilities—to be at least 2. By comparing current liabilities (those closest to maturity and thus those that must be paid back first) to current assets (a company's most liquid assets, such as cash and cash equivalents, accounts receivable, etc.), one gets an idea of a company's liquidity. The higher the current ratio the better, as high liquidity means less risk that the firm will get into financial trouble.

Keep in mind, however, that certain circumstances may create a high current ratio when, in fact, that company is facing problems. Receivables are current assets, for example, and a company with an uncommonly large amount of receivables may be having trouble collecting them. Inventory, another current asset, may be high because the company can't sell its products.

On the other hand, a low current ratio suggests the company is relatively illiquid and could have trouble paying off its current liabilities. This criterion is not required for public utilities and major telecoms because, according to Graham, this working capital factor takes care of itself in these industries as part of the continuous financing of their growth through sales of bonds and shares that these types of companies typically engage in.

Current Ratio

    1. Current ratio ≥ 2 Pass

    2. Current ratio < 2, and company is a utility or telecom   Pass

    3. Current ratio < 2, and company is not utility or telecom   Fail

Long-Term Debt in Relation to Net Current Assets When buying part of a private company, another issue you'd be wise to look at is debt. Graham didn't want companies to have excessive long-term debt. As such, the method we base on his approach calls for a firm's long-term debt to be no greater than its net current assets, which is its current assets minus its current liabilities, or its "working capital." In essence, the investor should ask himself (or herself), "If this company were to liquidate its assets today, would it be able to pay off all its short-term liabilities and long-term debts?" If a company can answer "yes" to that question, that's a sign that it is financially secure.

Long-Term Debt in Relation to Net Current Assets

    1. Long-term debt $\leq$ Net current assets   Pass

    2. Long-term debt $>$ Net current assets   Fail

Long-Term EPS Growth While Graham is known as the "father of value investing," growth did play a role in his stock picks. But unlike many other investors, Graham wasn't concerned with using historical earnings growth as a means to predict strong future growth. Instead, he used growth as another indication of financial stability. Our Graham-based model looks for signs of growth, requiring a firm's earnings to have grown by at least 30 percent over the past 10 years, with no negative EPS years in the last five years. (Again, this isn't an indication that the company's earnings will jump dramatically in the future, but instead a sign that the firm has been a consistent, solid performer—the type of lower-risk investment Graham liked.)

To calculate growth rate, Graham did not just compare the earnings for the first and last years of the 10-year period. Instead, he averaged the earnings for the first three years of the 10-year period and compared it to the average earnings for the last three years of the period.

And remember: Earnings can't be negative for any of the most recent five years. Even one year of losses in the past five means the company fails this test, a sign of just how serious Graham was about limiting risk.

Long-Term EPS Growth (Past 10 Years)

1. ≥ 30%, and no negative annual EPS in last five years   Pass

2. < 30%   Fail

3. ≥ 30%, with negative annual EPS in any of last five years   Fail

Price-Earnings Ratio Graham didn't just want to know what the true value of a company was; he also wanted to know how its real value compared to the value that Wall Street had given it (i.e., its share price). He targeted stocks that he believed were worth substantially more than their market values, believing that Wall Street would eventually recognize that these stocks were being undervalued and buy them. As mentioned in our discussion of "margin of safety," this meant that even if the company performed worse than hoped, its stock price drop would be tempered, or even negated altogether, by investors adjusting to its previous undervaluation.

In order to assess how a company's real value compared to the value Wall Street had placed on it, Graham analyzed its price-earnings ratio. Graham abhorred speculation; and the higher the P/E, the more speculative the stock is because there is less profit per share supporting the price. Graham thus wanted a stock's P/E to be "moderate," which he defined in *The Intelligent Investor* as having a P/E of no more than 15.

It's important to note that while most people use trailing 12-month earnings in determining the "earnings" part of the P/E ratio, Graham preferred to use the average of the last three years' earnings, so that's what our Graham-based model uses. This expanded time frame gave the risk-averse Graham a more conservative idea of what the company's earnings had been like.

Price-Earnings Ratio (P/E)

1. P/E ≤ 15   Pass
2. P/E > 15   Fail

Price-Book Ratio Another way Graham compared a company's real value to the value ascribed to it by Wall Street was through the price-book ratio. The P/B ratio divides the stock's price by its book value—total assets minus intangible assets minus liabilities. Put another way, it is tangible assets less the money the company owes. Keep in mind that Graham was into "reality"—real things, like tangible assets, not intangibles such as so-called "goodwill."

Graham wanted the P/B ratio to be reasonable. How he determined what was "reasonable" may sound a bit bizarre, but given Graham's track record, we're certainly not going to question it. Basically, he thought that when you multiply a stock's P/B ratio by its P/E ratio, the product should be no greater than 22. For example, suppose a stock's price is $30, its book value per share is $20, and its earnings per share are $3. Its P/B ratio is thus 30 divided by 20, or 1.5, while its P/E ratio is 30 divided by 3, or 10. Multiply the P/B (1.5) by the P/E (10) and you get 15, which would be good enough for Graham because it is not greater than 22.

Price-Book Ratio (P/B)

1. P/B × P/E ≤ 22   Pass
2. P/B × P/E > 22   Fail

Total Debt-Equity Ratio (D/E) For industrial companies, total debt—both long-term and short-term debt but not other liabilities—must not exceed total equity. That is, a firm's total debt-equity ratio can't be greater than 100 percent.

For utilities (including regulated phone companies and railroads), however, the company can safely have a much larger long-term debt (LTD) compared to equity. Their long-term debt-equity ratio can be as high as 230 percent.

Total Debt-Equity Ratio

1. Industrial companies—D/E ≤ 100%   Pass
2. Utilities, phone companies, railroads—   Pass
   LTD/E ≤ 230%
3. Industrial companies—D/E > 100%   Fail
4. Utilities, phone companies, railroads—   Fail
   LTD/E > 230%

Continuous Dividend Payments Dividends were also very important to Graham. He liked to see that a firm had been paying dividends uninterrupted for the last 20 years. The dividend could rise or fall from year-to-year, so long as the company was paying a dividend in some amount in each year of the past two decades.

But while dividend payments were a key component of most stocks' overall returns in Graham's time, things have changed today. Now, many companies—even very strong, financially conservative firms—just don't pay dividends, often because they'd rather reinvest their earnings in the company, or because they want to buy back shares, which increases the value of shares held by existing investors. When developing Validea.com, we thus found that including a 20-year continuous dividend criterion left us with very few—if any—stocks that would pass our Graham-based model. Because of that, we've chosen not to include this criterion in our model. If you look at the model's five-year performance figures at the end of this chapter, you'll see that the strategy has worked extremely well without a continuous dividend criterion.

 **Click It!**

To find current examples of stocks that pass the Graham-based Value Investor approach, log on to www.guruinvestorbook.com. Every day, the free site will feature three stocks that get approval from our Graham method, with links to detailed analysis of why those stocks score so well.

The Graham–Based Model Performance

We began tracking a portfolio of stocks picked using the Graham-based method in July 2003—some 54 years after *The Intelligent Investor* was published. But while the book had been in print for more than half a century, the strategy it details (as we interpret it) still appears to work.

In the five years since its inception, the 10-stock version of our "Value Investor" portfolio has gained 140.4 percent, more than six times the 21.4 percent gain of the S&P 500 during that time. The strategy came out of the gate quite strong, gaining 45.1 percent in the partial 2003 year, compared to 11.1 percent for the S&P. Its greatest full-year gain was 2006, when it jumped 26 percent (compared to the S&P's 13.6 percent). The portfolio's only down year was 2007, when it dropped 8.1 percent in an unusually momentum-stock-driven market, while the S&P gained 3.5 percent.

The 20-stock version of our Graham portfolio has done even better, gaining 146.3 percent since its inception (also July 15, 2003), handily beating the S&P 500's 21.4 percent gain. Its best year was in 2004, when it gained 34.6 percent compared to the S&P's 9 percent gain. Its worst year was in 2007, but its losses were much less severe than those of the 10-stock portfolio that year. It dropped 1.4 percent, compared to the S&P's 3.5 percent gain.

Both the 10-stock and 20-stock portfolios have been more volatile than the S&P, but they are by no means roller-coaster rides. The 10-stock version has a beta of 1.23, as does the 20-stock version (The market,

Table 3.1   Model Portfolio Risk & Return Statistics

	10-Stock	20-Stock	S&P 500
Annualized Return	19.2%	19.7%	4.0%
Total Return	140.4%	146.3%	21.4%
Best Full Year	26.0% in 2006	34.6% in 2004	13.6% in 2006
Worst Full Year	−8.1% in 2007	−1.4% in 2007	3.0% in 2005
Beta	1.23	1.23	1.0
Accuracy	56.8%	55.8%	N/A

Note: Returns statistics are from July 15, 2003 to July 15, 2008. See Appendix A for additional return disclosure and explanation.
Source: Guru Model Portfolio Tool, *Validea.com*

by definition, has a beta of 1.0; stocks with betas above 1.0 have been more volatile than the market, while those with betas below 1.0 have been less volatile).

While the Graham-based portfolios are fairly well diversified, there are a few areas of the market in which the model won't tread. As mentioned in the previous section, we've excluded technology stocks from eligibility in this model because Graham, in his time, found them too risky for his taste. The other category of stocks you won't find in our Graham-based portfolios are financials. Unlike tech stocks, we don't explicitly forbid the Graham-based model from picking financials. But because of the low-debt requirements that the Graham strategy uses, it is almost impossible for financial companies—which inherently carry large amounts of debt because of the nature of their businesses—to get high marks from the strategy. The lack of tech and financial stocks seems to agree quite well with the model, and as of July 2008, its 10-stock portfolio's returns ranked second out of our eight original strategies since their inceptions, while the 20-stock version ranked first. (See Table 3.1.)

Graham's Key Investment Criteria

- Look at the sector or industry the company is in, and its sales. Be sure the firm is not a technology company, and that its sales are sufficiently high.
- Look for a current ratio of at least 2.0.
- Make sure long-term debt does not exceed net current assets.
- Look for steady EPS growth over the past decade.
- Make sure that the price-earnings ratio using average three-year earnings is greater than 15.
- Look at the price-book ratio in combination with the P/E ratio.
- Look for continuous dividend payments.

Chapter 4

John Neff

The Investor's Investor

If investing is entertaining, if you're having fun, you're probably not making any money. Good investing is boring.

—GEORGE SOROS

I magine that you are interested in investing a good chunk of money, and you're reading up on various mutual funds to see if you can find some good prospects. You come across one fund that is described as "relatively prosaic, dull, conservative." Would you keep on reading about it, or move on to the next one?

If you're like most investors, you'd probably take a pass on this stodgy-sounding fund. After all, most people enter the stock market with dreams of hitting it big by getting in early on the next Apple, Google, or Starbucks. They're looking to invest in companies with exciting new products or technologies, the types of firms that get more than their fair share of media buzz.

Relatively prosaic, dull, and conservative is, however, exactly how John Neff described the Windsor Fund, which he managed for more than 30 years—and, despite the fact that the fund held the type of beaten up or unexciting stocks that most investors ignored, he didn't have any trouble finding people to invest with him. In fact, Neff was known for being a top choice of many professional fund managers who were looking to invest their own money.

Why did so many of the pros entrust their savings to Neff and his bland fund? The answer is simple: Because Windsor's results were anything but prosaic and dull. According to Neff's book, *John Neff on Investing,* Windsor averaged a 13.7 percent average annual net return while Neff was at the helm from 1964 to 1995, handily beating the S&P 500's 10.6 percent average return during that time. Over 30-plus years, a 3.1 percent yearly spread like that is huge: A $10,000 investment (with dividends reinvested) in Windsor the year Neff took the reins would have been worth more than $564,000 by the time he retired—more than twice what it would have been worth if invested in the S&P 500 for the same period (about $233,000).

Throughout his three-decade-plus tenure, Windsor was routinely featured in the top 5 percent of all U.S. mutual funds, according to "*Barron's* Roundtable" which appeared in *Barron's* on January 22, 2007. But despite this track record—which, considering the length of his tenure, may be the greatest ever for such a large fund—Neff remains largely unknown outside of Wall Street circles. So, just who is he, and why did he focus so much on stocks that many wouldn't give a second look?

Who is John Neff?

In his book, *John Neff on Investing,* Neff himself indicates that who he is and his choice of overlooked investments are, at least to some degree, intertwined. Born in 1931, Neff said his early years taught him that success is never automatic. His parents divorced when he was just four years old and it was only his grandfather's tireless work ethic that kept Neff and his mother's family from feeling the terrible effects of the Great Depression.

In addition to the value of hard work, Neff also learned a number of business-related lessons as he grew up. His family was full of entrepreneurs, and their successes—such as a chain of grocery stores his great-aunt and great-uncle ran in the 1930s—taught him about the importance of bargain shopping and managing money wisely. Their failures, meanwhile—like a store his uncle would later start up using money borrowed from John's grandmother—taught him other lessons, one of which was: "When it comes to money, emotional attachment can fool you." His uncle's failed venture also taught him that "just because a company is down it is not always a wise investment."

Neff didn't see his father until 14 years after his parents' divorce. When his father did seek him out again, he was hoping to make amends—and to offer young John a job working at his own business, Neff Equipment, a distributor of lubrication equipment and air couplings for automobiles and other machines. It wasn't the sexiest business, but it was successful, and that taught Neff another lesson: "[It] taught me that you don't need glamour to make a buck," he wrote. "Indeed, if you can find a dull business that makes money, it is less likely to attract competition." Neff says his father also was good at talking his suppliers into giving him discounts, which put his father in good position to offer his customers good deals; that also helped him appreciate the importance of seeking out bargains.

All of these experiences seem to have manifested later in Neff's life in the way he approached investing. For instance, bargain-hunting and sympathy for those who were struggling were apparent in his penchant for focusing on downtrodden, unloved stocks. Perseverance and intense work ethic, meanwhile, were part of the rigorous research and analysis he used to pick winners from this beaten-up group. So was the strength of conviction it took to stick with stocks that others shunned.

As part of his rigorous approach, Neff continuously searched the newspapers for companies with low price-earnings ratios (i.e., the least popular stocks in the market), also keeping tabs on those that had just posted new lows or were getting hammered in the press. From these shunned firms, he used a series of quantitative measures to identify those that were good bets to rebound. In the early 1990s, for example, Windsor reaped huge gains on Citibank, a firm that Neff believed had become significantly undervalued when a financial crisis sent most of the bank's fearful investors heading for the hills. "Perseverance, sympathy for the woebegone, frugality, stubbornness, and integrity, together with an inclination to flout convention and a penchant for rigorous analysis," Neff wrote of the lessons he learned growing up "These qualities formed the building blocks of a successful investment strategy."

It's important to note, however, that while Neff may have had a natural inclination to focus on these firms, there was also logic and good financial reasoning behind such an approach. "Woebegone regions have always lured me, for one very compelling reason," he explained. "Swept up by flavors of the moment, prevailing wisdom frequently undervalues good companies. Many—but not all—that languish out of favor deserve better treatment. Despite their solid earnings, they are rejected and ignored by investors caught in the clutch of groupthink." Sound familiar? That concept is central to the value investing approach that Benjamin Graham, discussed in Chapter 3, is credited with creating. Not surprisingly, the finance professor Neff credits with being his mentor while he attended the University of Toledo, Sidney Robbins, was himself a Graham disciple.

Low P/E Investing: There's Gold in the Market's Dregs

The first part of Neff's approach—identifying the "woebegone"—is fairly easy. Check the financial section of the newspaper and you'll find the companies whose stocks are near their 52-week lows, and those that are making headlines for negative reasons.

The challenge, of course, comes in the second part: separating the stocks that are unfairly being beaten down because of overreaction from those that deserve their low prices. To do this, Neff started with the P/E ratio. In fact, while others have categorized him as a "value investor" or a "contrarian," Neff wrote that he prefers a different label: "'Low price-earnings investor.' It describes succinctly and accurately the investment style that guided Windsor while I was in charge."

The P/E ratio, which divides a stock's per-share price by the per-share earnings the company generates, has probably been the most well-known and widely used stock variable throughout history. But because Neff views it as so critical, let's step back and remember just what it signifies. One of the common explanations of the P/E ratio is that it tells you how much investors are willing to pay for every dollar in earnings that a company is generating. That's true, but Neff also notes that the P/E is also a measure of what kind of growth investors are expecting from a company in the future.

For example, take two stocks, one with a P/E of 50 and the other with a P/E of 10. Earnings drive stock prices, so if investors are willing to pay five times as much for one company's dollar of current earnings as they are for the other company's dollar in current earnings, they must be expecting that the first company will grow earnings much more rapidly than the second.

This idea of expectations was key for Neff. Much like David Dreman, the great contrarian investor we'll read about in the next chapter, Neff found that high-flying growth stocks with high P/Es had so much expectation built into them that they often fell at the slightest sign of disappointment. Low P/E stocks, however, have little anticipation or expectation built into their price. Therefore, any improvement in performance is likely to boost the attention they get, while they suffer little if their results don't meet Wall Street's already low expectations. "Indifferent financial performance by low P/E companies seldom exacts a penalty," Neff wrote. "Hints of improved prospects trigger fresh interest. If you buy stocks when they are out of favor and unloved, and sell them into strength when other investors recognize their merits, you'll often go home with handsome gains."

Because of that, Neff says Windsor usually targeted stocks that "had the stuffing beaten out of them," with P/E ratios that were 40 to 60 percent below the market average.

Growth: Steady, Sustainable, Sales-Driven

While the P/E ratio is generally a good sign of a company's value, low P/Es aren't always a good thing. "Moribund or badly run companies deserved to languish, of course," Neff wrote.

One way Neff separated the moribund and badly run low P/E firms from those that were truly undervalued was by looking at

---

Ahead of the Curve

One intriguing side note regarding Neff's P/E focus is that his book was published in the late 1990s, at the height of the tech stock bubble. During that time, many investors ignored earnings, preferring instead to try to successfully speculate on what would become the next Microsoft or Dell and collect a windfall. Not Neff. In his book, he predicted that even the most successful tech stocks of the day couldn't possibly keep up their dramatic growth. And, he said, day traders who tried to make quick, easy money off tech firms "eerily suggest the investors of 1929. A dazed and confused public has been persuaded that investing is easy and that stock prices only go up." Not long after Neff's book was released, the tech bubble burst and a bear market began, devastating many investors who hadn't heeded his warning.

---

earnings growth. "Low P/E companies growing faster than 7 percent a year tipped us off to underappreciated signs of life," he said, "particularly if accompanied by an attention-getting dividend."

But while many investors look for as much growth as possible, hoping that the huge gains will continue, Neff believed that too much growth wasn't a good thing. He thought that very high growth rates could be dangerous because they usually come with high price tags even though investors can't count on them continuing forever. He thus preferred consistent, reasonable growth; anything higher than 20 percent usually involved too much risk. To a lesser degree, he also looked for stocks whose earnings for each of the past four quarters had been greater than the corresponding four quarters from the year earlier.

Future earnings predictions, as determined by analysts' estimates, were also important to Neff (though they are subject to change). "Looking ahead, we sought evidence of reasonable and sustainable growth rates poised to catch investors' attention in a sober marketplace," he wrote. "Growth rates less than 6 percent or exceeding 20 percent (our customary ceiling) seldom made the cut. Higher growth rates entailed too much risk for our appetite." Again, Neff wanted solid, steady-as-they-go firms, not the red-hot high-flyers.

In terms of the time frame he used for calculating growth rates, Neff says Windsor focused on the past five years. "We were always poised to react to events that occurred in a shorter time frame, but, ultimately, long-term financial results drove Windsor's long-term investment performance," he said.

There was another key part to Neff's earnings growth mindset at Windsor. Profit margins, he believed, can only grow so high. Eventually, a company must grow its sales if it wants to keep growing its earnings. Our Neff model thus requires that sales growth be greater than 7 percent per year, or at least 70 percent of EPS growth.

Don't Forget the Dividend

When talking about returns, most investors and publications focus only on capital gains, the returns you get from buying a stock at a certain price and watching its price rise. But Neff believed that this view overlooked a key part of how investors can make money: dividends.

While stock prices are subject to the whims of the market, good companies rarely cut their dividends, according to Neff. And since stock prices almost always sell on the basis of expected earnings growth rates, shareholders essentially get these periodic dividend payments for free. Thus, a key part of Neff's approach was looking for stocks with strong dividend payments. In fact, he estimates that Windsor's focus on dividend-paying stocks netted it about 2 percent per year over the S&P's return, attributing for more than half of his fund's average annual outperformance of the market.

Neff wasn't opposed to nondividend payers, as long as their prices were good and he thought that their earnings would grow enough. But to make sure that all income possibilities were taken into account, he focused on total return (EPS growth rate plus dividend yield). He found he could target stocks that were giving a lot of bang for their buck by comparing the total return to the stock's P/E ratio; the model we base on his writings approves when the total return/price-earnings ratio figure is at least double either the market average or the stock's industry average.

Willingness to be Heavily Weighted in a Few Industries

From a more general perspective, one thing that is important to note about Neff's style is that he was willing to focus large portions of his portfolio in a relatively small number of industry groups. In his 2000 book *Money Masters of Our Time*, author John Train notes that automotive firms made up more than 22 percent of Windsor's holdings in 1988, while financials represented an even bigger 37 percent. That year, the 10 largest positions represented more than half of Windsor's assets, according to Train. "One justification for these high concentrations is that he isn't taking far-out gambles," Train noted, however. "Since he buys only the very cheapest merchandise, should something go wrong, it hasn't far to fall."

One final area Neff examined: free cash flow. He believed that—particularly in an era in which earnings are more and more susceptible to accounting gimmickry—it was important to make sure firms had positive cash flows, which can help them buy back stock, pay dividends, or make acquisitions.

Discipline and Dedication

Over the years, of course, Neff's portfolio did a lot more rising than falling, making him one of the most successful investors in history—and probably one of the richest. But if you saw him walking down the street, you might not know it. "Modest, gray, and unspectacular" is how John Train described Neff in *Money Masters of Our Time*. "He looks and acts not at all the Wall Street hotshot, but the Midwestern executive: nice house, a little way out of town; wife of over 30 years; simple, unfashionable, and slightly messy clothes; no magnificent paneled office, just the disorderly, paper-strewn den one expects of a college department head."

"In his private life," Train continues, "[Neff] operates with the same philosophy that he applies to buying stocks. His house has few frills except for a tennis court, on which he plays a ferocious game on Saturdays. He likes to describe how cheaply he has bought equipment or clothing, shopping for his footgear at Lou's Shoe Bazaar and his jackets at Sym's, a discounter."

Just as success apparently didn't alter Neff's understated personal style, it also didn't appear to change the intense, hardworking approach that helped him achieve his initial success. In the foreword to *John Neff on Investing*, Charles D. Ellis (former managing partner of the consulting firm Greenwich Associates) writes:

> In addition to being original, independent, and very rational in his evaluations, John knew more because he worked longer and harder. . . . At home (or wherever he might be visiting), every Saturday at 1:00 P.M., John retires to the privacy of his room to read—again—every word in every issue of the *Wall Street Journal* for the preceding week of business. This is only one evidence of the remarkable self-discipline with which this unique professional prepares himself for the very competitive work of professional investment management.

In addition, Train also noted that Neff worked 60 to 70 hours a week, including about 15 hours each weekend.

What's crucial to note, however, is that Neff didn't just show discipline in his intense work schedule and research. He also demonstrated it in his willingness to stick to his strategy when times got tough, or when other flash-in-the-pan strategies were producing better short-term gains. To Neff, investing was a race to be won by the slow and steady, not those seeking big, easy rewards. Yes, occasionally you'll be lucky and reap a windfall from a stock pick, he wrote. But for the most part, he says, investing is "a four-yard gain and a cloud of dust," a term used to describe football teams whose offenses advance the ball not with long, flashy but risky 30- or 40-yard passing plays, but instead with simple, persistent low-risk running plays that gain a few yards at a time. "My investment style can give investors a lucrative edge over the long haul," Neff wrote. "But if you can't roll with the hits, or you're in too big a hurry, you might as well keep your money in a mattress." That's wise advice—no matter what investment strategy you follow.

The Toughest Task

The most difficult decision for an investor, Neff says, isn't deciding which stocks to buy, but deciding when to sell. "Beyond picking good low P/E stocks, Windsor's performance rested equally, if not more, on a firm selling strategy," he wrote. "You can be right as rain about a stock's potential, but if you hold on too long, you may end up with nothing."

We agree. (In fact, we've even dedicated an entire chapter—Chapter 14—to knowing when to sell.) But while many of the gurus give detailed advice on how to buy stocks, few give advice about when to sell, despite the importance of that decision.

Neff does, however, and discipline plays a key role in his selling strategy. He says one problem investors run in to is that they fall in love with a winning stock and hold onto it too long—"particularly when [their] contrarian stance has been vindicated." Many investors also fear that they will sell winners too soon and miss out on even greater gains—a fear Neff didn't succumb to at Windsor. "Instead of groping for the last dollar, we gladly left some upside on the table," he wrote. "Catching market tops was not our game. This was preferable to getting caught in a subsequent downdraft, which is never a pretty picture."

Neff says that Windsor sold stocks for two main reasons: deterioration in the stock's fundamentals (particularly in its earnings estimates or five-year growth rates), or the stock's price approached the firm's expectations. Windsor developed these price expectations for each stock it owned, using earnings estimates and the projected expansion of the stock's P/E ratio. It also adjusted these targets based on market climate. "We did not let absolute numbers beguile or dazzle us," Neff wrote.

Our own selling strategy differs from Neff's in some regards, as you'll see in Chapter 14. But we agree that one of the most important things an investor can do is stick to a firm selling strategy—whatever the details of that strategy may be.

Neff's Strategy: Step by Step

About the John Neff Strategy

The Track Record:	Neff's Windsor Fund (operated first under Wellington Management Company and later under the Vanguard Group) averaged a 13.7 percent annual return, net of fees, from 1964 through 1995, significantly outpacing the S&P 500's 10.6 percent average return during that period. That represents one of the best—if not the best—track records of all-time for such a large fund over such a long duration.
Risk:	Fairly Low. Neff focused on stocks whose prices had already been beaten down, so even if the company performed poorly its stock didn't have much further to fall. In addition, he focused on companies that paid strong dividends, income you can count on even when the stock isn't climbing.
Time Horizon:	Variable. Neff wrote that Windsor was willing to hold stocks for three, four, or even five years if their fundamentals remained intact. However, he also said that every stock Windsor owned was for sale; if one of his holdings' fundamentals and/or price changed so that he believed it no longer had good appreciation potential, he might sell after holding it for only a month—and he sometimes earned impressive profits doing just that.
Effort:	Moderate. Neff was a voracious researcher, and his quantitative method is fairly stringent. Modern stock screening technology makes some of that easier for today's average investor, however.

As you've seen, the stocks John Neff focused on weren't the type that generated a lot of discussion at cocktail parties or the office water cooler. They were instead those that were avoided by the majority of other investors, sometimes because they came from struggling industries or were the victims of bad headlines, and other times because they were flat-out boring companies. In that sense, Neff could certainly be considered a contrarian. But his reliance on the price-earnings ratio as a way to identify undervalued stocks led him to prefer another label—"low-price-earnings investor."

We'll thus begin the explanation of our Neff-based model with the critical variable Neff included it in that self-description—the P/E ratio.

Price-Earnings Ratio (P/E) Neff first and foremost focused on firms with below average P/E ratios. His rationale: Stocks with high P/E ratios have higher expectations, as shown by the fact that investors are willing to pay a higher price now for the company's future earnings. If the firm fails to meet those high expectations, the stock will fall— even if performance is reasonably good. Stocks with low P/Es, on the other hand, have much lower expectations. Any improvement in the company's performance will likely lead to the stock rising. Meanwhile poor performance isn't likely to hurt the stock too much, since expectations were already so low.

Neff wrote that the stocks the Windsor Fund bought usually had P/Es that were 40 to 60 percent below the market average, so that is the range we use in our Neff-based model. This identifies stocks that are unpopular on Wall Street. The criteria below will detail how Neff used other fundamental tests to make sure a low-P/E stock wasn't unpopular for good reason—that is, it was simply a dog.

P/E Ratio

1. ≥ 40% of market average and ≤ 60% of market average   Pass
2. >60% of market average   Fail
3. <40% of market average   Fail

EPS Growth Rate One way Neff separated promising low-P/E firms from others was by looking at EPS growth. He believed that very high growth rates could be dangerous because they usually come with high price tags even though investors can't count on them continuing forever. He preferred consistent, reasonable growth. Low P/E companies growing faster than 7 percent "tipped us off to underappreciated signs of life," he wrote; growth higher than 20 percent usually involved too much risk, however.

EPS Growth

1. ≥ 7% and ≤ 20%   Pass
2. <7%   Fail
3. >20%   Fail

Future EPS Growth Rate When it came to the future, Neff acknowledged that it is impossible to predict with certainty what earnings will be. However, he indicated that Windsor looked for stocks with reasonable and sustainable growth rates that would eventually catch investors' eyes.

According to Neff's strategy, companies with forward-looking growth rates less than 6 percent seldom made the cut. For our Neff-based model, we use that 6 percent figure. To confirm a company's historical growth rate, we make sure the consensus future growth rate estimate of analysts is greater than 6 percent for both the current fiscal year and the long term.

Analysts' Consensus EPS Growth Estimate

1. >6% for current year AND >6% for long term   Pass
2. ≤ 6% for current year AND/OR ≤ 6% for long term   Fail

Sales Growth Neff believed that profit margins could only expand for so long. "Eventually," he wrote, "attractive companies must demonstrate sales growth." Neff didn't specify exactly the sales growth rate he liked to see, so, in keeping with the general spirit of his growth discussion, our Neff-based model requires a firm's sales growth rate to be at least 70 percent of its EPS growth rate.

There is a caveat, however. A company shouldn't be penalized if it has a nonsales-driven spike in EPS, so long as its sales growth is reasonably strong. If a firm's sales growth rate is less than 70 percent of its EPS growth rate, it can thus still pass this criterion if its sales growth rate is greater than 7 percent.

Sales Growth

1. ≥ 70% of EPS growth rate   Pass
2. <70% of EPS growth rate but > 7%   Pass
3. <70% of EPS growth rate and ≤ 7%   Fail

Total Return/Price-Earnings Ratio To measure total return, Neff added a stock's EPS growth rate and its dividend yield. He liked a stock's total return/price-earnings ratio to be at least twice the market average—or at least twice its industry average—so those are the two ways a stock can pass this part of our Neff-based model. This criterion, the comparison of a stock's total return to its P/E ratio, was heavily relied on by Neff to establish that a stock was cheap compared to its industry or the market. It also gives weight to Neff's belief in the added attractiveness of dividend payments, which he believed many investors overlooked. Note, however, that Neff did not require that all his stocks have dividends (typically one third of his stocks did not have dividends).

Total Return/Price-Earnings Ratio*

1. ≥ (Market total return/price-earnings ratio) × 2   Pass

2. ≥ (Industry total return/price-earnings ratio) × 2   Pass

3. (Market total return/price-earnings ratio) × 2 *and*   Fail
   < (Industry total return/price-earnings ratio) × 2

*For reference purposes, at the time of this writing, the market's total return is 0.76 (an average of all stocks in the S&P 500) and the market's average P/E is 17.29 (again using the S&P 500).

Note: The following two categories are minor criteria and count for substantially fewer points than the criteria listed above because Neff gave them less emphasis. Failing these criteria will not prevent a stock from receiving strong interest; nonetheless, they are areas to which Neff paid attention.

Free Cash Flow Neff believed that—particularly in an era in which earnings are more and more susceptible to accounting gimmickry—it was important to make sure firms had positive cash flows, which can help them buy back stock, pay dividends, or make acquisitions. If a company has a positive cash flow, it passes this part of our Neff model.

Free Cash Flow (per share)

1. > 0   Pass

2. ≤ 0   Fail

Earnings per Share Persistence Neff liked it when a stock's earnings per share for each of the past four quarters had been greater than the corresponding four quarters from a year earlier, showing consistent growth. That's the standard our Neff-based strategy uses.

EPS By Quarter (Q1 = most recent quarter; Q5 = 5 quarters ago)

1. Q1 > Q5, and Q2 > Q6, and Q3 > Q7, and Q4 > Q8   Pass
2. Q1 ≤ Q5, or Q2 ≤ Q6, or Q3 ≤ Q7, or Q4 ≤ Q8   Fail

 Click It!

If the Low P/E Investor approach appeals to you and you're looking for some Neff-type picks, visit www.guruinvestorbook.com. The free site lists three stocks that pass our Neff model every day, a good way to get ideas when building your portfolio.

The Neff-Based Model Performance

Our Neff-based model was not among the eight original Guru Strategies that we began tracking in 2003. It came on board a bit later, at the start of 2004, and since then it has performed quite well.

The 10-stock Neff portfolio was up 30.6 percent since its inception, more than tripling the 9.3 percent return of the S&P 500 during that time. The 20-stock model hasn't fared quite as well, but its 15.4 percent gain still outpaces that S&P figure. Both the 10- and 20-stock portfolios have incurred relatively low volatility, with betas of 1.14 and 1.16, respectively.

The 10-stock portfolio's best year in terms of percentage gain was 2006, when it jumped 22.3 percent compared to the S&P's 13.6 percent. Its first two years were even better in terms of performance versus the S&P, however: In 2004, it more than doubled the index, and in 2005 its 15 percent gain was more than five times that of the S&P. The 2007 year was its worst, as the value-centric portfolio dipped 1.9 percent compared to the S&P's 3.5 percent gain amid a major momentum market. The 20-stock portfolio also beat the market rather handily in its first three years before dropping 10.6 percent in 2007.

Much like Neff himself, the Neff-based model will often tread into areas where most investors aren't going because of its low-P/E focus, and often it will load up heavily in these areas. In January 2008, for example, when the subprime mortgage and credit crises had sent financials tumbling, the 10-stock Neff portfolio added five financials. When this happens, however, the model gets these types of unloved stocks at bargain prices, meaning that—just as was the case with many of Windsor's picks—they don't have a long way to fall if they don't bounce back. (See Table 4.1.)

Table 4.1   Model Portfolio Risk and Return Statistics

	10-Stock	20-Stock	S&P 500
Annualized Return	6.1%	3.2%	2.0%
Total Return	30.6%	15.4%	9.3%
Best Full Year	22.3% in 2006	21.6% in 2006	13.6% in 2006
Worst Full Year	−1.9% in 2007	−10.6% in 2007	3% in 2005
Beta	1.14	1.16	1.0
Accuracy	53.0%	51.8%	N/A

Note: Returns statistics are from Jan. 2, 2004 to July 15, 2008. See Appendix A for additional return disclosure and explanation.
Source: Guru Model Portfolio Tool, Validea.com.

Neff's Key Investment Criteria

- Focus on stocks with price-earnings ratios that are 40 to 60 percent of the market average—that is, unpopular stocks. People aren't expecting much from these companies, so any increased performance can lead to big gains, while poor performance doesn't hurt that much.
- Look for modest, steady, consistent, sales-driven growth.
- Use the total return/price-earnings ratio to see how much bang a stock will give you for your buck and find deep values.
- Look for stocks that pay nice dividends; because stock prices usually are driven by earnings, you often can essentially get dividend payments for free.
- Try to find firms with positive cash flows.
- Diversification is okay to a degree. But you should be willing to go where the best opportunities are regardless of industry or sector popularity.
- Stay disciplined. You beat the market by making slow and steady gains over time, not by trying to reap huge windfalls on certain stocks.

Chapter 5

David Dreman

The Great Contrarian

A crowd always thinks with its sympathy, never with its reason.
—WILLIAM R. ALGER (1822–1905), MINISTER,
THEOLOGIAN, AND WRITER

B y now, you've probably begun to notice a major similarity
among these legendary gurus—they are contrarians who tend
to operate against conventional wisdom. If most investors are
rushing to buy a particular stock, you'll likely find the gurus selling or
avoiding it. Similarly, when most investors are steering clear of a stock,
you'll likely find investors like Graham and Neff taking a closer look at
it. And, over time, their willingness to go against the grain has earned
them millions.

So, when one investor from among this prestigious value-driven group is specifically known for being—as *Kiplinger's* magazine once put it—"the consummate contrarian," you know he must have a serious penchant for swimming upstream—not to mention the ability to do it well.

That consummate contrarian is David Dreman, and, when it came to the stream that is the stock market, he swam it just about as well as anyone. Dreman, an author, long-time *Forbes* columnist, and chairman and chief investment officer of Dreman Value Management, has made an incredibly successful career out of picking gems off the market's trash heap. His Kemper-Dreman High Return Fund was one of the best-performing mutual funds ever, ranking number one out of 255 funds in its peer groups from 1988 to 1998, according to Lipper Analytical Services. And when Dreman published *Contrarian Investment Strategies: The Next Generation* in 1998, the fund had been ranked number one in more time periods than any of the 3,175 funds in Lipper's database.

Who Is David Dreman?

The son of the chief trader at a large commodity firm in Winnipeg, Canada, Dreman started on the road to investment management at an early age. Born in 1936, he has long been fascinated with the stock market, and would often accompany his father to floor of the exchange as a youngster. According to Dreman Value Management's website, while at the exchange he was able to observe first hand the dynamics of a very active market—and the reaction of the traders and the markets in general.

After graduating from the University of Manitoba, Dreman began his career working as a security analyst at his father's trading firm in Winnipeg. He later served as head of research at Rauscher Pierce Refsnes in New York and as a senior investment officer with J&W Seligman.

In 1977, Dreman opened his own firm. Soon he was posting impressive results by focusing on stocks that were overlooked, "beaten up," or sometimes in the midst of an outright crisis. He loaded up on these stocks, and unloaded them when the market valued them at about the same level it valued most stocks.

For example, in 2000, while other investors fled in droves from tobacco giant Altria (formerly Philip Morris) after the company was targeted in major lawsuits, Dreman swooped in. A few years later, when Tyco was dealing with its embarrassing CEO fiasco, Dreman snatched up its shares, too. He took some heat for those decisions, but by sticking to his unpopular belief that those firms had value, he ended up netting huge gains. In a way, Dreman built his portfolio with all the kids nobody else wants in gym class; then he proceeded to watch his team beat the stuffing out of the more popular challengers.

The Contrarian Strategy: Psychology Meets Investing

Dreman, whose company now manages more than $20 billion in assets, embraces his contrarian reputation. He uses the word "contrarian" in the title of several of his books on investing, and the jacket of *Contrarian Investment Strategies* refers to his yacht, named *The Contrarian*. While there may well be a naturally rebellious side to him, there are also some very concrete, intelligent, and observant reasons that Dreman adopted his swim-against-the-tide approach.

More so than perhaps any other guru we'll examine, Dreman is a student of investor psychology. In fact, his first book, written in 1977, was titled *Psychology and the Stock Market* (unless otherwise noted, however, all quoted material for this chapter comes from *Contrarian Investment Strategies,* which also deals heavily with investor psychology). This makes Dreman particularly worth reading because he presented not only an implementable, proven strategy for investing; he also addressed the psychological reasons that many investors fail. Being aware of these dangers is useful, whether you are using Dreman's strategy or a different one.

In *Contrarian Investment Strategies,* Dreman essentially states that he believes there are relatively simple, proven strategies you can use to beat the market—particularly contrarian approaches—yet most investors "cannot follow through" and stick to these strategies. Why can't they?

According to Dreman, investors cannot follow simple strategies to beat the market because they are prone to overreaction, and, under certain well-defined circumstances, overreact predictably and systematically. For instance, if a stock is considered "good"—it's one of the "hot" stocks you read about in the paper, hear about on cable TV, or get tips about from your friends and coworkers—investors consistently overprice it. If a stock is "bad"—its price has been dropping, the company is making negative headlines, there are concerns about its industry's future—investors underprice it. What's more, this overvaluing of the supposed "best" stocks and undervaluing of the supposed "worst" often goes to extremes.

Dreman also found that the market is driven by how investors react (or, perhaps more to the point, overreact) to "surprises." These frequent surprises include earnings reports that exceed or fall short of expectations, government actions that might affect a stock, or news about new products. What's more, he believed that these surprises were often precipitated by analysts—mainly Wall Street analysts—who were more often than not wrong about their earnings forecasts. He writes:

> There is only a 1 in 130 chance that the analysts' consensus forecast will be within 5 percent for any four consecutive quarters.... To put this in perspective, your odds are ten times greater of being the big winner of the New York State Lottery than of pinpointing earnings five years ahead. (Dreman's emphasis)

When you put investors' tendency to overreact together with the frequent surprises in the market, you get to the crux of why Dreman believed so much in a contrarian approach. Surprises occur a lot, he believed, and because the "best" stocks are often overvalued, good surprises can't increase their values that much more. Bad surprises, however, can have a very negative impact on them. On the other hand, because they already tend to be undervalued, the "worst" stocks don't have much further down to go when bad surprises occur. When good surprises occur, however, they have a lot of room to grow. And, Dreman found, the effect of an earnings surprise continues for an extended period of time.

His conclusion: Buy out-of-favor stocks because surprises (positive and negative ones) are commonplace. If you own favorites, you'll get clobbered by negative surprises but won't get much upside by positive surprises; whereas if you own out-of-favor stocks, you'll hardly be penalized for negative surprises but will be rewarded handsomely by positive ones.

This sounds logical, but Dreman found that even people who had an idea of this concept often didn't follow it. Part of the explanation for that, he found, was that people tend to be overly optimistic. They have unrealistic optimism about future events, thinking such events will come out better than they realistically are likely to be. In other words, they view themselves in an unrealistically positive light and they have unrealistic confidence in their ability to control a situation. For example, they may believe that having lots of information will shield them from surprises in the market because they have studied everything worth studying and therefore know all that's worth knowing.

An example Dreman gives regarding how this overoptimism can play out is the securities analyst who knows that high-flying stocks will drop from the skies faster than a pelican diving for a fish if earnings come in below the Street's expectations. Yet the same analyst will still recommend high flyers because he is confident he knows enough about the stocks he has recommended so there is no chance they will experience negative surprises. That might happen to other analysts, he thinks, but not to him. Of course, given the unpredictability of the market and events surrounding it, there's a good chance it will happen to him.

The bottom line for Dreman is that investors should never underestimate the probability of a negative surprise occurring, because they occur quite often, and can send an overvalued stock tumbling.

Taking Advantage

If all of this negativity is getting you down, don't worry: There's good news in all of this. Because so many investors have the same emotional and psychological responses to the market, Dreman believes that the wise investor can beat the market by going against the grain and focusing on stocks that are priced lowest in relation to certain fundamentals. History backs this idea up, he notes, saying:

> The findings show that companies the market expects the best futures for, as measured by the price/earnings, price-to-cash flow, price-to-book value, and price-to-dividend ratios, have consistently done the worst, while the stocks believed to have the most dismal futures have always done the best. (Dreman's emphasis).

Dreman goes further than just identifying unloved stocks with these four measures. He also wants to make sure that a firm is financially strong; he's interested in companies whose stocks are selling on the cheap because of overreaction and fear—not because there are real problems with the firm. He thus looks at a variety of other fundamental factors—return on equity, profit margins, debt-equity ratio, and yield— to make sure a company is standing on solid financial footing. (We'll look in more detail at all of the criteria Dreman uses in the "Step by Step" section of this chapter.)

Better for the Bear

One of the benefits of Dreman's strategy is that stocks meeting any of the four contrarian indicators he cites—low price-earnings, price-cash flow, price-book, or price-dividend ratios—tend to outperform the market and their more popular counterparts during bear markets. Dreman supported this contention by measuring the average quarterly returns for each of the four contrarian groups—low P/E, low P/CF, low P/B, and low P/D stocks—in all of the quarters in which the market was down from 1970 to 1996. He found that stocks in each of the four contrarian categories beat the market, on average, in those down-market quarters—and that they beat high P/E, high P/B, high P/CF, and high P/D stocks by even more. Here's a look at just how much better the contrarian methods fared when the going got rough:

Average Quarterly Return During Down-Market Quarters, 1970–1996

Low price-dividend stocks:	−3.8 percent
Low P/E stocks:	−5.7 percent
Low price-cash flow stocks:	−5.8 percent
Low price-book value stocks:	−6.2 percent
Market average:	−7.5 percent
High P/E stocks:	−9.5 percent (approx.)
High price-book value stocks:	−9.5 percent (approx.)
High price-cash flow stocks:	−9.5 percent (approx.)
Low-yield (high price-dividend) stocks:	−12.2 percent

Dreman also found that his contrarian approach had broader applications. He once told *Fortune* that he focused not only on individual contrarian companies, but also on industries that have characteristics similar to out-of-favor companies. "What makes High-Return [one of his funds] different from most funds is that I can, and will, take big positions in certain sectors," he said. "I don't load up on one stock, but I will buy many stocks in the same industry when it looks like an industry is in crisis and trading at ridiculously cheap levels."

As an example, he pointed out that banks "were literally being given away" in 1990, so he bought those and did well with them. This could be a strategy individual investors might pursue: Find an industry that is out of favor and buy several of its members. If you try this kind of industry play, follow Dreman's overall contrarian strategy, which is looking for the most unpopular stocks, defined as those fitting his four contrarian characteristics—low price-earnings, low price-book, low price-cash flow, or high yields.

Another important point to remember is that Dreman buys for profit over the relatively longer term—two to three years—and his studies show that it is even profitable to hold as long as eight years. So if you follow this strategy, you need to be prepared to sit with stocks that are out of favor with the market for a couple of years in order to hold the stock when it turns around and makes its move.

How to React to a Major Market Crisis

One final note on Dreman's take on investor psychology involves "crisis investing." While most investors flee the market at the sign of a crisis—be it economic, political, governmental, or some other type—Dreman, not surprisingly, will do the opposite. "A market crisis presents an outstanding opportunity to profit, because it lets loose over-reaction at its wildest," he wrote. "People no longer examine what a stock is worth; instead, they are fixated by prices cascading ever lower.... Further, the event triggering the crisis is always considered to be something entirely new." He goes on to say, "Buy during a panic, don't sell."

In *Contrarian Investment Strategies,* Dreman provides a table that shows what he calls "11 major postwar crises." These include the Berlin blockade, Korean War, Kennedy assassination, Gulf of Tonkin crisis, 1979–1980 oil crisis, and 1990 Persian Gulf War. He shows how, one year after all but one (the Berlin Blockade, when the market dropped), the market was up between 22.9 percent and 43.6 percent, except for a 7.2 percent rise after the Gulf of Tonkin crisis. The average gain was 25.8 percent. Two years after the crisis, the average gain was 37.5 percent. It's worth noting that following the September 11 terrorist attacks, which occurred after Dreman wrote *Contrarian Investment Strategies,* it took just one month for the S&P 500 to climb back to pre-September 11 levels; a year after the attacks, however, the index had fallen below pre-September 11 levels, the dot-com meltdown no doubt being a factor.

Dreman's analysis doesn't take every single crisis into consideration, but he analyzed most of the major ones between the end of World War II and the writing of his book, and his argument is compelling. Bad news often gives the market the jitters, only to have it recover when the bad news turns out not to be as devastating as first feared, and the savvy investor can take advantage of that knowledge.

Redefining Risk

One of the more intriguing parts of Dreman's philosophy is his take on the concept of risk. Traditionally, investors view "risk" as being synonymous with "volatility." In other words, they believe that to get higher returns, they must be willing to stomach bigger short-term swings in a stock's price.

Dreman, the contrarian, not surprisingly disagrees. "It has been known for decades that there is no correlation between risk, as the academics define it, and return," he writes. "Higher volatility does not give better results, nor lower volatility worse." Studies have shown, he says, that there is not necessarily any stable long-term relationship between risk and return, and often there is no relationship between the return achieved and the risk taken. "Volatility is not risk," he says, warning, "Avoid investment advice based on volatility."

So if volatility is not risk, what is? To Dreman, risk was the chance that you might not meet your long-term investment goals. And the greatest enemy of reaching those goals: inflation. He writes:

> An all-encompassing strain of risk permanently entered the investment environment for the first time after World War II. The virulent new risk is called inflation. Nothing is safe from this virus, although its major victims are savings accounts, T-bills, bonds, and other types of fixed-income investments....

One of the points Dreman is making is that investors usually use Treasury bills as their benchmark for risk. These are considered risk-free because their nominal value can't go down. For Dreman, though, T-bills and bonds are in fact highly risky because of their susceptibility to inflation. For example, if you buy a 10-year T-bill that pays 3 percent in interest per year, and inflation is creeping up at, say, 2 percent per year, the real value of your investment at maturity will end up being significantly less than 3 percent greater than the price you paid for it. In the case of low-interest-paying T-bills, higher inflation could even mean that your investment loses value, in terms of real purchasing power, over its lifetime.

> *The major risk is not the short-term stock price volatility that many thousands of academic articles have been written about. Rather it is the possibility of not reaching your long-term investment goal through the growth of your funds in real terms. To measure monthly or quarterly volatility and call it risk—for investors who have time horizons 5, 10, 15, or even 30 years away—is a completely inappropriate definition.* (Dreman's emphasis)

Dreman says a realistic definition of risk recognizes the potential loss of capital through inflation and taxes, and includes:

1. The probability your investment will preserve your capital over your investment time horizon.
2. The probability your investments will outperform alternative investments during the period.

In the short term, stocks fluctuate unpredictably, so if you're saving to buy a house or a car within the next two years or so, bonds and T-bills are a good choice. But over the long term, stocks far more often than not outperform alternative investments like bonds or T-bills, according to Dreman.

In fact, Dreman's research shows that inflation-adjusted returns for stocks—which, unlike bonds or T-bills have the ability to produce increasing earnings streams—have consistently outpaced those of bonds and T-bills since the start of the 1800s. The gap has widened since the mid-1920s, when inflation began to have a more significant impact.

What's more, from 1946 to 1996, according to Dreman, compound returns after inflation for stocks were better than those of bonds 84 percent of the time if your holding period was five years. Stocks also outperformed T-bills in 82 percent of those five-year periods. Using 10-year periods, stocks beat bonds 94 percent of the time and T-bills 86 percent of the time. When you look at 20-year holding periods, stocks beat both bonds and T-bills 100 percent of the time.

To Dreman the lesson is clear: Using his definition of risk, stocks are actually the safest investment out there over the long term. Investors who put some or most of their money into bonds and other investments on the assumption they are lowering their risk are, in fact, deluding themselves. "Indeed," he writes, "it goes against the principle we were taught from childhood—that the safest way to save was putting our money in the bank."

Dreman's Strategy: Step by Step

About the David Dreman Strategy

The Track Record: Dreman's Kemper-Dreman High Return Fund was one of the best-performing mutual funds ever, ranking as the best of 255 funds in its peer groups from 1988 to 1998, according to Lipper Analytical Services. At the time Dreman published *Contrarian Investment Strategies: The Next Generation,* the fund had been ranked number one in more time periods than any of the 3,175 funds in Lipper's database.

Risk:	Fairly Low. Dreman focused on stocks whose prices had already been beaten down, so even if the company performed poorly its stock didn't have much further to fall. In addition, he focused on companies that paid strong dividends, income you can count on even when the stock isn't climbing.
Time Horizon:	Dreman's time horizon is two to eight years; if a company has not turned things around largely within two years, he usually sells and moves on.
Effort:	Relatively low to medium.

Now that we have a general understanding of the principles that govern Dreman's investment philosophy, let's look at how we can implement this guru's strategy for investing in stocks. Because Dreman's approach incorporates a variety of different variables, many of which accomplish different general tasks, we've broken our Dreman-based methodology down into a few main categories: contrarian indications; size and earnings; and strong financial position and favorable ratios.

Look for Contrarian Indications

Dreman believed that investors' penchant for overreaction often makes popular stocks overpriced and unpopular stocks underpriced. Because of that, popular stocks have a long way to fall if they don't meet expectations, and little room to climb in the event they meet or exceed expectations. Because unpopular stocks are often already undervalued, however, they have a lot of room to climb if the company meets or exceeds expectations, and not much room to fall if the company disappoints. By focusing on unpopular stocks that had strong underlying businesses, Dreman thus believed he limited his risk and increased his chance at picking winners.

The first main part of the Dreman methodology is thus to find "contrarian" stocks—those that are undervalued based on their fundamentals. Dreman did this by comparing a stock's price to four different financial variables that measured the strength of a company's underlying business: earnings, cash flow, book value, and dividend yield. In order to eliminate weak companies, we have stipulated that a stock should pass at least two of the following four major contrarian criteria in order to receive some interest from the Dreman-based model.

Price-Earnings Ratio If a stock is producing high earnings relative to the price you're paying for its shares, that's an indication of a good value. Dreman conducted studies from 1970 to 1996 that showed stocks with P/Es in the bottom 20 percent of the market had an average annual return of 19 percent versus 15.1 percent for the market. His studies also showed that low P/E stocks have higher returns than high P/E stocks (they returned 12.3 percent) while exposing the investor to less risk.

Since Dreman's studies targeted stocks in the bottom 20 percent of the market according to P/E, that's the standard we use for this criterion.

P/E Ratio

1. In bottom 20% of market   Pass
2. Not in bottom 20% of market   Fail

Price-Cash Flow Ratio A strong cash flow indicates a company is taking in a good deal more money than it is sending out, a great sign. If a firm's stock price is low relative to the cash flow it is generating, therefore, that's another signal that it's being undervalued and fits the contrarian bill.

As with the P/E ratio, Dreman looked for stocks with P/CF values in the bottom 20 percent of the overall market, so that's the standard a stock has to meet in this criterion of our Dreman-based model. In studies conducted from 1970 to 1996, Dreman showed that stocks that had P/CF ratios in the bottom 20 percent of the market returned 18 percent, versus 15.1 percent for the market. His studies also proved that lower P/CF stocks have greater returns than higher P/CF stocks, while incurring less risk.

Dreman defines cash flow as "after-tax earnings, adding back depreciation and other noncash charges. It is a measure of a company's real earnings power, as well as an indicator of its financial viability."

In applying Dreman's strategy to our model portfolio, price-cash flow ratio is a particularly good measure for finding bargain cyclical companies during a recession, when the traditional P/E ratio tends to get very high or is not calculable because a firm has no earnings.

Price-Cash Flow Ratio (P/CF)

1. In bottom 20% of market   Pass
2. Not in bottom 20% of market   Fail

Price-Book Ratio Book value is another indication of what a company's business is really worth, so by comparing book value to share price you can get an idea of whether the stock is an undervalued, contrarian pick.

According to Dreman, book value is the value of a company's common stock less all liabilities and preferred shares. Our Dreman-based model looks for stocks with a P/B value in the bottom 20 percent of the overall market, because that's again what Dreman used in his research. In studies of stock market returns from 1970 to 1996, he found that stocks with P/B ratios in the bottom 20 percent of the market had an average annual return of 18.8 percent versus 15.1 percent for the market. His studies also proved that low P/B stocks have greater returns than high P/B stocks while incurring less risk.

Price-Book Ratio (P/B)

1. In bottom 20% of market   Pass
2. Not in bottom 20% of market   Fail

Price-Dividend Ratio The final way Dreman looked for stocks whose fundamentals were strong compared to their stock prices—i.e. those that were contrarian picks—was by looking at the price/dividend ratio. As with the other three contrarian indicators, our Dreman-based model looks for stocks in the bottom 20 percent of the market in terms of P/D ratio, since that's what Dreman used in his book. (Looked at another way, the yield—the dollar amount of dividends for the last four quarters divided by the current share price—should be in the top 20 percent.) Dreman conducted studies from 1970 to 1996 that showed stocks with P/D ratios in the bottom 20 percent of the market had an average annual return of 16.1 percent versus 15.1 percent for the market.

Dreman was cautious about investing on the basis of this criterion, as it is mainly for income-seeking investors, who are better off investing in stocks that pass this criterion rather than investing in bonds. For investors with different objectives, this is a very useful criterion that should be used in conjunction with Dreman's other criteria. We use it in our model in conjunction with the three other contrarian indicators.

Price-Dividend Ratio (P/D)

1. In bottom 20% of market   Pass
2. Not in bottom 20% of market   Fail

Size and Earnings

Knowing that a stock achieves "contrarian" status wasn't enough for Dreman to invest in it. He found that size and earnings power also had a big impact on the returns of contrarian picks.

Market Cap Dreman believed that the investor is exposed to less risk of accounting gimmickry when investing in larger firms. In addition, he believed that larger companies are more in the public eye and tend to have more staying power. He thus focused his stock picking on medium-sized to large-sized companies (the largest 1,500 companies in the market), so that's a requirement of our Dreman-based model. At the time of this writing, the minimum market capitalization a company must have to get into the group of the 1,500 largest companies is about $1.87 billion, but that figure will fluctuate.

Market Cap

1. Among 1,500 largest publicly traded stocks   Pass
2. Not among 1,500 largest publicly traded stocks   Fail

Earnings Trend Dreman liked to see a rising trend in the reported earnings for the most recent quarters. In the model we base on his writings, we require the most recent quarter (Q1) to have greater earnings than the previous quarter (Q2).

Earnings Trend
1. EPS Q1 > EPS Q2   Pass
2. EPS Q1 ≤ EPS Q2   Fail

EPS Growth in the Immediate Past and Future For noncyclical companies only, Dreman liked earnings to have grown more than the S&P 500's earnings grew in the immediate past, and he also made sure of the likelihood that the firm's earnings would not plummet in the near future.

For the past EPS growth, he looked at the past six months. The company's growth rate over that period (i.e., from Q3 to Q1) and its estimated growth rate for the current year both had to be greater than the same figures, respectively, for the S&P 500. To pass this test on our Dreman model, a stock must meet both those standards.

EPS Growth in the Immediate Past and Future

1. EPS growth from Q3 to Q1 > S&P 500 growth Q3 to Q1 *and*   Pass
   projected growth for this year > S&P 500 growth for this year
2. EPS growth from Q3 to Q1 ≤ S&P 500 growth Q3 to Q1 *and/or*   Fail
   projected growth for this year ≤ S&P 500 growth for this year

Note: Dreman suggests that cyclical companies are better evaluated using a price-cash flow ratio.

Keep in mind that sometimes stock prices are irrationally battered down from a temporary depression in earnings. Dreman sees these occurrences as opportunities for buying good stocks at cheap prices. To determine whether a depression in earnings is a temporary feature or the result of long-term weakness in the company, the first criterion we use is that the projected EPS growth rate for the next few quarters should be greater than that projected for the same quarters for the S&P 500. It is also desirable if the estimated EPS growth rate for the next year (compared with the current year) should be greater than that of the S&P 500.

The next criterion in this "dip" situation is that projected EPS in either of the next two quarters should be greater than the quarter before the earnings dip. Put another way, Dreman wanted to see that earnings will more than bounce back quickly, indicating that the dip is projected to not be long term. He used conservative (low) EPS estimates, if available. One important note in comparing earnings estimates to actual historical earnings: Estimates are usually based on fully diluted earnings before extraordinary items. That means when you compare estimates with historical earnings, you must be sure you are using the fully diluted historical earnings before the extraordinary items.

If, using the low estimate, the EPS for the next quarter, or the quarter after, is greater than the company's actual EPS two quarters ago, then we can infer that even the most conservative analyst thinks the company's EPS will improve next quarter or the quarter after. In other words, the stock is turning around and moving above and beyond the earnings dip.

Alternatively, if the projected EPS for the next two quarters is not greater than the EPS in the quarter before the dip, it is possible that the dip in earnings is part of a long-term sickness in the company. Thus it would not pass this criterion.

Look for Strong Financial Position and Favorable Ratios

The final part of the Dreman methodology involves looking for as many healthy financial ratios as possible to ascertain the financial strength of the company. Dreman wanted to be sure he was investing in strong firms whose stocks were being beaten down because of irrational fear or negative hype—not firms whose stocks were struggling because of long-term financial problems. The criteria detailed below help make sure a company is on strong financial footing.

Current Ratio According to Dreman, a prospective company must have a strong current ratio, which measures the ratio of current assets to current liabilities. The current ratio is often an indicator of a company's ability to pay its current (one year or less) debts. Dreman wanted to see a current ratio higher than the average of the company's industry, or greater than 2. He feels this criterion is a good identifier of financially strong companies. If a company passes either of those standards (or both), it passes this test in our Dreman-based model.

Current Ratio

1. > Industry average or > 2   Pass
2. ≤ Industry average *and* ≤ 2   Fail

Payout Ratio A good indicator that a company has the ability to raise its dividend is a low payout ratio, which is the percent of a company's earnings that it pays out in dividends. Dreman found that if the recent payout ratio is less than the stock's 5- to 10-year historical average, there is a lot of room for the company to increase its dividend. Our Dreman model targets firms whose current payout ratios are lower than their historical payout ratios.

Payout Ratio

1. < Average historical payout ratio   Pass
2. ≥ Average historical payout ratio   Fail

Note: If payout ratio is > 40 percent and ≤ 80 percent and company is an electric or water utility, the stock passes. This is low for these types of companies.

Return on Equity Dreman said that return on equity is an important way to measure how profitable a business is. A stock should have a high ROE, as this helps to ensure there are no structural flaws in the company. Dreman said the ROE should be greater than the ROE earned from the top one-third of the 1,500 largest-cap stocks and considered anything over 27 percent to be staggering. Our model calls for a stock to meet that first part (being in the top third of the 1,500 largest-cap stocks), and gives bonus points if the stock's ROE is above 27 percent.

Return on Equity (ROE)

1. In top third of 1,500 largest-cap stocks   Pass
   (as ranked by ROE)

2. > 27%   Pass—Best case

3. All others   Fail

Pretax Profit Margins Dreman believed profit margins were an important financial ratio because the higher and more stable they are, the better regarded the business is. As such, he looked for pretax profit margins of at least 8 percent and considered anything over 22 percent to be very impressive. This model thus looks for stocks to have pretax profit margins of at least 8 percent, and gives bonus points for anything over 22 percent.

Pretax Profit Margins

1. > 22%   Pass—Best case

2. ≥ 8%   Pass

3. < 8%   Fail

Yield Dreman found that contrarian stocks can often provide high dividend yields in addition to offering better appreciation potential than in-favor stocks. As such, he theorized that an above-average and growing dividend yield improved performance when used in conjunction with the primary rule of buying contrarian stocks. In the model portfolio that we developed, we consider high to be at least 1 percent higher than the yield of the Dow.

Yield

1. ≥ Dow yield + 1 percentage point   Pass
2. < Dow yield + 1 percentage point   Fail

Debt-Equity Ratio The company must have a low debt-equity ratio, which indicates a strong balance sheet. This is another way to make sure there are no major structural holes in a firm because high debt can lead to financial problems.

In the Dreman-based model we have determined a low debt-equity ratio to be less than 20 percent. Please note that we don't apply this ratio to financial companies such as banks because they inherently carry a lot of debt due to the nature of their businesses.

Debt-Equity Ratio (D/E)

1. = 0   Pass-Best Case
2. > 0 but ≤ 20%   Pass
3. > 20%   Fail

 Click It!

At this book's companion website, www.guruinvestorbook.com, you can view three stocks every day that pass our Dreman-based contrarian investor model. The free site also provides links to our analysis of just why a stock passes muster with the Dreman strategy.

The Dreman-Based Model Performance

Since we started tracking it in July 2003, our Dreman-based model has been one of our best performers. The 10-stock portfolio has gained 79.2 percent over the first five years, almost four times the S&P 500's gain during that time. Three times (2003, 2004, and 2006) it has returned over 30 percent, and one of the years it didn't (2005) its 18.4 percent return was more than six times greater than the S&P's gain (3 percent). The value-centric portfolio struggled in the unusually momentum-driven market of 2007, losing 12 percent, its only negative year. Our 20-stock Dreman-based portfolio has also fared quite well, gaining 77.5 percent since its July 2003 inception. Its best year percentage-wise was 2004, when it jumped 30.5 percent (compared to the S&P's 9 percent gain); but its best year in relation to the broader market was 2005, when it gained 21.5 percent—more than seven times the S&P's 3 percent gain. The portfolio's worst year was also 2007, when it dropped 7.8 percent.

Table 5.1 Model Portfolio Risk and Return Statistics

	10-Stock	20-Stock	S&P 500
Annualized Return	12.4%	12.1%	4.0%
Total Return	79.2%	77.5%	21.4%
Best Full Year	34.3% in 2006	30.5% in 2004	13.6% in 2006
Worst Full Year	−12.0% in 2007	−7.8% in 2007	3% in 2005
Beta	1.01	1.0	1.0
Accuracy	62.7%	61.8%	N/A

Note: Returns statistics are from July 15, 2003 to July 15, 2008. See Appendix A for additional return disclosure and explanation.
Source: Guru Model Portfolio Tool, Validea.com.

One interesting thing to note about the Dreman model is its lack of volatility. Since their inceptions, the 10- and 20-stock portfolios have betas of 1.01 and 1.0, respectively. This means that they have essentially been no more volatile than the broader market. Of course, given his take on volatility and risk, Dreman probably wouldn't pay much attention to these figures, as he focused much more on the long term than on short-term volatility. But for average investors who might not be as experienced in the market, or for those who tend to let their emotions get the best of them when investing, this model's lower volatility could make it an attractive choice.

Like Dreman himself, our Dreman-based model tends to gravitate toward firms from unloved industries. Over the past year, the portfolios have featured a number of financials, a group that has been dogged by the subprime mortgage crisis; as well as a bunch of firms from the energy sector, which has been dealing with a variety of issues (high costs of extracting oil, the push for alternative fuels, etc.). Some patience is often required in this model, as it can take time for the market to come around on beaten up industries. Over the long run, though, our model's success seems to back up Dreman's view that contrarian strategies can reap excellent gains if you stick with them. (See Table 5.1.)

Dreman's Key Investing Criteria

LOOK FOR CONTRARIAN INDICATIONS

The stock should pass two or more of the following criteria:

- Price-earnings (P/E) ratio is in bottom 20 percent of market.
- Price-cash flow (P/CF) ratio is in bottom 20 percent of market.
- Price-book (P/B) ratio is in bottom 20 percent of market.
- Price-dividend (P/D) ratio is in bottom 20 percent of market.

LOOK AT SIZE AND EARNINGS

- Pick from the 1,500 largest-cap stocks.
- Look for an increasing earnings trend.
- EPS growth in the immediate past and future should be greater than the market average.

LOOK AT THE FINANCIAL RATIOS

- Current ratio should be at least 2, or greater than the industry average.
- Payout ratio should be lower than historical average.
- Return on equity (ROE) should be in the top third of the 1,500 largest stocks.
- Pretax profit margins should be at least 8 percent.
- Yield should be significantly higher than the Dow.
- Debt-equity (D/E) ratio should be no greater than 20 percent.

Chapter 6

Warren Buffett

The Greatest Guru

Common sense is genius dressed in its working clothes.
                                    —RALPH WALDO EMERSON

I buy expensive suits. They just look cheap on me.
                                    —WARREN BUFFETT

The "Oracle of Omaha." The Richest Man in the World. The Greatest Investor of All Time. There are a lot of superlatives that can be used to describe Warren Buffett. But when you sort through all the hype—something Buffett himself excels at when investing—Warren Buffett is, simply put, a sensible, rational businessman who is very, very good at what he does. While many of today's celebrities are famous more for the way they market themselves than for their actual accomplishments, the reason Buffett has become the investing world's most famous member is, plain and simple, his track record. Over a 32-year period, his firm, the holding company Berkshire Hathaway, has averaged a 24 percent annual return for investors. That's 24 percent a year, on average, over *more than three decades*—perhaps the greatest track record ever.

Of course, personal style has added to Buffett's legend, but only in terms of its relative absence. While his net worth of $62 billion makes him the richest man in the world, Buffett's primary residence remains the gray stucco Nebraska home he purchased for $31,500 nearly 50 years ago, according to *Forbes*. His folksy Midwestern manner and penchant for simple pleasures—a cherry Coke, a good burger, and a good book are all near the top of the list—have been well-documented, offering a stark contrast to Wall Street's glamour and glitz. Yes, he travels by private jet, but he certainly isn't one for excess; after being married for the second time a few years back, the *New York Times* reported that he, his new bride, and two others dined not at a five-star restaurant but instead at Bonefish Grill, a seafood restaurant chain where you can get a center-cut filet mignon for less than $20.

Much like his personal style, Buffett's investing approach isn't flashy or eye-catching. A disciple of Ben Graham, Buffett has earned his billions by using a strict conservative philosophy that targets well-established, conservatively financed firms that have decade-long track records of success. You won't find him jumping from high-flying tech stock to high-flying tech stock. Instead, he invests in simple businesses with simple products that people can't or don't want to live without—Coca-Cola, Wal-Mart, Anheuser-Busch, and Burlington Northern Santa Fe Corp. (the railroad-transportation giant) are all major holdings of Berkshire—and then he holds on to them for years and years and years.

While many investors will try to pitch complicated, almost unintelligible investment schemes, Buffett breaks investing down to its core. He's not interested in speculation or hype; if a company is making the "next big thing", you probably won't see him buying it. He'd rather buy a proven, stable thing. His primary concerns are simple: What a business is really worth, and at what price can he get its stock (or the entire company). He doesn't try to capitalize on small day-to-day stock market movements the way traders do; instead, he focuses on a company's business—Is it financially sound? Is it likely to keep growing for years and years into the future? Is management doing a good job?—because he knows that, over time, the stocks of firms with strong businesses and good long-term prospects are likely to rise considerably, regardless of what those stocks are doing today or tomorrow or next week. Berkshire's annual letter to shareholders doesn't even measure performance by stock price changes. While the firm's numbers are often quite impressive on that basis, Buffett knows stock fluctuations, even year-to-year fluctuations, are subject to irrational investor behavior that can't be predicted. So instead, the letter lists Berkshire's annual percentage change in per-share book value. Focus on the business, and the stock will follow—that's the idea.

Buffett's brilliance is thus remarkable in its simplicity and sensibility. When you hear him speak, you don't get the sense that he is incredibly more intelligent than other investors, that he possesses some sort of extraordinary mind that can comprehend facts and figures that others can't; instead, you get the sense that he is the only sane man standing in the room full of crazies that is Wall Street. You hear what he has to say about business and you don't think, "Wow. How did he come up with that?" You think instead, "Gosh, why didn't I think of that?"

That's because Buffett, as much as anyone in the world, realizes that being a great investor is more about mindset than brainpower. "You have to have the right temperament," Money's Jason Zweig quoted him as saying at a May 2008 press conference. "I tell the students who come visit me that if you have more than 120 or 130 I.Q. points, you can afford to give the rest away. You don't need extraordinary intelligence to succeed as an investor. You need a philosophy and the ability to think independently. It doesn't make any difference what other people think of a stock. What matters is whether you know enough to evaluate the business." It's a basic concept, but amid all of the greed and fear and emotion that permeates Wall Street, it's one that is easily lost.

For all its simplicity and common sense, Buffett's approach is incredibly difficult for most investors to follow—not for its logistical intricacy or mathematical complexity, but because of the way it requires you to be so unemotional and rational in your decision-making—something that, as we discussed in Chapter 1, most humans fail miserably at. Buffett, however, has a rare ability to put emotions aside when investing. Asked by PBS' Susie Gharib in a May 2008 interview what makes his father so successful, Peter Buffett, the youngest of Buffett's three children, had this to say:

> I think it's because he's removed emotion from his decision-making. He is not colored by anything he thinks somebody else is doing, somebody else might want, some feeling he has about something that might not be rational. Ultimately, it's because he is clear and unemotional, dispassionate about his relationship to those numbers on the page and the information he's taking in.

Who Is Warren Buffett?

Buffett's common sense business acumen manifested itself not long after he was born on August 30, 1930, in Omaha. According to Warren Boroson in *J.K. Lasser's Pick Stocks Like Warren Buffett,* Buffett was supposedly six years old when he started buying six-packs of Coke for 25 cents and reselling them for 30 cents. At 11, he bought his first stock, three shares of Cities Service Preferred. He paid $38 a share, watched them drop to $27, held on until the stock rebounded, and sold for a $6 profit at $40. He learned that patience could be a virtue when the stock subsequently hit $200.

At 14, with savings from his two newspaper routes, Buffett reportedly bought 40 acres of Nebraska farmland for $1,200, which he leased. While still in high school, he bought pinball machines that he installed in barbershops and, by graduation, had earned $10,000, which is the equivalent of more than $100,000 in today's dollars.

Buffett came by his stock market interest honestly. His father, Howard Buffett, came from a line of grocers but decided to become a stockbroker. (Howard Buffett also had other aspirations as well—in 1942 he ran for Congress as a Republican and won.)

Not surprisingly, Buffett headed off to college with business on his mind. He first attended the University of Pennsylvania's Wharton School but transferred to the University of Nebraska, graduating in 1950. A voracious reader, Buffett picked up a book during his last year at Nebraska that would turn out to have a dramatic impact on his life, *The Intelligent Investor* by Ben Graham. Buffett became a big fan of Graham's. When Harvard turned him down for its MBA program, it probably did not come too much as a letdown. Instead Buffett attended Columbia University, where Graham taught, and became Graham's star student. To this day, he speaks with great reverence about Graham.

After earning his master's degree, Buffett began working at his mentor's New York firm. In 1956, he returned to Omaha and started his own investment partnership. His partners each put in $25,000 (supposedly, Buffett invested $100), and he appointed himself general partner. With the money he raised, Buffett began to buy stocks. He did well, earning a 29.5 percent compounded annual rate of return between the start of the partnership and its dissolution in 1969 versus 7.4 percent for the Dow. One of his investments in the 1960s was in a struggling textile mill in Massachusetts called Berkshire Hathaway. As Berkshire's textile business faded in the face of foreign competition, Buffett used its assets to buy other businesses

Over the years, Buffett built Berkshire up—and up and up and up. Today, the firm owns 76 operating businesses that combined have more than 230,000 employees and took in more than $13.2 billion in net earnings in 2007—a far cry from that struggling textile mill. Among its subsidiaries are a number of insurance companies, including GEICO, and an array of other businesses, such as Fruit of the Loom, Benjamin Moore, NetJets, and Shaw Industries. So revered is Berkshire that its annual meeting has become known as "Woodstock for capitalists." In 2008, the Omaha event drew about 30,000 people, many of whom were no doubt there to hear Buffett's trademark investment wisdom—and his trademark wit.

Warren's Wisdom

While Warren Buffett's fame is largely due to his incredible track record, the public's infatuation with him has also grown because of his straight-shooting wisdom and trademark quick wit. Here's a sampling of the sage advice and witty commentary that the man called the "Oracle of Omaha" has given over the years:

"It takes 20 years to build a reputation and five minutes to ruin it. If you think about that, you'll do things differently." (Quotedb.com)

"Investors should remember that excitement and expenses are their enemies. And if they insist on trying to time their participation in equities, they should try to be fearful when others are greedy and greedy only when others are fearful." (Berkshire Hathaway 2004 Letter to Shareholders)

"[It] comes about from having an investment philosophy grounded in the idea that a stock is a piece of a business. If you look at it that way, there's no reason to get excited whether some analyst is recommending it or the company is splitting the shares two-for-one, or whatever. The only way to drive the extraneous thoughts out of your mind is to have a philosophy. And for us that philosophy comes from Benjamin Graham and *The Intelligent Investor*, especially chapters 8 and 20. It's not very complicated stuff." (2008 Press Conference at Berkshire annual meeting)

"Our favorite holding period is forever." (Berkshire Hathaway 1988 Letter to Shareholders)

"I've reluctantly discarded the notion of my continuing to manage the portfolio after my death—abandoning my hope to give new meaning to the term "thinking outside the box." (Berkshire Hathaway 2007 Letter to Shareholders, explaining Berkshire's plans for his succession)

The Man behind the Fortune

How does Buffett feel about his cult status? Well, while he'll talk publicly about Berkshire and the markets, Buffett doesn't talk a whole lot about himself. But in April and May 2008, PBS television ran "Meet the Buffetts," a series of interviews with his three children that delved into the man behind the empire a bit. During her interview, Susie Buffett, the oldest of the three, was asked what her father thinks of his following. "I think he finds it sort of amusing and sweet and he appreciates that people feel that way," she responded. "Although I'm not sure he would even now say he thinks it's deserved or you know, that it really actually makes any sense that people think that much of him. I do."

The "Meet the Buffetts" feature also gave some more interesting insights into the richest man in the world. For example, Susie Buffett was also asked why her father, with all of his money, didn't indulge himself more. "Because that's not what he's interested in doing," she said. "If he wanted to have 20 houses or six yachts or, you know, fly to Paris every other week, he would do it. He doesn't like to do that. He likes to sit in his house, play bridge on his computer, hang out with my son, and my dad and I go to the movies almost every Sunday. You know, it's what he likes to do. He's doing what he likes to do."

Peter Buffett had similar thoughts. "My father isn't actually trying to make money," he said. "He loves what he does and the money just keeps coming out. The money is the byproduct. And it's a great score-card. It tells him he is doing a great job and he is the best at what he does. He is not making it to spend it or to make himself happy or look better to his friends."

Indeed, while Buffett by no means lives a pauper's lifestyle, he certainly doesn't seem to have the need to throw his money around the way many of his fellow billionaires do. Most of his wealth—about 99 percent, he stated in Berkshire's 2007 letter—remains tied up in Berkshire stock. And in July 2006, he announced that he'd begin gradually giving away about 85 percent of his Berkshire shares to five charities: the Bill & Melinda Gates Foundation (Buffett is good friends with the couple), three foundations that are each headed by one of Buffett's children, and the Susie Buffett Foundation, named after Buffett's late wife. About five-sixths of the shares—which altogether were worth about $37 billion when Buffett made his announcement—were earmarked for the Gates' foundation. (See Carol J. Loomis, "Warren Buffett Gives Away His Fortune," *Fortune,* June 25, 2006.)

Bet You Didn't Know This about Buffett

While Buffett's heartland America, salt-of-the-earth image is well known, his personal life has had at least one major unconventional streak that caught our eyes. After his first wife, Susan, left the couple's home and moved to San Francisco in the late 1970s after raising their three children, Buffett remained married to her, and the two remained close, according to a September 2006 *New York Times* article written by Jeff Bailey and Eric Dash ("How Does Warren Buffett Get Married? Frugally, It Turns Out.") But Susan Buffett introduced her husband to a friend, Latvian-born Astrid Menks, with whom she had worked at an Omaha restaurant. Warren and Astrid became longtime companions, while Astrid and Susan Buffett remained very close; according to Roger Lowenstein's "Buffett: The Making of an American Capitalist" (1995), friends would even receive cards from the Buffetts signed "Warren, Susie and Astrid." In 2006, two years after his first wife passed away, Buffett married Astrid, in a small ceremony.

The Patient Investor Strategy: Buy (with Great Care)-and-Hold (for a Long, Long Time)

As intriguing as Buffett the person is, what should really be of interest is learning how he made his fortune, so let's get down to business.

First off, be aware that Buffett is the lone guru we follow who hasn't written a book or paper that discloses his quantitative investing strategy. Our Buffett-based model is based on *Buffettology*, a 1997 book written by Buffett's former daughter-in-law, Mary Buffett, who worked closely with Warren. David Clark, a longtime friend of the Buffett family, coauthored the book.

Before we get into the more quantitative parts of Buffett's approach that Mary Buffett lays out, let's look at some of Buffett's broader investing principles. While he hasn't written his own book, Buffett will from time to time divulge parts of his approach—one of the best sources of these tidbits is his annual letter to Berkshire Hathaway shareholders—so for these we can go straight to the horse's mouth. (The annual letters can be found online on Berkshire's website at www.berkshirehathaway. com/reports.html).

In the company's 2007 letter, for example, Buffett reiterated that Berkshire was looking to make some significant acquisitions, and laid out six qualities that he and the company wanted to see in potential buys:

1. Large purchases (at least $75 million of pretax earnings unless the business will fit into one of our existing units).
2. Demonstrated consistent earning power (future projections are of no interest to us, nor are "turnaround" situations).
3. Businesses earning good returns on equity while employing little or no debt.
4. Management in place (we can't supply it).
5. Simple businesses (if there's lots of technology, we won't understand it).
6. An offering price (we don't want to waste our time or that of the seller by talking, even preliminarily, about a transaction when price is unknown).

This is classic Buffett: He wants to invest in (or outright buy) companies that have solid, reliable, conservatively financed businesses involving simple products or services—and he doesn't want to play games trying to do so. Tell him what the price is, and he'll analyze the heck out of the company and see if he thinks it's a good deal. If it is, he'll snatch it up; if not, he'll pass.

Two other critical (and interrelated) qualities Buffett looks for in companies: an "enduring moat" and a "durable competitive advantage," both of which he also discusses in his 2007 letter.

By having an *enduring moat*, Buffett means that a company must have some quality that makes it almost impossible for a competitor to overtake it—regardless of how much money that competitor is willing to spend trying to do so. "The dynamics of capitalism guarantee that competitors will repeatedly assault any business "castle" that is earning high returns," Buffett wrote in Berkshire's 2007 letter. "Therefore a formidable barrier such as a company's being the low-cost producer (GEICO, Costco) or possessing a powerful world-wide brand (Coca-Cola, Gillette, American Express) is essential for sustained success. Business history is filled with "Roman candles," companies whose moats proved illusory and were soon crossed."

The Coca-Cola example is a great one. Coca-Cola, whose stock is a long-time holding of Buffett's and whose cherry cola is a long-time favorite of his, is one of the world's most famous companies—maybe even its most famous. It's not just the sheer volume of Coca-Cola products that are sold all over the world; it's the fact that Coke is such a recognizable product that it has become ingrained in the fabric of our culture. In fact, we sometimes refer to just about any dark-colored cola as a Coke, even if it's made by another brand. Because it has such incredible brand recognition, it's hard to imagine a new company taking over Coke's market leadership—regardless of how much it was willing to spend on advertising or its products. It wouldn't be able to cross that enormous brand-name "moat" that Coca-Cola has built over the years.

While Coke's brand recognition and enormous popularity is largely responsible for its moat, it's only one type of *durable competitive advantage* a company can have over its competitors. Another can be the quality of the products or services it offers. In his 2007 letter to shareholders, Buffett says that that is the case with FlightSafety, a Berkshire-owned firm that trains pilots. According to Buffett, FlightSafety is known as being the best at what it does—and when people are looking to learn to fly, they want to learn from the best. "Going to any other flight-training provider than the best is like taking the low bid on a surgical procedure," Buffett wrote. New competitors to FlightSafety thus aren't likely to make much headway because they can't match the reputation of FlightSafety.

When discussing this concept in *Buffettology*, Mary Buffett says that Buffett looks for "consumer monopolies"—a market position that is virtually unassailable and gives the company power and leverage in the marketplace. We have found the word *monopoly* conjures up a much stricter requirement for companies—in particular that they have overwhelmingly dominant market share—than the requirement that Buffett necessarily uses. Many of Buffett's investments, including recent ones, aren't anywhere near classic monopolies. Virtually all have many competitors in the market such as Dairy Queen Restaurants, Shaw's Carpets, or even American Express. To us, Buffett places a lot of weight on what most people call brand image; he looks for a very strong, well-recognized brand, usually a consumer brand that may be regional (like See's Candy or Dairy Queen). Occasionally, he does buy businesses that sell commodities—GEICO, Shaw's—but only if he believes they have the lowest production cost in their industry. And remember: Banks are also a commodity industry.

Mary (to avoid confusion, we'll often refer to her and Warren by their first names throughout this chapter) describes how Warren determines if a company has a consumer monopoly in this way: "Warren has developed a conceptual test to determine the presence of . . . a consumer monopoly. In testing for the presence of a consumer monopoly, he likes to ask this question: *If he had access to billions of dollars (which he does) and his pick of the top fifty managers in the country (which he does), could he start a business and successfully compete with the business in question?* . . . If the answer is a resounding no, then the company in question is protected by some kind of strong consumer monopoly" (Mary's emphasis).

To go further, Buffett looks at how much damage a competitor could inflict even if he didn't care about making money. Mary cites such companies and products as Coca-Cola, the *Wall Street Journal,* Wrigley's gum, and Hershey chocolate bars as examples of companies and products largely impervious to competition, even competition willing to fight the good fight without making any money. (Interestingly, Berkshire bought into Wrigley's in 2008, more than a decade after Mary Buffett cited it as being Buffett-like in its imperviousness to competition).

In *Buffettology,* Mary Buffett specifically lists a few broad categories of businesses that tend to get Warren's attention:

- A business that makes products that wear out fast or are used up quickly, or makes products that merchants have to carry or use to stay in business. Crest toothpaste, Gillette razor blades, and Doritos corn chips are all good examples. Supermarkets, convenience stores, and drugstores have to carry some or all of these products, which means the makers of these products are good investment prospects.
- Communications businesses that provide a repetitive service that manufacturers must use to persuade the public to buy their products. When there were only three television networks, each made a bunch of money, which prompted Buffett to invest in Capital Cities and then ABC, says Mary. Strong local newspapers are another example (Berkshire owns the *Buffalo Evening News*).
- A business that provides repetitive consumer services that people and businesses are consistently in need of. Credit card companies or tax preparation services are examples.
- A business whose main product has not changed much over time nor is expected to change much in the foreseeable future, as this is a

major, major component in being able to have predictable earnings in the future. Auto insurance doesn't change much; candy doesn't change much; and the same for burgers, Coke, carpet, and so on. (Buffett himself noted in Berkshire's 2007 letter, "A moat that must be continuously rebuilt will eventually be no moat at all.")

- Companies that don't have to spend a lot on capital expenses, such as facilities upgrades, or research and development. Those are major expenses that can cut into profits.

One more quality that can give a company a moat is strong management—but not strong management that is dependent on a single star manager. "If a business requires a superstar to produce great results, the business itself cannot be deemed great," Buffett wrote in the 2007 Berkshire letter. "A medical partnership led by your area's premier brain surgeon may enjoy outsized and growing earnings, but that tells little about its future. The partnership's moat will go when the surgeon goes. You can count, though, on the moat of the Mayo Clinic to endure, even though you can't name its CEO."

By the Numbers

Of course, many of the qualities we examined thus far—enduring moats, durable competitive advantages, strong management—are broad concepts, not quantitative tests. But that doesn't mean those concepts aren't included in our Buffett model. In *Buffettology*, Mary Buffett lays out a number of quantitative tests that Warren uses to measure whether or not a company does have some of the characteristics we mentioned above.

For example, while there is no single, definitive way to measure whether a company has a durable competitive advantage, companies that do have these advantages tend to have certain fundamental qualities, such as *high returns on equity*. According to Mary, Warren looks for firms whose returns on equity have consistently been above average. In her book, she says an ROE of 12 percent is about average, and that firms that have produced ROEs over 15 percent in each of the past 10 years are the type that Warren seeks out.

Another example: Mary says that one way Warren assesses whether a firm's management is strong is by looking at its use of *retained earnings*.

He measures how much a stock's earnings per share have risen in the past 10 years, and then divides that by the total amount of earnings it has retained (per share) over that span. This gives you an idea of the kind of return management is producing for shareholders using the company's retained earnings; if the return is 12 percent or more, Warren sees that as a sign management is doing a good job.

Buffett uses another quantitative measure—*free cash flow*—to get an idea if a company is one that has a lot of capital expenses. Companies that spend a lot on facilities upgrades and research and development tend to use up a lot of cash, and Warren doesn't like that. If a firm has a negative free cash flow, Buffett thus shies away, according to Mary.

Buffett also turns to numbers when trying to make sure a company is the type of stable and conservatively financed firm he likes to invest in (remember, Buffett's mentor was the ultraconservative Ben Graham). He wants to see that *earnings per share* have increased reasonably consistently over the past decade, and he wants a firm's debt to be no more than five times its annual earnings. Those qualities make it easier to predict future earnings, and having the best possible idea of a company's future is very, very important to the conservative-minded Buffett.

According to Mary, Warren uses criteria such as ROE, use of retained earnings, free cash flow, and several others to determine if a company is strong enough for him to invest in it. Then, he uses some more numbers to determine the other half of the equation: whether the company is selling at the right price. Buffett is interested in a company's intrinsic value and will buy only when a company's stock is selling at a price that makes sense, given that intrinsic value. Mary says of this concept: "To Warren the intrinsic value of an investment is the projected annual compounding rate of return the investment will produce." Buffett is looking at what finance types call *future value*—in this case, what the company will be worth at some specified time in the future, say, 10 years or more.

Let's say a stock is currently selling for $21 and you project that in 10 years it will sell for $65. Is this a good, bad, or indifferent performance? Using a financial calculator, you can quickly calculate the stock's annual compound rate of return. First (all financial calculators work similarly), you would punch in 21 and PV for present value (the stock's value today; we need to change the sign to a minus sign by pressing +/- after you type in 21 but before you press PV, to indicate that this is a cash outflow used to purchase an investment). Then press 65 and FV for future value (the stock's expected price in the future), 10 and n for the number of periods (the periods in this example are years and their number is 10). Then press CPT i to compute the compound interest rate, which ends up being 11.96 percent (note: in addition to a financial calculator you can also use a "rate" function in Excel). This means we project the stock will earn for us 11.96 percent each year (on average), compounded, over the next 10 years. Buffett would then look at this and decide if this rate of return is worth the investment.

How does he know what the stock will be worth in the future? That's the tough part. "Warren focuses on the predictability of future earnings," Mary writes, "and he believes that without some predictability of future earnings, any calculation of a future value is mere speculation, and speculation is an invitation to folly. Warren will make long-term investments only in businesses whose future earnings are predictable to a high degree of certainty. The certainty of future earnings removes the elements of risk from the equation and allows for a sound determination of a business's future value." Buffett is interested in looking into the future and seeing where a company is likely to go and what it will be worth when it gets there. Then he looks at what it's selling for now. If it is selling for a price that will provide him with a good return over the long term, he'll buy.

To predict where a stock will be in the future, Buffett uses not just one, but two different methods to estimate what the company's earnings and stock's rate of return will be 10 years from now. One method involves using the firm's historical return on equity figures, while another uses earnings per share data. (We'll examine how to use these methods in greater detail in the "Step by Step" section in just a bit.) This notion of predicting what a company's earnings will be in 10 years may seem to run counter to Buffett's nonspeculative ways. But while using these methods to predict a company's earnings for the next 10 years in her book, Mary Buffett notes: "In most situations this would be an act of insanity. However, as Warren has found, if the company is one of sufficient earning power and earns high rates of return on shareholders' equity, created by some kind of consumer monopoly, chances are good that accurate long-term projections of earnings can be made."

One note here: Technology doesn't interest Buffett because, he claims, he doesn't understand it and because future earnings of tech companies tend to be highly unpredictable as a result of technical surprises and rapid product cycles, so he makes no attempt to calculate a tech stock's long-term future value.

One last variable that Buffett views favorably is stock buybacks, or repurchases. These occur when a company thinks its stock is so low priced that it is a good investment, and it goes into the public markets and buys back shares of its own stock. By doing so, it decreases the number of shares in the market. Under the law of supply and demand, if demand is constant and supply decreases, prices should go up, which is what companies are counting on when they repurchase their shares. These programs are generally announced publicly.

The Buffett Strategy: Step by Step

About the Warren Buffett Strategy

The Track Record:	Berkshire Hathaway, the holding company that Buffett has run for decades, posted a 24 percent average annual return over a 32-year period.
Risk:	Relatively low. Buffett targets companies that are trading at a discount compared to the intrinsic value of their business. Generally, they are large firms with long histories of success, which also limits risk.
Time Horizon:	Forever. Yes, Buffett believes you should spend a lot of time identifying the right companies to invest in, wait until their price is right, and then buy and hold . . . and hold and hold. He's held some of his investments for decades.
Effort:	"Highly selective" best describes Buffett's approach to identifying companies he will invest in. He requires in-depth analysis of every company he looks at. On the front end, therefore, a considerable amount of effort is required to use Buffett's strategy. But on the back end— the time after you make the purchase and are holding it (usually for years)—there's very little effort.

There are two major stages in making a Buffett investment decision. The first is determining whether a particular company is a Buffett-type company, that is, whether it fits within Buffett's "realm of confidence"—a company whose high returns can be predicted with a fair amount of certainty. The second stage is determining whether the price a company's stock is currently selling for will allow a commensurate high return that is better than your other options.

Note: Buffett is not into diversification (owning stocks in several industries). He concentrates his investments in a few stocks. Such a strategy would usually be considered risky, but not in his case because he does such a thorough analysis of his investments before he buys; he waits until the price is low; he looks for companies with superior market positions; and he holds for so long. All of these help lower his risk level.

First Stage: "Is This a Buffett-Type Company?"

While Buffett has generated some of the most incredible returns in history, the types of companies he targets are often simple and unexciting. To him, stability and simplicity trumps excitement any day. A few nonquantitative ways to target "Buffett-like" stocks:

- **Look at the nature of the company's business.** Buffett invests only in companies that have strong brand recognition, not quite correctly called consumer monopolies, or companies that other firms must go through to conduct a major business project or campaign, which he calls *toll bridge companies*. Only a handful of companies have the size, depth, and reach that meet Buffett's requirements. Examples include Coca-Cola, Gillette, the *Washington Post*, McDonald's, and American Express.
- **Look to see if the company has the ability to pass on costs.** See if the company has the ability to adjust prices to inflation, which helps companies make money no matter what type of economic climate exists at the time. This particular function cannot be automated. It can be performed simply, though, by asking whether over the past decade or two or three the company has been able to substantially raise the price of its main product, such as newspapers that originally cost 25 cents per copy but now cost 75 cents. The companies mentioned above fit the bill.
- **Look at the complexity of the product.** Buffett likes companies that are easy to understand. He wants to be able to comprehend the exact business of the company (Lynch and Graham take very

similar approaches.) Products that Buffett considers understandable include soft drinks, razors, diapers, and ice cream. Although Buffet tended to disengage in technology investments, we believe that certain major technology products, such as personal computers, are at least fairly understandable in today's technologically advanced society.

Earnings Predictability Now, let's begin the quantitative part of the Buffett approach, starting with earnings. Buffett likes to invest in companies that have steady, predictable earnings growth. In order to determine if earnings look predictable, our model checks to see if any year's earnings per share (EPS) is negative in the past decade. If so, with one exception, it fails Buffett's predictability criterion. However, it is important to note that a possible exception is if earnings were negative in the most recent fiscal year. If earnings were otherwise predictable but there is a loss or a sharp drop in earnings in the most recent fiscal year that he thinks is "temporary," Buffett might see that as an opportunity. Bad news like an earnings drop can substantially lower the price of the company temporarily to the "strike zone," where it is attractive to invest in or acquire. That temporary qualification, however, does call for a lot of contrarian business judgment because media articles about the company at the time are likely to paint a dismal outlook. However, the bad news may also be a recession in an industry or a dramatic drop in the popularity of an industry, whereby all stocks in the industry are well off their highs, in which case there is substantially less concern about permanent flaws in a specific company.

Earnings Predictability (Y1 is the EPS for the most recent fiscal year; Y10 is the EPS 10 years ago)

1. $Y1 \geq Y2 \geq Y3 \geq Y4 \geq Y5 \geq Y6 \geq Y7 \geq Y8 \geq Y9 \geq Y10$ and no years with a negative EPS.   Pass—Best Case

2. $Y1 \geq Y2 \geq Y3 \geq Y4 \geq Y5 \geq Y6 \geq Y7 \geq Y8 \geq Y9 \geq Y10$ (except for dips from a prior year's earnings that total no more than 45 percent). No years with a negative EPS.   Pass

3. All other combinations   Fail

Note: We believe the above method reflects Buffett's general approach to assessing earnings predictability, and it is thus the method we use in our Buffett-based model. Mary Buffet does, however, provide additional examples where a stock passed the earnings predictability test. For one thing, she says it is acceptable that EPS could be negative or involve a sharp decline in the most recent year (Y1), providing EPS had been highly predictable in the rest of the past decade, as that may provide a good buying opportunity for a firm with a good long-term track record. She also gives two other examples of when dips may be tolerated: In one, the firm H&R Block had a one-time EPS dip of 35 percent, but otherwise had predictable earnings increases over the past ten years. In the other, Gannett, the firm had two EPS dips in the past decade, but the dips totaled less than 20 percent.

Level of Debt Buffett likes conservatively financed companies. Nonetheless, he has invested in companies with large financing divisions and in firms with rather high levels of debt. He seems to exclude from this criterion financially oriented companies such as American Express, Salomon, and Wells Fargo, as well as insurance companies such as GEICO.

Buffett is different from other gurus in determining what level of debt is considered conservative. Whereas other gurus use a debt-equity ratio, Buffett wants to see that the long-term debt of a company can be paid off from net income in five years or less, with less than two years preferred.

If a company is not in finance, banking, or insurance, all of which require a firm to take on high levels of debt because of the nature of their businesses, then the Buffett-based model uses the following debt criteria:

Long-Term Debt

1. ≤ 2 times earnings   Pass—Best case
2. > 2 and ≤ 5 times earnings   Pass
3. > 5 times earnings   Fail

Note: If you look at Mary's examples in terms of traditional LTD-equity, the highest level Buffett invested in for a nonfinancial company was about 46 percent.

Return on Equity Buffett likes companies with a 10-year average return on equity (ROE) of at least 15 percent or better and, ideally, ROEs consistently above 15 percent each year, which is better than average. (U.S. corporations have, on average, returned about 12 percent on equity over the last 30 years.)

If the 10-year average ROE is greater than or equal to 15 percent, Buffett would consider this high enough to pass. A high return on equity indicates management has done a great job allocating retained earnings, leaving shareholders with a solid, above-average return.

A 10-year average ROE lower than 15 percent is unacceptable and suggests that management is not doing a good job allocating retained earnings. This test, too, is a cornerstone of Buffett's methodology and cannot be compromised.

Return on Equity (Averaged over the Last 10 Years)

1. ≥ 15%   Pass
2. < 15%   Fail

Return on Total Capital (ROTC) Because some companies can be financed with debt that is many times their equity, they can show a consistently high ROE, yet still be in unattractive price-competitive businesses. To avoid such firms, for nonfinancial companies Buffett also looks for a consistently high return on total capital. This model requires a firm's average 10-year ROTC —defined as the net earnings of the business divided by the total capital in the business, including both equity and debt—to be at least 12 percent.

Return on Total Capital Averaged over the Last 10 Years

1. ≥ 12%   Pass
2. < 12%   Fail

Capital Expenditures Buffett likes companies that do not require major capital expenditures. That is, the company does not need to spend a ton of money on major upgrades of plant and equipment or on research and development to stay competitive. He thus looks for free cash flow to be a positive number.

Free cash flow greater than zero is wonderful, indicating that the company is generating more cash than it is consuming. On the other hand, free cash flow equal to zero or negative is a bad sign, indicating that the company is spending more money than it is taking in.

Free Cash Flow

1. > 0 Pass
2. ≤ 0 Fail

Use of Retained Earnings Along with measuring return on equity, another way Buffett assesses management's performance is by looking at its use of retained earnings. Mary Buffett writes that one way to do this is to take "the per share earnings retained by a business for a certain period of time, then compare it to any increase in per share earnings that occurred during this same period." We're interested here in seeing if management is using retained earnings properly—that is, to increase shareholder wealth.

To figure this out, Buffett looks at the total amount of retained earnings for a specified period and compares it to any gain in EPS over the same period. Specifically, this variable looks at the earnings gain from ten years back to the present. That is, it takes the difference between last year's fiscal earnings and earnings for the fiscal year ten years ago, and divides that figure by the total amount of retained earnings over that same period. This then gives a rate of return.

It is more than acceptable to Buffett if use of retained earnings provides a return of 15 percent or better. Essentially, management is doing a great job putting the retained earnings to work. If return on retained earnings is less than 15 percent but greater than or equal to 12 percent, management has proven it can earn shareholders a decent return on the earnings they kept. Buffett prefers 15 percent or better but nonetheless has invested in companies where the return on retained earnings is between 12 percent and 15 percent.

Buffett would consider unacceptable use of retained earnings that provides a return of less than 12 percent as management is not profitably allocating retained earnings. Essentially, investors would be better off if the company paid all earnings out to shareholders and let them invest the earnings on their own.

Utilization of Retained Earnings

1. ≥ 15%   Pass—Best case
2. ≥ 12% and < 15%   Pass
3. < 12%   Fail

This concludes Buffett's first-stage analysis. When he gets positive responses to all of the above criteria, which confirms that the company being looked at is a "Buffett-type company," only then does he proceed with the second stage, a price analysis. The price analysis will determine whether the stock is at an attractive enough price to be purchased.

Second Stage: "Is This Buffett-Type Company Attractively Priced?"

Once you have determined that the firm is a Buffett-type company, you need to let the market price determine whether to invest in the company, as your initial price heavily determines the returns you can make over the long run. There are always alternative options for investments (one of which is Treasury bonds) and a goal of Buffett's is determining that the current price of the company is more attractive than bonds.

There are four major parts to the second-stage analysis. First, you need to compute the "initial rate of return" to see if the initial return is at least as much as a long-term Treasury bond, before even considering any future price appreciation. Second, you need to find out your expected annualized return using something Buffett calls the ROE method. Third, you find your expected annualized return using another tactic that Buffett calls the EPS growth method. The fourth and final step is to average both returns to create the final return and see if that would be high enough to excite Buffett.

The Initial Rate of Return The first number we need to find is our initial rate of return. You'll look at the company's initial rate of return and see if it is at least as much as a long-term Treasury bond yield. To calculate the initial rate of return, the EPS is divided by the current market price. This is also known as the Earnings Yield.

Initial Rate of Return = Earnings per Share/Price per Share

(Keep in mind that the "initial rate of return" we're talking about here is assessing how much bang for your buck you're getting in terms of a company's *earnings*—not terms of its dividends or stock price appreciation. The assumption is that usually, the return you get on a stock should be in the neighborhood of its earnings yield.)

Next, compare the initial rate of return with the long-term Treasury bond yield.

With the initial rate of return determined, compare it with the long-term (10-year) Treasury bond yield. Buffett favors companies with an initial rate of return that is as good as or better than the long-term Treasury bond yield, which at the time of this writing is a relatively low 3.87 percent. However, he has occasionally invested in companies with lower initial rates of return than the long-term T-bond yield as long as the company's yield is expected to expand rapidly.

If the initial rate of return is greater than or equal to the long-term T-bond yield, the company is an obvious choice. That's because the firm's earnings yield is starting out at or above the return of a T-bond, plus it should grow over time (earnings should grow in future years while the price per share you paid for the stock will remain the same, causing the earnings yield to expand); the return of the bond, on the other hand, doesn't grow—it remains static. If the initial rate of return is less than the long-term bond yield, Buffett prefers to avoid the stock.

Initial Rate of Return

1. ≥ Long-term T-bond yield   Pass
2. < Long-term T-bond yield   Fail

The Return on Equity Method We'll now describe how to find the expected rate of return using Buffett's ROE method. Several steps are needed to arrive at this number.

Step 1. Find the Percent Average ROE After Payout

Take a firm's total equity on its most recent balance sheet and divide by shares outstanding. This gives you *equity per share*.

Next, we need to look up the return on equity (ROE) for the last 10 years, including the estimated ROE for the current year (if available). We sum the ten ROEs and divide by 10. This gives a 10-year *average ROE*.

The next step is finding the average payout. Again, this is a simple average. Find the dividend payout ratio (the percent of earnings that the company pays out as a dividend) for each of the last 10 years (including the estimated payout for the current year, if available), and average them. This gives you the *average payout percent*.

Then we can find the Percent Average ROE After Payout. To do so, perform the following calculation with the numbers you found just a minute ago.

Percent Average ROE After Payout = Average ROE × (1−
(Average payout percent)

What you have just found is the expected growth rate of a company's equity, after reducing it for dividends the company is expected to payout.

Step 2. Project the Equity in 10 years

This is where it gets a little tricky. We need to do a time value of money calculation, so get your calculator ready. Our PV, or present value, is the *equity per share* that we already calculated. Our time period, or n, is 10 years. We'll be solving for FV, or future value; that is, we'll be finding out how much equity per share we can expect a company to have ten years from now.

To find that future value, the Buffett method uses the *Percent Average ROE After Payout* that we just found in the previous step. That's the "i" in the time value of money equation:

PV =   Current equity per share

n =   10 (the time period, or 10 years)

i =   Percent Average ROE After Payout
             (from above)

After inputting those values, solve for *FV* (future equity per share) by pressing the keys CPT FV on your business calculator.

Step 3. Convert the Future Equity into a Future EPS

Now, take the future equity per share and multiply it by the 10-year historical average ROE we found in Step 1. This gives you the expected future EPS for 10 years from now.

Future EPS (in 10 years) = future equity/share (in 10 years) ×
10-year average ROE

Step 4. Calculate the Future Stock Price

We're getting closer. Now that we have the future EPS, we can figure out the future expected stock price. Remember, a stock's price is equal to its EPS times its P/E ratio. Since we have the stock's future EPS (from Step 3), what we now need to find is its expected P/E ratio. To do so, look up the stock's price-earnings ratio in each of the past 10 years and average those figures. (The assumption here is that the stock's P/E ratio ten years from now should be in line with its 10-year historical P/E.)

Now, take the expected future EPS from Step 3 and multiply it by the average P/E for the past 10 years. (*Note:* To be conservative, we actually use the lower of the current P/E or the average P/E for the past 10 years.) This gives you a projected future stock price.

Future Stock Price (in 10 years) = EPS (in 10 years) ×
historic P/E ratio (or
current P/E ratio, if lower)

Step 5. Calculate the Future Dividends and Add to the Future Stock Price to Get the Future Stock Price With Dividends

As you know, price appreciation is only part of what investors get from stocks. The other part is dividend payments. Now that we've found the future stock price, we need to do another calculation to find the total dividend pool so we can add that to the stock price to really get an idea of how much bang you can expect the stock to give for your buck over the next 10 years.

To start, take the company's estimated EPS for the current year and multiply by the historical average EPS growth rate to figure out the projected EPS in each year for the next 10 years. Then multiply each year's projected EPS by the average payout percent we found in Step 1. This gives you the amount of dividends you can expect to earn for each year. Sum up all the years' dividends and add the total for the ten years to the future stock price from Step 4. Now you have the future stock price with dividends.

Future Stock Price (with Dividends) = future stock price +
total dividend payouts
(10 years)

Step 6. Calculate Your Expected Rate of Return Based on the Average ROE Method

Now we can move to the final part of this method, which is to find our expected return. To do so, do a time value of money calculation with your financial calculator. This is pure plug-and-chug. Enter the following values in your calculator to solve for i, which is the expected return:

PV = Current stock price

FV = Future stock price + Total dividend pool

n = 10 (the time period, or 10 years)

Solve for i (or your expected return using the ROE method) by pressing CPT I on your business calculator.

- If the expected return using the ROE method is greater than or equal to 22 percent, you have an exceptionally good return. Buffett would consider this absolutely fantastic.
- If the return is less than 22 percent but greater than or equal to 15 percent, Buffett would consider this a good return.
- If the return is less than 15 percent but greater than or equal to 12 percent, you have a return slightly below what Buffett prefers. However, he has invested in companies like this before, as it is still a solid return. For instance, he invested in McDonald's in 1996 when the return was expected to be 12.6 percent.
- Anything below 12 percent is unacceptable.

Expected Return (ROE Method)

1. ≥ 15%   Pass—Best case
2. ≥ 12% and < 15%   Pass
3. < 12%   Fail

The EPS Growth Method Now we enter the third major part of this second-stage analysis. We'll find the expected rate of return using another tactic that Buffett calls the average EPS growth method. We need to take a couple of steps to get to this number.

Step 1. Calculate the expected future stock price (with dividends) based on the average EPS growth method

First, we'll have to find our future stock price, using the EPS growth rate, rather than the equity growth rate used above. If you take the historical average EPS growth rate, you can project the EPS in 10 years. Basically take 1 + EPS growth and raise it to a factor of 10, then multiply by the current year (Y0) estimated EPS. The number you get is EPS in Year 10.

EPS in 10 yrs. $= (1 + \text{EPS growth rate})^{10} \times \text{Current year EPS}$

Now multiply EPS in Year 10 by the more conservative of the 10-year average P/E, which we found earlier in the ROE method, or the current P/E. This equals the future stock price.

Future Stock Price (in 10 yrs.) $=$ EPS in 10 yrs. $\times$ 10-year average P/E (or current P/E, if lower)

Add in the total expected dividend pool. First, take the projected EPS in each of the next 10 years (which we calculated in Step 5 of the ROE method by using the historical average EPS growth rate). Multiply each year by the average payout percent (which we found back in Step 1 of the ROE method), starting with the EPS the year after the current year. This gives you a payout dollar amount for each year. Add these ten numbers together to get a total dividend amount, and add that total to the future stock price we just calculated. Now you have your expected stock price, with dividends, in Year 10.

Future Stock Price (with Dividends) = future stock price + total dividend payouts (10 years)

Step 2. Calculate your expected rate of return based on the average EPS growth method

With the stock price in Year 10, you can figure out your expected return based on the current price and the future expected stock price, including the dividend pool. To do so, you'll need to break out your financial calculator again to do a time value of money calculation.

Enter the following values into your calculator to solve for i, which will be your expected return using the EPS growth method:

PV	=	Current stock price
FV	=	Future stock price with total dividend pool (calculated in Step 1)
n	=	10 (time period, or 10 years)

Solve for *i* (or your expected return using the EPS growth method).

- An expected return greater than or equal to 22 percent is an exceptionally good return.
- A return below 22 percent but greater than or equal to 15 is a good return.
- A return below 15 percent but greater than or equal to 12 percent is acceptable. Buffett likes to see a 15 percent return or better but nonetheless would consider this a good, solid return.
- Anything below 12 percent is too low for Buffett to have interest.

Expected Return (EPS Growth Method)

1. ≥ 15%	Pass—Best case
2. ≥ 12% and < 15%	Pass
3. < 12%	Fail

Averaging the Predicted Future Returns Now we've come to the fourth and final part, where we average the two expected rates of return. This will give you a final expected rate of return, which determines whether you should invest in the stock.

Average final return = (Expected return of ROE method + Expected return of EPS method) ÷ 2

- A return of 22 percent or more is an exceptional return.
- A return less than 22 percent but greater than or equal to 15 percent is a good return.
- A return less than 15 percent but 12 percent or more is still acceptable. As mentioned, Buffett likes to see a 15 percent return but has nonetheless invested in companies with this expected return.
- Any return below 12 percent, however, is unacceptable to Buffett.

Range of Expected Returns

1. ≥ 15%	Pass—Best case
2. ≥ 12% and < 15%	Pass
3. < 12%	Fail

 Click It!

To find current examples of stocks that pass the Buffett-based Patient Investor approach, log on to www.guruinvestorbook.com. Every day, the free site features three stocks that get approval from our Buffett method, with links to detailed analysis of why those stocks score so well.

The Buffett-Based Model Performance

We began tracking our Buffett-based model in early December 2003, a few months after the inceptions of our eight original models. Since then, our 10-stock Buffett portfolio has performed fairly well, gaining 21.2 percent compared to the S&P 500's 14.5 percent. The 20-stock portfolio hasn't fared as well, however. It gained 7.9 percent, lagging the S&P 500 by almost 7 percentage points. Of all of the 10- and 20-stock portfolios we track that are based on the gurus covered in this book, it's the only one that has not beaten the market since its inception. Keep in mind, however, that we've been tracking this portfolio for less than five years, which, to an extremely long-term investor like Buffett, would be relatively short.

Our Buffett model tends to select a wide variety of stocks, but two of the groups that seem to get the most interest are financials and retailers. The Buffett-based portfolios we track also tend to hold stocks for longer than many of our other guru-based portfolios. Sometimes, they'll hold onto a stock for a couple years before selling.

One question we often get is how stocks that Buffett is buying (or owns) stack up against our Buffett-based model. The results are mixed. As of May 2008, for example, Johnson & Johnson—of which Berkshire owns more than 64 million shares—got approval from our Buffett method. A recent Berkshire investment, Burlington Northern Santa Fe Corp., however, got a low score, failing to meet our return on equity, return on total capital, use of retained earnings, and expected return tests.

There are a few reasons for such a discrepancy. First, our model measures where a company's fundamentals stand right now, not where they were when Buffett bought the company or its stock. Second, Buffett, with all of his experience and access, may have non-fundamental reasons for investing in a firm that he thinks trump any fundamental shortfalls. And third, investors can and will change their strategy over time. It has been 11 or so years since *Buffettology* was published, and Buffett may have changed his strategy since then. If he has, however, he hasn't said how. And we feel comfortable sticking with our *Buffettology*-based method, because it was a proven winner over such a long period of time. We use the model not as a way to predict Buffett's future moves, but instead as a way to take advantage of the strategy he used to find his past investments, many of which have been extremely profitable.

While we believe our Buffett-based model accurately reflects the stock selection process that Mary Buffett lays out in *Buffettology*, it's important to note that Buffett manages his portfolio much differently than we manage ours. All of the model portfolios we discuss in our guru chapters are rebalanced every 28 days, because we've found that, in general, our quantitative strategies produce the best results with that rebalancing time frame. Buffett doesn't use scheduled rebalancings, however. He's a true buy-and-hold investor.

One other difference to note: Buffett might consider tech companies' future earnings to be unpredictable in the long run because they continually cannibalize and make obsolete their own products, but we feel comfortable letting our model select tech stocks. There are two reasons we feel this way:

1. Many have now shown a long track record of steady earnings increases.
2. The nature of their newer products requires a level of historical compatibility with their older products that assures a steady supply of future customers.

And while Buffett might feel that he doesn't understand the products these companies make, we feel that most people have a basic understanding of technology as today's widespread use of computers is transforming them into common, everyday appliances. The lack of knowledge and the complexity of technology are no longer reasons to ignore this very important segment of the market. (See Table 6.1.)

Table 6.1 Model Portfolio Risk and Return Statistics

	10-Stock	20-Stock	S&P 500
Annualized Return	4.3%	1.7%	3%
Total Return	21.2%	7.9%	14.5%
Best Full Year	37.3% in 2004	27.5% in 2004	13.6% in 2006
Worst Full Year	−12.2% in 2007	−7.7% in 2005	3% in 2005
Beta	1.11	1.08	1.0
Accuracy	55.4%	52.8%	N/A

Note: Returns statistics are from Dec. 5, 2003 to July 15, 2008. See Appendix A for additional return disclosure and explanation.
Source: Guru Model Portfolio Tool, Validea.com.

Buffett's Key Investing Criteria

- Look for companies with commanding market shares.
- Invest as though you were buying the entire company, not just buying shares.
- Make sure the company has a long history of increasing *earnings per share* (EPS)
- Make sure the company is conservatively financed by comparing debt to earnings, and by making sure it has free cash flow.
- Assess the job management is doing by looking at *return on equity* (ROE), use of retained earnings, and *return on total capital* (ROTC).
- Compare the stock's initial rate of return to the long-term Treasury bond yield.
- Look into the future. Estimate the stock's future value using both the ROE method and the EPS growth method, and then determine if it is a good buy today.
- Know the industry.
- Do your homework up front. Study and thoroughly analyze the companies in which you place your faith—and your money.
- Don't rush out to buy the stock of a good company. Be sure it is priced low enough that it is likely to provide you with a good return.
- After you buy, put the stock in the back of your mind. You are holding for the long term, and unless you have made a poor choice of investment or something totally unforeseen occurs, plan on keeping the stock through thick and thin. This is a stock you may well pass on to your children or grandchildren.

Part Three

THE GROWTH LEGENDS (WITH A VALUE TWIST)

S tudies have shown that over the long term value stocks beat growth stocks. But by no means is growth a bad thing. In fact, some of the best investment strategies of all time focus on growth, or they are value approaches that incorporate a growth component. Mutual fund great Peter Lynch, money manager and author Kenneth Fisher, and billionaire newsletter champ Martin Zweig all targeted stocks that had strong earnings growth, while making sure they didn't pay too much for them. And they didn't just post impressive returns; they were also innovators. Each developed a groundbreaking new ratio—Lynch the P/E/growth, Fisher the price-sales, and Zweig the puts-calls—that would become a permanent part of investment parlance. But what really drew us to them was their track records. By combining growth and value criteria, these gurus' approaches use a bit of the best of both investment strategy worlds—helping them produce some of the best results in investing history.

Part Three

THE GROWTH LEGENDS (WITH A VALUE TWIST)

Chapter 7

Peter Lynch

The Star "GARP" Manager

The heights by great men reached and kept
Were not attained by sudden flight,
But they, while their companions slept,
Were toiling upward in the night.

—HENRY WADSWORTH LONGFELLOW,
"THE LADDER OF ST. AUGUSTINE"

As you've seen, we're big believers in focusing on the numbers when it comes to beating the stock market. And when it comes to the great Peter Lynch, you don't need to look too far past these three pairs of numbers to understand why he's known as one of history's greatest investors:

- **15.8 and 29.2**. From 1977 to 1990, the period that Lynch oversaw Fidelity Investments' Magellan Fund, the S&P 500 returned an average of 15.8 percent per year. Magellan, on the other hand, averaged a 29.2 percent annual return—nearly doubling the S&P for more than a decade.

- **20 and 14.** The first number, 20, is the amount of money, in millions of dollars, that Magellan managed when Lynch took over; the second, 14, is the amount, in billions of dollars, that it managed when he left—a 700-fold increase.
- **$10,000 and $280,000.** If you had put $10,000 into Magellan the day Lynch began overseeing the fund, you'd have had $280,000 by the day he retired 13 years later—putting you a lot closer to being able to retire!

Those numbers are impressive—very impressive. In fact, they make for one of the best investing track records of all time, and they are a big part of why Lynch remains one of the most well-known and frequently quoted investors in the world today, even though he retired nearly two decades ago.

But while Lynch's staggering track record is no doubt a big part of his appeal, there are other reasons he is so revered in the investing world. A big part of his popularity is due to the fact that, despite having been one of the greatest—and richest—professional investors ever, Lynch's investment philosophy is one that just about anyone can understand and use. His approach is grounded in common sense and he speaks with a down-to-earth sensibility, as well as a trademark sharp wit.

One of Lynch's Many Pearls of Wall Street Wisdom

"[Invest in] a business that any idiot can run—because sooner or later, any idiot is probably going to run it."

One Up on Wall Street, Lynch's best-selling 1989 book, captured his common sense approach—no fancy, esoteric theories, high level math, or technical jargon; just simple and very insightful investment advice. While it was extremely well received in the investment community, the book was really aimed at the "everyman"—average Joes and Janes who were neither rich nor well schooled in finance and didn't have access to the sophisticated information and technical resources available to professional investors. Lynch didn't just believe that these everyday investors could do well on Wall Street; he believed that they actually held some distinct advantages over professional investors—advantages that we'll discuss in this chapter.

Who Is Peter Lynch?

Lynch's own investing journey had humble beginnings. He was born on January 19, 1944, in Newton, Massachusetts. When he was 10, his father, who had worked as a mathematics professor at Boston College and later as an auditor at the John Hancock Insurance Company, died of cancer. To earn money, Lynch began caddying at a private golf club in the Boston area. The 1950s were a good time for the stock market, and many club members were investing—including D. George Sullivan, a big-wig at Fidelity Investments. Little did Lynch know that, in addition to making himself some cash, his caddying would also make him a contact—Sullivan—who would shape his amazing career.

While walking the fairways and greens, young Lynch heard the talk about stocks and became intrigued. As he grew up, his interest in stocks was reflected in his educational endeavors. He graduated from Boston College with an undergraduate degree in finance, and he would later earn an MBA from the University of Pennsylvania's famed Wharton School.

It was during his senior year at Boston College that Lynch's old caddying job began to pay dividends. At the urging of Sullivan, the "hapless golfer, great guy, and good tipper" who was now Fidelity's president, Lynch applied to Fidelity for a summer job. While he was one of 75 other candidates who were seeking just three open positions, Lynch got one of the jobs. "In helping D. George Sullivan find his ball," Lynch wrote in *One up on Wall Street*, "I was helping myself find a career. I'm not the only caddy who learned that the quickest route to the boardroom was through the locker room of a [country] club."

Following his summer gig at Fidelity, Lynch headed off to business school at Wharton. In addition to coming away from Wharton with an MBA, he also came away with something more precious: his wife, Carolyn. The two met at Wharton, and were married in 1968 while Lynch was serving a two-year tour of duty in the army, which was required because he was part of the ROTC program.

By the time Lynch met Carolyn, he had been following stocks for years and knew investing was where he wanted to spend his professional life. In fact, so consumed was Lynch with investing (at a time when that was fairly uncommon) that on his first date with his future wife, he reportedly talked only about investing. That evidently wasn't a turnoff for Carolyn—then or now. The couple eventually married, had three children, and remains together today.

In 1969, after completing his tour in the army (for part of which he was stationed in Korea), Lynch joined Fidelity full-time as an analyst, at times following textiles and then the metals industry. About five years later, he became the firm's research director, while continuing as an analyst. Then, on May 31, 1977, he took over the Magellan Fund. When you consider the track record he was about to establish, it's incredible to think that Magellan was the first fund that Lynch had ever managed.

But while Lynch would indeed soon begin to put together that legendary track record, his tenure at Magellan didn't begin well. Through the 1950s and much of the 1960s, the stock market had performed nicely, but it then turned down and suffered during the 1970s, and Magellan wasn't immune to the problems. In an interview on the Public Broadcasting System program *Frontline*, Lynch said: "The first three years I ran Magellan, I think one-third of the shares were redeemed. I mean there was very little interest. People didn't care." Not an auspicious beginning.

But Lynch was a performer, and it wasn't all that long before he turned things around. The fund began to do well, with the stock market taking a sharp turn up in the beginning of 1982, and the press—and then the investing public—took increasing interest in the Magellan Fund based on its performance under Lynch. Lynch's success didn't come easy—he worked at least six days a week and sometimes part of Sunday, even though he is a devout Catholic—but Magellan investors reaped the awards.

Eventually, however, Lynch's workload took a toll, he says, and he retired on May 31, 1990—13 years to the day from when he took over

Magellan. Though only 46 (the same age at which his father died), he quit to spend time with his wife and three children. He left Magellan having steered the fund through not only good markets, but also through down times—including the trough of the 1970s and the great thud of 1987—and he walked away at the height of his success, which no doubt added to his aura.

Since his retirement, Lynch has kept busy, and he remains a vice chairman of Fidelity. But while he spent his career compiling his fortune, today much of his work involves using his money to help others. According to a 2005 *Boston Globe* article titled "Peter Lynch's Guide to Philanthropy," Lynch became very active in philanthropy after retiring from Fidelity, and he gives large sums of money to a variety of causes, both through his family's individual contributions and groups like the Lynch Foundation, a charity he developed. In addition to giving away money, he works to raise money, the article noted, citing his fundraising efforts with the Inner-City Scholarship Fund, a Catholic Schools Foundation program that gives scholarships to low-income children attending urban Catholic schools in the Archdiocese of Boston. Lynch began chairing the fund in the early 1990s, helping to raise more than $55 million for scholarships between then and 2005.

P/E/G Investing: Start With What You Know . . .

Few in history have managed a mutual fund with such great success over a lengthy period of time, let alone one that became as large as Magellan. How did Lynch do it?

Interestingly, a big part of his approach involved something that is not at all exclusive to being a renowned professional fund manager: He invested in what he knew. Lynch believed that if you personally know something positive about a stock—you buy the company's products, like its marketing, etc.—you can get a beat on successful businesses before professional investors get around to them. Focus on where you shop, what you buy, the industry in which you work, and where you live, and you can get a jump on big stock market winners over time.

Lynch is fond of telling how this belief led him to one of his better investments: Hanes, the maker of L'eggs pantyhose. Years ago, quality pantyhose were typically sold in department stores or specialty shops, where women shopped about once every six weeks. Poorer-quality pantyhose were sold in grocery and drug stores, where women usually shopped weekly. Hanes saw an opportunity here: Sell higher-quality pantyhose made of heavier fabric with a better fit, in the most convenient places—namely grocery and drug stores. The company was really selling convenience as much as pantyhose.

While Hanes test marketed the product in Boston, Lynch's wife, Carolyn, bought a pair, liked them, and the rest, as they say, is history. Impressed with his wife's approval of the product, Lynch researched the company, bought its stock, and made six times what he paid—a "six bagger" in Lynch-speak. This is a simple, compelling story that most everyone can understand and picture themselves doing. That's one of the more important reasons for Lynch's appeal: His approach is direct, everyday-like, and seemingly simple enough for all of us to undertake if we want.

. . . But End With Fundamentals

But while it has been a much-discussed part of his approach, having personal knowledge of something good about a company's business was by no means the only part of Lynch's strategy. In fact, in the revised version of *One up on Wall Street* (2000), he said many had misinterpreted his buy-what-you-know tip, leading him to write this "disclaimer."

> Peter Lynch doesn't advise you to buy stock in your favorite store just because you like shopping in the store, nor should you buy stock in a manufacturer because it makes your favorite product or a restaurant because you like the food. Liking a store, a product, or a restaurant is a good reason to get interested in a company and put it on your research list, but it's not enough of a reason to own the stock! Never invest in any company before you've done the homework on the company's earnings prospects, financial condition, competitive position, plans for expansion, and so forth.

As always, Lynch's caution is full of common sense. Just because you've had a pleasant experience with a company doesn't mean that all—or even many—of its other customers have. Using your personal experiences as a jumping-off point is a good first step in searching for stocks, but in the end you need to make sure that the business—and in particular its fundamentals—is strong. Remember, Lynch retired, in part, because he spent at least six days a week studying companies. If he could have sat back and looked around his neighborhood for little-known businesses that were doing well, he might still be managing Magellan today.

One thing that makes Lynch a bit different from our other gurus is that he broke stocks down into different categories, and applied different fundamental tests to them depending on which category they fell into. The three main classification groups he used were (1) "fast-growers," which increase earnings at a rate of 20 percent or more per year while maintaining relatively low levels of debt (example: Apple); (2) "stalwarts," large, prominent companies that have annual sales in the multibillion dollar range and experience 10 to 19 percent annual earnings growth (example: Wal-Mart); and (3) "slow-growers," which tend to be large and aging companies that pay dividends and have single-digit earnings growth (example: Tomkins PLC, the engineering and manufacturing conglomerate, a slow-grower at the time of this writing). We examine each of these categories in more detail in the "Step by Step" section of this chapter.

Other Opportunities

Although Lynch focused on fast-growers, stalwarts, and slow-growers, he also considered other types of stocks. Here's a look at some of the other categories he used:

Cyclicals: These include auto manufacturers, airlines, tire companies, steel and aluminum companies, chemical companies, large semiconductor companies, and defense companies. They tend to do well when the economy is doing well and falter when the economy heads south. For Lynch, timing is everything with cyclicals. You want to get in when they are on the upswing and get out before they go down. Lynch strongly suggests that you need to work in some profession connected to the industry if you are going to have a successful edge in

detecting early signs that the business is picking up or falling off—which seems to make this a tough way to go about
picking stocks for most people.

Turnarounds: These companies are in trouble and attempt-
ing to turn their situation around. Turnaround candidates
make up lost ground very quickly. Lynch lists five types of
turnarounds:

1. Bail-us-out-or-else: Buy on hopes that the government
   will help bail out the company, as demonstrated by
   Chrysler (a Lynch winner) in the early 1980s.
2. Who-would-have-thunk-it: A company that surprises
   the market by being able to successfully turn around.
3. Little-problem-we-didn't-anticipate: A company that has
   a minor problem that is perceived by the market to be
   worse than it really is.
4. Perfectly-good-company-inside-a-bankrupt-company:
   A quite healthy part of a sick company.
5. Restructuring-to-maximize-shareholder-values: This
   refers to the way companies rid themselves of unprofit-
   able subsidiaries, so what's left is the good stuff.

Lynch pays particular attention to the cash on hand and the
long-term debt for turnarounds. He likes to see more cash than
debt, and he likes to see that the type of debt is not bank debt
or corporate paper (which are due on demand), but instead
funded debt like corporate bonds.

Asset plays: These companies are sitting on something valuable
that you know about but the Wall Street crowd has overlooked. A supermarket chain might have stores it has owned
for decades. The stores' value is on the books at original cost,
which is a fraction of their present value. That represents a
potential hoard of cash, which is not seen on the balance
sheet if the company were to sell these stores. Lynch asks:

- What are the firm's assets and how much are they worth?
- How much debt is there to detract from these assets?
- Is there someone waiting on the sidelines to buy the assets?

Lynch's Famous P/E/G Ratio

While Lynch looked at several fundamental variables that in some cases differed depending on the stock's classification, one variable stood out above all others and across all categories—and it was one that he created himself: the P/E/growth, or "P/E/G," ratio. While the P/E ratio (which compares a company's per-share price to its per-share earnings) may be the most well-known stock market variable, Lynch found that looking at the P/E by itself was less useful than looking at it in comparison to a company's growth. The rationale: Higher P/E ratios are okay, provided that the firm is growing at an appropriate pace. If a company's P/E ratio was about even with or less than its growth rate (i.e., its P/E divided by its growth rate is 1.0 or lower), Lynch saw that as acceptable. If the P/E was half or less of the growth rate, that really piqued his interest.

Lynch found that the P/E/G was a great way to identify growth stocks that were still selling at a good price. In fact, the P/E/G ratio became the most important fundamental variable he considered when looking at a stock, and his reliance on it is one of the things he is most known for in the investing world. His P/E/G-focused approach is an example of "GARP"—Growth At a Reasonable Price—investing, another term that became an essential part of the stock market lexicon in large part due to Lynch.

To show how the P/E/G can be more useful than the P/E ratio, Lynch has cited Wal-Mart, America's largest retailer. In *One up on Wall Street,* he notes that Wal-Mart's P/E was rarely below 20 during its three-decade rise, which wouldn't be considered low. Its growth rate, however, was consistently in the 25 to 30 percent range, generating huge profits for shareholders despite the P/E ratio not being particularly low. That also proved another one of Lynch's tenets: that a good company can grow for decades before earnings level off.

When determining a P/E/G, Lynch looked at historical data because he feels that using the estimated future growth rate is just guessing. We agree, so in our model we use the average of the three-, four-, and five-year growth rates to determine the P/E/G—not projected future earnings growth rates.

While Lynch looked at the P/E/G for all stocks, he did make a distinction between calculating the P/E/Gs of fast-growers and those of stalwarts and slow-growers. Because dividends are often important to companies with moderate or slow growth, he adjusted the P/E/G calculations for dividend yield when examining stalwarts and slow-growers. For fast-growers, which typically reward shareholders not with dividends but with growth in stock value, he did not incorporate dividend payments into the P/E/G.

For example, take a stalwart or slow grower with a P/E of 14, a dividend yield of 4 percent, and a growth rate of 12 percent. To figure out the P/E/G, divide the P/E (14) by the sum of the growth rate and dividend yield (12 + 4 = 16). The P/E/G is thus 14/16, or 0.88, which comes in under the Lynch-based approach's 1.0 upper limit, a good sign.

Generally Speaking

Before we get into the other, more detailed quantitative parts of Lynch's strategy, there were a number of other broad qualities that served as a jumping-off point for Lynch—many of which aren't what you'd expect. In fact, Lynch notes that a lot of them are just the types of characteristics that make many analysts and investors wary of a stock. Here's a sampling of some of those qualities that he discussed in *One up on Wall Street*:

- **A Boring Company Name**. Lynch believed that if you get in early enough with a company that has a boring name, you will probably get a few bucks off the stock's price just because of the name. One example he cites is "Bob Evans Farms."
- **A Dull Business**. Like another of our gurus, Warren Buffett, Lynch downplayed tech stocks. He believes if a company with terrific earnings and a strong balance sheet also does dull things, it gives you a lot of time to purchase the stock at a discount.
- **A Disagreeable Product Line**. A firm that makes intestinal byproducts or manufactures a machine that washes greasy auto parts is a good example.
- **Spin-off Status**. Lynch's reasoning is that large companies don't want spin-offs to get into trouble because that would reflect poorly on the parent company, so the parent sends

the spinoff into the world with a strong balance sheet and preparation to succeed on its own.

- **Relative Anonymity**. If a stock isn't well-known, isn't owned by institutions, isn't followed by analysts, that's a good thing because you can get deals on stocks flying under the radar.
- **Focus of Rumors**. Another way you can get discounts on a stock is if rumors abound about it. An example Lynch gives is a company rumored to be involved with toxic waste and/or the Mafia. "Or better yet," he writes, "toxic waste *and* the Mafia."
- **A Depressing (Not Depressed) Industry**. The mortuary business is a good example. Lynch claims Wall Street tends to ignore companies that deal with mortality.
- **A No-Growth or Slow-Growth Industry**. These industries don't get the attention of professional investors, so they can slip under the radar.
- **A Niche**. Lynch liked niche companies because they often have little if any competition.
- **Products That Must Be Repurchased**. Drugs, soft drinks, razor blades, and cigarettes are examples. People have to keep coming back to buy more and more of these items.
- **A User (Not Maker) of Technology**. Lynch's thinking: Technology helps companies that are heavy technology users to cut costs, while at the same time the companies benefit from falling technology prices.
- **Insiders Are Buyers**. Lynch believes there's no better tip-off to the probable success of a stock than that people in a company are putting their own money into it. Even though insider buying excites him, he considers insider selling usually meaningless because there are many reasons why insiders sell (to buy a house, pay for a child's college tuition, buy a sailboat), but there is only one reason why insiders buy: They think the stock is undervalued and will eventually go up.
- **Company Is Buying Back Shares**. By buying back shares and decreasing total shares outstanding, earnings per share can be "magically" increased, which can in turn affect the stock price significantly.

- **"Idiot Proof."** This goes back to the quote we referenced earlier. Lynch liked a business to be simple enough that even managers who weren't the brightest bulbs couldn't wreck it.

  Remember that these qualities are simply characteristics that led Lynch to look deeper into a stock and its fundamentals because companies that had these qualities tend to be undervalued. He wouldn't invest in a company simply because it had one or more of these characteristics, though; in fact, many of the firms in which he ended up investing possessed few or none of these.

A True Disciplinarian

There's one more point about Lynch's general approach—and it's a crucial one that is shared by many of the other gurus we follow. It's simple in theory, but in practice it is one of the hardest things for an investor. Lynch recognized something discussed earlier: that the stock market was unpredictable in the short term, even to the smartest investors. Over the long term, however, good stocks rise like no other investment vehicle, something Lynch also realized. His philosophy: Use a proven strategy and stay in the market for the long term and you'll realize those gains; jump in and out and there's a good chance that you'll miss out on a chunk of them.

That, of course, means resisting the temptation to bail when the market takes some short-term hits and good stocks fall in value—no easy task. But as Lynch once said, "The real key to making money in stocks is not to get scared out of them."

Another One of Lynch's Many Pearls of Wall Street Wisdom

Lynch once said in an interview with PBS that putting money into stocks and counting on having nice profits in a year or two is "just like betting on red or black at the casino. . . . What the market's going to do in one or two years, you don't know."

Lynch's Strategy: Step by Step

About the Peter Lynch Strategy

The Track Record: From the time Lynch took over Fidelity's Magellan Fund in 1977 until the time he retired in 1990, Magellan averaged a 29.2 percent annual return—almost double the S&P 500 average of 15.8 percent. In the last five years of his tenure, the fund beat 99.5 percent of all other funds, according to *Barron's*.

Risk: This strategy is for investors willing to take on a moderate amount of risk. Lynch wasn't really low-risk because he did focus to a degree on fast-growers, but he also avoided the higher-risk areas of the market during his day, such as technology stocks. He considered a nice cross section of stocks, including large companies, which makes his approach suitable for many investors in terms of risk. Also, Lynch suggests focusing on companies you know, which is reassuring to many investors and helps hold down the anxiety level.

Time Horizon: Just as with risk, Lynch is suitable for a variety of investors in terms of time horizon. You can ride his fast-growers for anywhere from 3 to 10 years, but he also has strategies for shorter-term gains, like his stalwarts, which can produce gains of 30 percent to 50 percent in one to two years.

Effort: Because Lynch has an uncommonly wide range of choices and focuses on a range of fundamentals—but holds onto his investments for at least a medium length of time, usually years—his strategy requires a moderate amount of effort on the part of the investor.

Now, let's get down to the nitty-gritty. If buying what you know and the other factors listed above were merely jumping-off points for Lynch, just how did he end up picking stocks?

As mentioned previously, Lynch first broke them down into six different categories: fast-growers, stalwarts, slow-growers, turnarounds, cyclicals, and asset plays. Each of these six categories has value, but Lynch focuses primarily on fast-growers, stalwarts, and slow-growers. Because of our ability to automate the analysis in these three primary categories, we'll focus only on them—but keep in mind there can be good reasons to hold the other types (in particular, Lynch was successful with turnarounds and held a good number of them in his portfolio), although they require special sophistication and finding evaluative data is difficult.

- **Fast-growers**. These were Lynch's favorite type of investment. Such companies have been growing EPS at a rate of 20 percent per year or better over the long term. This seems very straightforward, but there are some areas where we've had to make our best interpretation: For example, Lynch doesn't say what time frame should be used to calculate growth rate. Is it over three years? Five years? To get the best picture of a company's long-term growth history, we use an average of the three-, four-, and five-year EPS growth rates, which we've found to work quite well.
- **Stalwarts**. Stalwarts are companies whose annual EPS growth is in the 10 to 19 percent range (again we use the average of the three-, four-, and five-year EPS figures), and which have sales in the multibillion-dollar range. (Lynch talks a lot about fast-growers, but stalwarts are what he focuses on most in his writings because, in part, fast-growers such as Wal-Mart and Home Depot eventually become stalwarts. Think of stalwarts as well-established companies that still have good growth potential.)
- **Slow-growers**. Slow-growers have an annual EPS growth rate of less than 10 percent (calculated by our model in the same way as it is for fast-growers and stalwarts). These tend to be large and aging companies that pay dividends and are expected to grow slightly faster than the Gross National Product. Lynch focused more on fast-growers and stalwarts than slow-growers; if such stocks appeal to you, invest in them primarily for their dividends.

Determining the Classification

1. EPS growth < 10%   Slow-grower
2. EPS growth ≥ 10% and < 20%   Stalwart
3. EPS growth ≥ 20%   Fast-grower

Because Lynch used different criteria for different classifications of stocks, we'll break the criteria-by-criteria portion of this analysis into three parts: The first section details the criteria he used on all stocks, regardless of their classification. The second section then lists the criteria that are specific to each of the three categories. Finally, the third section includes two "bonus" criteria, which apply to all stocks regardless of their classification.

So if, for example, you're analyzing a fast-grower, you'd use all of the tests in the "For All Stocks" section; then in the second section, you'd only apply the tests under the "Fast-Growers" heading. And last but not least, you'd see if the stock passes the two bonus criteria in the third section.

Part 1: For All Stocks

Whether a stock was a fast-grower, stalwart, or slow-grower, the most important test Lynch applied to it was the P/E/Growth ratio. But that wasn't the only test he used across all categories of stocks. Here's how Lynch used the P/E/G, and those other important tests.

P/E/Growth Ratio Lynch famously used the P/E/G to identify growth stocks selling on the cheap—this is why his strategy is a considered a Growth At a Reasonable Price (GARP) approach. To determine a stock's P/E/G, you divide its price-earnings ratio by its historical growth rate. The rationale: The faster the stock is growing earnings, the higher the P/E an investor should tolerate. The lower the P/E/G, the better, because that means you're getting more earnings growth for your dollar.

For stalwarts and slow-growers, Lynch adjusted the growth portion of the P/E/G for yield because those types of stocks tend to have strong dividend payouts. To do this, simply add the growth rate percentage to the dividend yield percentage. For example, if the stock has a growth rate of 15 percent and a dividend yield of 3 percent, the "G" part of the P/E/G is 18.

P/E/Growth Ratio (P/E/G) for Fast-Growers

1. > 0 and ≤ 0.5   Pass—Best case
2. > 0.5 and ≤ 1   Pass
3. > 1   Fail

Yield–Adjusted P/E/Growth Ratio (P/E/G) for Stalwarts and Slow–Growers

1. > 0 and ≤ 0.5 Pass—Best case
2. > 0.5 and ≤ 1 Pass
3. > 1 Fail

Change in Inventory-to-Sales Ratio Another variable Lynch examined when assessing a stock was the ratio of its inventory to its sales. He makes an important observation here. His view of inventory contains quite a bit of common sense, yet few other gurus mention it. (*Note:* Inventory-to-sales criteria do not apply to nonmanufacturing companies, such as service and financial companies.) Lynch saw it as a red flag when inventories increase faster than sales. Inventory piling up indicates the demand for products isn't what the company expected. In our Lynch-based model, we interpret Lynch as giving an allowance of up to 5 percentage points (inventory/sales ratios can increase up to 5 percentage points from last year to this year). Example: If a company's inventory-to-sales ratio is 10 percent one year, it can be no higher than 15 percent the next year to pass this test.

The bottom line for Lynch: If inventories increase less than sales, the same rate as sales, or a small amount faster than sales, the company passes this test; but if inventories increase substantially more quickly than sales, the firm fails the test.

Change in Inventory-to-Sales Ratio

1. If a financial or service company   Not applicable
2. Change in inventory/sales is negative   Pass—Best case
3. Change in inventory/sales = 0   Pass
4. Change in inventory/sales is positive but ≤ 5 percentage points   Pass—Minimum
5. Change in inventory/sales is positive and > 5 percentage points   Fail

Total Debt-Equity Ratio Lynch also liked companies that were conservatively financed, and he measured this with the debt-equity (D/E) ratio. If a company's debt is less than or equal to 80 percent of its equity, it passes this test. If a firm has a debt-equity ratio greater than 80 percent, it fails. Keep in mind that there are some gradations here—the lower the debt-to-equity ratio, the better. Lynch especially liked companies whose debt was less than 50 percent of their equity.

Certain types of companies, such as financial institutions and utilities, generally carry large amounts of debt because of the nature of their business. For utilities, a debt-equity ratio over 80 percent is acceptable. For financials, Lynch considers other criteria, which makes him unique; other gurus also like low-debt companies but don't make explicit provisions for companies that naturally carry large amounts of debt.

Total Debt-Equity Ratio (D/E)

1. If a financial or service company   N/A (See tests below for financial firms)
2. D/E < 30%   Pass—Best case
3. D/E ≥ 30% and < 50%   Pass—Normal
4. D/E ≥ 50% and < 80%   Pass—Mediocre
5. D/E ≥ 80%, and firm is a utility   Pass
6. D/E ≥ 80%, and firm is not a utility company   Fail

Ratios for Financial Stocks The other areas Lynch examines when it comes to financial stocks are:

- **Equity-to-Assets Ratio.** This is a measure of financial health. If the ratio is 5 percent or greater, a stock passes the test.
- **Return on Assets.** The ROA is a measure of profitability. A financial firm's ROA should be at least 1 percent according to this model.

Equity-to-Assets Ratio (E/A)—Financial Companies Only

1. E/A ≥ 5%   Pass
2. E/A ≥ 13.5%   Pass—Best case
3. E/A < 5%   Fail

Return on Assets (ROA)—Financial Companies Only

1. ROA ≥ 1%   Pass
2. ROA < 1%   Fail

Part 2: Category-Specific Tests

Now, on to the different variables that Lynch applied to different classifications of stocks (i.e., fast-growers, stalwarts, slow-growers). Depending on what classification the stock you're analyzing falls into, find the appropriate section below and perform the additional tests listed in that section.

Fast-Growers

P/E Ratio If a fast-grower's sales are greater than $1 billion and the P/E ratio is less than 40, the stock passes muster. If the P/E is above 40, however, that's a bad sign because large firms have trouble maintaining high enough growth to support P/Es over that threshold. Smaller firms can have very high P/E ratios during their growth years, however, so fast-growers with annual sales of less than $1 billion are exempt from a maximum on their P/E ratios.

P/E for Fast-Growers

1. Sales > $1 billion and PE ≤ 40   Pass
2. Sales > $1 billion and PE > 40   Fail
3. Sales ≤ $1 billion   N/A

EPS Growth While Lynch liked fast-growing stocks, he also believed there is such a thing as too much growth. When a firm's historic growth rate is greater than 50 percent, he avoids it. Growth that high is unlikely to be maintained over the long run. Usually, companies growing at a rate greater than 50 percent per year are in hot industries. That's a Lynch no-no, because everyone already knows about them, and they could be overpriced.

To Lynch, long-term growth between 20 and 50 percent was acceptable, with 20 to 25 percent optimal. His thinking: These growth rates can be maintained.

EPS Growth for Fast-Growers

1. ≥ 20% and ≤ 25%   Pass—Best case
2. > 25% and ≤ 50%   Pass
3. > 50%   Fail

A Few Lynch Fast-Grower Tips

- Look to see if the company has duplicated its successes in more than one city or town to prove that expansion will work.
- Make sure the company still has room to grow.
- Notice whether expansion is speeding up or slowing down and if sales are "one-shot" deals (like a Sony PlayStation), as opposed to products customers buy continuously (such as Coke or Gillette razor blades).
- It is a big plus if few institutions own it and only a handful of analysts have ever heard of it. The less people know about it, the better, because then the stock may be undervalued.

Stalwarts

Sales A stock is considered a true stalwart if its earnings growth rate is between 10 and 20 percent and its annual sales are $2 billion or more. (*Note:* We actually interpret this criterion's threshold as $1.9 billion because a 5 percent difference in this rule of thumb just isn't meaningful.) If sales are less than $1.9 billion, it doesn't qualify as a true stalwart and is ignored.

Sales for Stalwarts

1. ≥ $1.9 billion	Pass
2. < $1.9 billion	Fail

Earnings per Share Lynch wanted stalwarts to be profitable, which means its earnings per share over the trailing 12 months will be positive. If it makes no money or loses money, it fails the test.

EPS for Stalwarts

1. EPS > 0	Pass
2. EPS ≤ 0	Fail

Slow-Growers

Sales Lynch likes slow-growers to be larger companies. If a company's annual sales are equal to or greater than $1 billion, it passes muster. If smaller than $1 billion, it fails.

Sales for Slow Growers

1. Sales ≥ $1 billion   Pass
2. Sales < $1 billion   Fail

Comparing Yield with the S&P 500's Yield A criterion Lynch uses with slow-growers is to compare the stock's yield with the yield of the S&P 500; if it is higher than the S&P 500, it passes this test but if not, it fails. (*Note:* Minimum acceptable yield is 3 percent. We interpret Lynch as putting this floor under the yield because a major reason for investing in slow growers is their yield. If they have too low a yield—irrespective of what the S&P 500's yield is—they aren't worth holding. Less than 3 percent just isn't worth it.)

Yield Compared with the S&P 500 Yield (for Slow-Growers)

1. Yield ≥ S&P Yield and ≥ 3%   Pass
2. Yield < 3%   Fail
3. Yield < S&P Yield and ≥ 3%   Fail

Part 3: Bonus Criteria

While these two criteria aren't mandatory, Lynch considered them to be a bonus when looking at stocks. They apply to all categories of stocks (both stocks listed in Parts 1 and 2).

Free Cash Flow per Share-to-Current Price Ratio Cash flow, notes Lynch, is the amount of money a company takes in as a result of doing business. Every company takes in cash. That's no big deal. A distinguishing factor among companies is that some companies have to spend more money than others to bring in their cash flow. That's why Lynch emphasizes free cash flow, which he defines as "what's left over after the normal capital spending is taken out. It's the cash you've taken in that you don't have to spend." Technically, free cash flow is:

Operating earnings + Amortization + Depreciation − The full amount paid for capital equipment

The more *free cash flow* (FCF) a company has, the better. Lynch looked at free cash flow per share compared to the stock's price. He gives the example of a company whose stock was $20 (and fairly priced according to his usual measures). But, in addition, it had $10 to $11 per share in total cash flow and $7 left over (free cash flow) after capital spending. If you divide the FCF ($7) by the price ($20), you get 35 percent, which is Lynch's threshold for becoming excited about a high FCF. Though this criterion is not required for Lynch's analysis of his various categories of companies, it is considered a bonus if free cash flow meets or beats the minimum of 35 percent or more of the stock price.

Free Cash Flow per Share-to-Current Price Ratio (Bonus)

1. ≥ 35%   Pass—Bonus

Net Cash per Share-to-Current Price Ratio Lynch likes to see a lot of net cash, which he defines as the cash and marketable securities found on the balance statement less long-term debt. If a company's stock is trading for $30, and it has net cash per share of $9 (30 percent), that's good. If it has $12 in net cash (40 percent), that's very attractive. And if it has $15 or more (50 percent +) and passes Lynch's other criteria, quick, mortgage the house and kids, your ship has come in. Note that instead of trying to find the cash per share and the price per share, one is able to use the total cash less the total long-term debt in the company as of its most recent statement and divide by market cap.

Net Cash per Share-to-Current Price Ratio (Bonus)

1. ≥ 30% and < 40%   Pass—Good
2. ≥ 40% and < 50%   Pass—Better
3. ≥ 50%   Pass—Best

 Click It!

If the P/E/G Investor approach appeals to you and you're looking for some Lynch-type picks, visit www.guruinvestorbook.com. The free site lists three stocks that pass our Lynch model every day, a good way to get ideas when building your portfolio.

The Lynch-Based Model Performance

Using the Lynch-based quantitative strategy that we've just outlined, we at Validea have been fortunate enough to see some Lynch-like results. Since we began tracking it on July 15, 2003, a 10-stock portfolio that includes stocks that score highest using our Lynch-based method has gained 73.5 percent (11.6 percent annualized)—more than tripling the S&P 500 gain of 21.4 percent (4.0 percent annualized). It's done so with a bit more volatility than the S&P (the portfolio's beta is 1.15, compared to the market beta of 1.0), but when you consider the results, the slightly higher volatility has certainly been worth it.

The 20-stock Lynch-based portfolio that we have tracked has done even better. Since its inception (also July 15, 2003), it has gained 88.8 percent (13.5 percent annualized), with essentially the same beta (1.18) as the 10-stock portfolio.

Both the 10- and 20-stock portfolios have beaten the S&P in five of the six years since we began tracking them (that includes the partial years of 2003 and 2008). The 10-stock portfolio's best year was 2004, when it gained 34.7 percent, compared to just 9 percent for the S&P. Its worst year: 2007, when it dropped 13.5 percent while the S&P rose 3.5 percent. The 20-stock model's best year was the partial year of 2003, when it gained 38 percent compared to the S&P's 11.1 percent. (Its best full year was 2004, when it jumped 24.8 percent compared to the S&P's 9 percent gain.) And while it lagged the S&P's 3.5 percent gain, the larger portfolio still gained 1.1 percent in 2007 (its worst year).

In terms of the types of stocks it targets, our Lynch-based model is somewhat similar to Lynch himself. It finds appeal in a wide variety of industries and sectors, and its highest-rated stocks tend to be fast-growers, with some stalwarts mixed in.

One difference in Lynch's own approach and our Lynch-based strategy is that we allow our model to roam the technology sector. Like Graham and Buffett, Lynch stayed away from tech stocks because he thought they were too risky. While that may have been true in the 1980s, technology has become a huge part of our economy today, and many tech stocks have now established long records of consistent success. That makes well-run tech stocks a lot less risky than the tech stocks of Lynch's era, so we feel it appropriate to include them in our universe

Table 7.1 Model Portfolio Risk and Return Statistics

	10-Stock	20-Stock	S&P 500
Annualized Return	11.6%	13.5%	4.0%
Total Return	73.5%	88.8%	21.4%
Best Full Year	34.7% in 2004	24.8% in 2004	13.6% in 2006
Worst Full Year	−13.5% in 2007	1.1% in 2007	3.0% in 2005
Beta	1.15	1.18	1.0
Accuracy	57.1%	58.7%	N/A

Note: Returns statistics are from July 15, 2003 to July 15, 2008. See Appendix A for additional return disclosure and explanation.
Source: Guru Model Portfolio Tool, Validea.com.

of investment options. One good example: Foundry Networks, a firm that designs, manufactures, and sells switching and routing solutions that are used by computer networks and has generated positive earnings per share for nine straight years. Our Lynch-based model targeted Foundry in the summer of 2006, and the stock yielded a 25.9 percent gain in the four months it was in the 10-stock portfolio. (See Table 7.1.)

Lynch's Key Investing Criteria

FAST-GROWERS

- Stock must have an EPS growth rate between 20 and 50 percent.
- Look for a P/E/G ratio below 1.0.
- Look to see if the company has duplicated its successes in more than one city or town.
- Look for a debt-equity ratio less than 80 percent (financial and utility companies are exempt).
- For financials, look for an equity-assets ratio of at least 5 percent and a return on assets rate of at least 1 percent.
- Notice whether expansion is speeding up or slowing down and if sales are from "one-shot" deals, or from products customers buy continuously.

- If sales are greater than \$1 billion, the P/E ratio should be less than 40; if sales are less than \$1 billion, no P/E restriction applies.
- The inventory-sales ratio should be decreasing, or increasing by only a small margin.
- Try to find stocks that few institutions own, and which are known by only a handful of analysts.
- If the free cash flow-price ratio and/or net cash-price ratio are very high, the stock gets bonus points.

STALWARTS

- STOCK MUST HAVE AN EPS GROWTH RATE BETWEEN 10 AND 20 PERCENT.
- Sales must be in the multi-billion dollar range.
- Look for a yield-adjusted P/E/G below 1.0.
- EPS should be positive.
- Look for a debt-equity ratio less than 80 percent (financial and utility companies are exempt).
- For financials, look for an equity-assets ratio of at least 5 percent and a return-on-assets rate of at least 1 percent.
- The inventory-sales ratio should be decreasing, or increasing only by a small margin.
- If the free cash flow-price ratio and/or net cash-price ratio are very high, the stock gets bonus points.

SLOW-GROWERS

- STOCK MUST HAVE EPS GROWTH RATE BELOW 10 PERCENT.
- Look for a yield-adjusted P/E/G below 1.0.
- Sales should be greater than \$1 billion.
- Yield should be higher than the S&P average, and at least 3 percent.
- Look for a debt-equity ratio less than 80 percent (financial and utility companies are exempt).

- For financials, look for an equity–assets ratio of at least 5 percent and a return on assets rate of at least 1 percent.
- The inventory–sales ratio should be decreasing, or increasing by just a small margin.
- If the free cash flow–price ratio and/or net cash–price ratio are very high, the stock gets bonus points.

Chapter 8

Kenneth L. Fisher

The Price-Sales Pioneer

Learning is always rebellion. . . . Every bit of new truth discovered is revolutionary to what was believed before.

—MARGARET LEE RUNBECK

I f you're at all familiar with the stock market, you almost surely have some knowledge of the price-earnings ratio. For decades, the P/E ratio has been the most frequently used and discussed stock analysis ratio. The P/E ratio is determined by dividing a stock's per-share price by the amount of per-share earnings it generates to give investors an idea of how much bang they are getting for their buck. As you've already seen, Ben Graham, John Neff, David Dreman, and Peter Lynch all used the P/E ratio in one way or another when analyzing stocks, and the statistic has become so widely used that it is often the only financial ratio included in newspapers' daily listings of stock quotes.

But when most people are focused on one thing, you'll usually find Kenneth Fisher focused on something else—and quite often to great benefit. That certainly was the case back in 1984, when Fisher's book *Super Stocks* turned the P/E-focused investment world on its head. While many investors relied heavily on the P/E ratio, Fisher believed there was a major hole in its usefulness. Part of the problem, he explained in *Super Stocks,* is that earnings—even the earnings of good companies—can fluctuate greatly from year to year. The decision to replace equipment or facilities in one year rather than in another, the use of money for new research that will help the company reap profits later on, and changes in accounting methods can all turn one quarter's profits into the next quarter's losses. And that can happen without regard for what Fisher thought was truly important in the long term: how well or poorly the company's underlying business was performing.

While earnings fluctuate, Fisher found that sales were far more stable. In fact, he found that the sales of what he called "super companies"—those that were capable of growing their stock price 3 to 10 times in value in a period of three to five years—rarely decline significantly. Because of that, he pioneered the use of a new way to value stocks: the *price-sales ratio* (PSR), which compared the total price of a company's stock to the total sales the company generated.

Fisher's innovative theory made for big news in stock market circles, and *Super Stocks* became a best seller. Since its publication, the price-sales ratio has become a major tool for many investors, and Fisher has built something of an empire in the investment world. With a net worth of $1.8 billion, he was one of the 300 richest Americans as of 2007, according to *Forbes.com,* and his money management firm, Fisher Investments, oversees about $45 billion in assets. In addition, Fisher has become one of the longest-running columnists in Forbes magazine's history, and he's written three more books on investing. And, through it all, Fisher remains very much a stock market rebel—though, as you'll soon see, now the reasons don't involve the ratio he made famous.

Who Is Kenneth L. Fisher?

While many of the gurus we've examined so far came from humble beginnings, Fisher's family was quite well-to-do. In fact, he comes from investing royalty: His father, the late Phillip A. Fisher, is considered by some to be the "Father of Growth Investing." The elder Fisher's book, *Common Stocks and Uncommon Profits* (1958), is something of a bible for growth-stock investing, and was the first investment book ever to make the *New York Times* list of bestsellers. Just how influential was it? Well, a young Warren Buffett was so impressed with the book that he traveled to California to meet Phillip Fisher and learn his strategies firsthand.

Kenneth Fisher, born November 29, 1950, first wanted to go in a different direction from his father—initially, he hoped for a career in forestry. Family pressure hooked him into the family business, however—though, as we'll soon see, forestry has managed to play a part in his investment career.

After graduating from California State University, Humbolt (now Humbolt State University), Fisher began working with his father. While he has spoken with great reverence for his father, the two apparently weren't the best coworkers. In an article in *Millionaire Magazine*, Fisher is quoted as saying about his working relationship with the senior Fisher: "It was something I figured out was not going to work very well. When I started with him, he was already 65 years old and, in that regard, was very habitual. At that point in time, he was not interested in chang- ing very much . . . and I am very much of a rebel." Nevertheless, Fisher no doubt learned from his father; his website states that Ken Fisher "is the only industry professional his father ever professionally trained."

Today, Fisher's money management firm handles more than $45 billion in assets, and has clients that include Fortune 500 companies, foundations and endowments, and thousands of high net worth investors. Its isolated location gives a clue about Fisher's rebellious nature. "In the financial world, people have a tremendous tendency to think all the same things that everyone else thinks," he once told *Millionaire* magazine. "It's actually very hard to build a corporate culture in the middle of an urban environment where people can, so freely, if you will, get their thoughts contaminated by all the people around them. So by having most of the firm [Fisher Investments] up here, we more easily establish a corporate identity and a corporate culture unique to us—which you can only get with the separation from a typi- cal downtown firm."

Interesting Fact

In 1973, Ken separated from his father professionally and created his own investment company, Fisher Investments Inc., located in Woodside, California, next to a lush forest preserve that is in splendid isolation from the financial world. He has conveniently placed his business and his home in the forest he learned to love as a youngster. Fisher has a huge collection of logging history, and, according to the Humbolt State University website, he is regarded as one of the world's foremost experts on 19th century logging, and has documented more than 35 abandoned logging camps in the northern Santa Cruz Mountains. In 2006, he established the Kenneth L. Fisher Chair in Redwood Forest Ecology at his alma mater. Fisher lives in Woodside with his wife of nearly 40 years, Sherrilynn. The couple has three grown sons, one of whom wrote a book about investing for teenagers while he was in his teens.

While his track record as a money manager is pretty good, Fisher may be most known for his work for Forbes magazine. He's been writing his "Portfolio Strategy" column for *Forbes* since 1984, making him the fourth-longest-running columnist in the prestigious magazine's history. In addition, he has authored or coauthored numerous other articles for such publications as *Financial Analysts Journal, Journal of Portfolio Management,* and *Research.*

Fisher has also published three books since *Super Stocks,* including *The Wall Street Waltz* (1987), *100 Minds That Made the Market* (1993), and *The Only Three Questions That Count* (2006). *The Only Three Questions That Count* details Fisher's investment strategy today, and you should be aware that his approach has evolved quite a bit since *Super Stocks.* (We examine how and why that evolution has occurred later in this chapter.) For our Fisher-based model, however, we stick with the approach that Fisher detailed in *Super Stocks.* There are a couple good reasons why. First, Fisher's *Super Stocks* strategy is largely quantifiable; he outlines several specific, quantitative criteria and guidelines, something he doesn't do as much of in his latest book about his new approach. Secondly, Fisher's publisher just released a new, updated edition of *Super Stocks* in 2007, which leads us to presume that Fisher believes there is still some value in his original approach. And thirdly, the strategy quite simply works. Our *Super Stocks*-based model has been our best performer over the past five years, another reason it remains quite relevant today.

Price-Sales Investing: A Revolutionary Approach

If you're going to understand why Fisher believed so strongly in using the PSR to identify undervalued stocks, you need to understand what he called "the glitch." Like some of the other gurus we've looked at, Fisher is a student of investor psychology, and one thing he believed investors did was raise expectations to unrealistic levels for companies that have periods of strong early growth. When these darlings of Wall Street have a setback—maybe their earnings drop, or maybe they continue to grow but simply don't keep pace with investors' lofty expectations—their stocks can then plummet as investors overreact and sell, thinking they've been led astray. (This is not unlike David Dreman's take on expectations and surprises.)

But while investors overreact, Fisher believed that these "glitches" are often simply a part of a firm's maturation. Good companies with good management identify the problems, solve them, and move forward. As they do, the firms' earnings and stock prices begin to rise again. If you can buy a stock when it hits a glitch and its earnings and price are down, you can make a bundle by sticking with it until it rights the ship and other investors jump back on board.

The trick is thus trying to evaluate a company during those periods when Wall Street is down on it because its earnings are in flux, or even negative, so that you can find good candidates for a rebound (remember, you can't use a P/E ratio to evaluate a company that is losing money, because it has no earnings). The answer, Fisher said, was to look at sales, and the PSR.

The PSR works similarly to the P/E ratio, except that sales are used in place of earnings. The PSR, Fisher wrote in *Super Stocks,* "is the total market value of a company divided by the last 12 months' corporate sales." To calculate the total value of a company, or its total market capitalization, you simply multiply its stock price by the company's total number of shares. It is, in a sense, what you would pay for the company if you wanted to buy the company in its entirety.

For example, if a company's stock is trading at $20 and it has 10 million shares outstanding, its market value or market cap is $20 × 10 million, or $200 million. If its sales last year were $250 million, its PSR is 0.80 ($200 million/$250 million = 0.80).

"Why should one consider price-sales ratios at all?" Fisher asked in *Super Stocks.* "Because they measure popularity relative to business size. Price/Sales Ratios are of value because the sales portion of the relationship is inherently more stable than most other variables in the corporate world."

His point is this: Earnings can be highly volatile, including the earnings of good companies, while sales rarely decline for top-flight businesses. They may be flat, but they generally tend to be less volatile than earnings. Earnings, however, can be moved quickly and dramatically by a wide variety of variables that do not necessarily portend how the company will perform, such as changes in accounting procedures or in the amount of research and development the company engages in. Wall Street focuses on earnings and abandons companies with earnings troubles, which is why Fisher liked to look at sales. A company with troubled earnings but strong sales is a company Fisher may well have wanted to own in his *Super Stocks* days.

Part of Fisher's thinking was that, if a company has a low PSR, even a slight improvement in its profit margins can produce a big gain in earnings, which will then drive the stock's price up since most investors react to earnings. Companies with high PSRs don't have this leverage.

Another part of Fisher's thinking was that investors should focus on causes, not results, when it came to evaluating a firm's prospects. "What is the bottom line?" he wrote. "To buy stocks successfully, you need to price them based on causes, not results. The causes are business conditions—products with a cost structure allowing for sales. The results flow from there—profits, profit margins, and finally earnings per share."

One more general note on Fisher's take on PSRs: He doesn't like looking at per-share numbers because he thinks it is important to focus on the overall business, including its size.

In terms of specifics, Fisher listed three rules regarding PSRs in *Super Stocks*:

Rule 1. Avoid stocks with PSRs greater than 1.5, and never buy those with a PSR in excess of 3. In this case, you are paying $3 for every $1 of sales. He admits stocks with such high PSRs can increase in price but only based on hype, not anything of substance.

Rule 2. Aggressively look for stocks with PSRs of 0.75 or less. Such a PSR means you are paying 75 cents or less for every $1 of sales. These are the stocks you want, and you should hold onto them for a long time, he says.

Rule 3. Once you've bought a stock with a desirable PSR (0.75 or less), sell it when the PSR reaches 3.00 (if you don't want to take much risk) or hold it even longer, to 6.00 or higher, if you are really a risk taker.

There are some variations on these rules, however. For example, Fisher found that different industries often behave differently, and one distinction he drew involved "basic industry" or "smokestack" stocks— those that "plug along without much fanfare making the essential materials and parts we all need in our daily lives," such as steel, auto, chemical, paper, mining, and machinery firms.

Because companies in these smokestack industries tend to grow slowly and don't earn exceptionally high margins, they don't generate a lot of excitement or command high prices on Wall Street, and their P/S ratios tend to be lower than those of companies that produce more exciting products. Fisher adjusts his P/S target for these firms. Similarly our Fisher-based model looks for smokestack firms with P/S ratios between 0.4 and 0.8; it is particularly high on those with P/S values under 0.4.

Fisher's research also indicated the following about PSRs:

- Big companies tend to have lower PSRs than smaller companies (lower PSRs are better).
- Pleasant surprises come mostly from stocks with PSRs of less than 1.
- Disappointments come from stocks with the highest PSRs just prior to reporting the poor results.

Beyond the PSR

While the PSR was key to Fisher's *Super Stocks* strategy, he warned not to rely exclusively on it. Terrible companies can have low price-sales ratios simply because the investment world knows they are headed for financial ruin. To be a true "super stock," a firm also had to have other strong fundamentals. Profit margins, debt ratios, earnings growth and free cash flows were all an important part of his *Super Stocks* quantitative approach. (We examine his specific criteria in the "Step by Step" section of this chapter.)

In addition, Fisher didn't believe in simply buying stocks that met quantitative screens. Some of his criteria were qualitative, and a material part of *Super Stocks* was devoted to explaining how to look at a company qualitatively and how to do qualitative research. For example, much like Warren Buffett seeks out companies that are surrounded by "economic moats" that protect them from competitors, Fisher looked for companies that had an "unfair advantage" over their competition, such as strong name recognition or an important patent. For our model, we of course must stick to the quantifiable criteria Fisher detailed, which are substantial and have proven quite successful to date.

One interesting way in which Fisher's *Super Stocks* approach differed from most of our other gurus' strategies is its treatment of firms in the technology and medical industries. Fisher saw research as a commodity, and to these types of companies, it was a valuable one. To measure how much Wall Street valued the research that a company did, he compared the value of the company's stock (its market cap) to the money it spends on research. Price-research ratios less than 5 percent were the best case, and those between 5 and 10 percent were still bargains. Those between 10 and 15 percent were borderline, while those over 15 percent should be avoided.

One final quantitative note: After the publication of *Super Stocks,* Fisher refined his PSR strategy's take on debt. He didn't want a firm to be mortgaged to the hilt, so he targeted companies with current assets at least double current liabilities and total equity at least half of total assets.

Fisher on How to Time the Market (Sort of)

In Chapter 2, we examined how market timing just doesn't work for the vast majority of investors. In *Super Stocks,* Fisher expresses a similar sentiment. "There is no end to the lengths people go to try to find the magic key to the stock market," he writes, adding that people have tried computers, astrology, demographic studies, sunspots, economics, technical analysis, tea leaves, and even "the skin of a dried lizard at sunset cast to the wind." But, he says, "at best, one could hope to be right about the stock market perhaps half the time. At worst, one is apt to be wrong most of the time. Stock-market seers run hot for a couple of years. Then most embarrass themselves."

But there's more. Even if you *could* predict the market's major moves, Fisher says it wouldn't be worth it. He studied how an investor would have fared had he correctly called every 100-point move of the Dow Jones Industrial Average for the five-year period ending December 31, 1982. Such an investor (which of course, probably doesn't exist) would have earned a compound rate of return of 51.5 percent. That sounds great, but, according to Fisher, it's no better than the return you could generate by buying a super stock. And, in the perfect-market-timing scenario, you also would be jumping in or out of the market 11 times during that span, resulting in significant trading costs. Plus, since the vast majority of those 100-point swings occurred in less than a year, you'd be taxed at higher short-term gains rates. Super Stocks make their gains over a three- to five-year period, generating long-term gains that are subject to lower tax rates.

Fisher does, however, offer a solution for how to time the market. His two rules:

1. When a company is selling at a (sufficiently) low PSR— *buy* it.
2. If you can't find companies selling at (sufficiently) low PSRs, *don't* buy stocks.

Of course, this isn't exactly market timing in the way most people think of it, because it looks at specific stocks rather than the entire market. But whether you call it market timing or not, it's certainly a lot better plan than those used by most investors who try to time the broader market's movements.

Source: Kenneth L. Fisher, *Super Stocks*, reissued edition (New York: McGraw-Hill, 2008).

Always Evolving

As we noted earlier, Fisher's investing approach has evolved in many ways since the original publication of *Super Stocks*. In the 1990s, for example, he began to focus more and more on the importance of investment style. Investors, he said, need to focus on style and to rotate their investment holdings to match the popular style of the time.

One interesting example of what Fisher meant by "style" involves his study of stock returns between January 1976 and June 1995. In this study, he broke stocks down into six styles: big-cap value, midcap value, small-cap value, big-cap growth, midcap growth, and small-cap growth. What he found was that these styles went in and out of favor periodically. From January 1976 to September 1978, for example, small cap value was the leading style, producing an annualized return of 42.69 percent. This beat the loser, big growth, by 37.84 percent. The spread of the best four styles over the worst two was big—23.25 percent—and the four best styles outperformed the S&P 500 by 23.41 percent.

The bottom line for the entire period studied (January 1976 to June 1995) was:

The annualized return for the best four styles at a given time	17.79%
Annualized market return (Wilshire 5000)	14.64%
Premium of best four styles over the market	3.15%

For Fisher, this was evidence that style selection was a crucial part of achieving excess returns in the market. If you could figure out when certain styles were going to be in favor, you could pick from a wide swath of stocks in that style and do well. To decide which style to pick, he would use certain economic indicators, such as the yield curve (which measures the relationship between shorter- and longer-term interest rates) and how the U.S. gross domestic product (GDP) compared to overseas GDP. Back then, he advocated focusing on what he believed the best four styles at a given time were, and avoiding the worst two. Focusing your investments only on what you believe is the best style at a given time could net you even better returns, but you risked losing a bunch if you picked the wrong style.

As Fisher focused more and more on style, he scrapped the PSR strategy he had detailed in *Super Stocks*. The reason? He believed that once the masses learned about it, the ratio had become priced into the market. Essentially, more people were focusing on low-PSR stocks, driving their prices higher and limiting the gains you could get from buying them. (We'll address this and its impact on our model in a bit.)

Today, Fisher remains focused very much on style, so much so that he says only about 10 percent of his strategy involves actual stock selection. He writes in *The Only Three Questions That Count* that about 70 percent of it involves assessing various economic, political, and sentiment drivers to determine asset allocation—that is, how to divvy up investment dollars among stocks, bonds, and cash. Another 20 percent is "sub-asset allocation," which involves deciding which countries, which sectors, which types of market capitalizations, and which styles (value or growth) to invest in. Only after he's determined how much of his portfolio to put in stocks and which categories of stocks he's interested in does he start looking at individual stocks. From there, he says, he goes category by category (one category might be "U.S. small-cap value industrials", for example), and picks a few stocks from each.

How does he pick those stocks? Part of it is fundamentals (in one example he mentions in "Three Questions," he even notes that a stock he liked was selling at a low price for its revenues—essentially meaning its PSR was low). But a big part of it is nonquantitative, as is the way he decides his asset allocation and sub-asset allocation. One of the key points in "Three Questions" is that, according to Fisher, "You can't make market bets and win long term unless you know something others don't." It's the same concept behind his reason for ditching his low-PSR approach: Once the masses are aware of an investment strategy, it gets priced into the market. That's why one of the three questions the book's title refers to is "What Can You Fathom That Others Find Unfathomable?"

One example Fisher gives of something he can fathom but most investors can't is the "presidential term cycle." Part of this phenomenon is that, historically, stock returns are much better in the third and fourth year of a president's term than they are in the first two years. Fisher surmises that investors are more hesitant in the first part of the term because that's when big changes can occur as the president begins to put his or her agenda into action. In particular, one thing that can occur is the redistribution of wealth through tax and other legislative changes, something that makes Wall Street very cautious. By the third and fourth years, however, the president has settled in and controversial legislation is unlikely because he or she is trying to get reelected or is simply tired and hanging on as their term winds down. Investors have more of an idea what they can expect, so they're more likely to be bullish, the theory goes.

Fisher is also a big proponent of looking at global economic indicators—not just those that reflect conditions in the United States. He uses the global yield curve (the spread between shorter- and longer-term interest rates) as a way to discern whether to focus on growth or value stocks, for example. "Simply put, the global yield curve tells you when to switch from value to growth and back," he writes. "After it has gone completely flat, you head into a period of growth stock dominance. After it gets very steep, you switch into value stock dominance. After it flattens, it's time to tilt to growth again." Fisher focuses on the global yield curve rather than the U.S. yield curve because, "If one country's yield curve inverts while the global yield curve remains positive, there are still opportunities for businesses, institutions, private clients, and so on to continue doing business globally." Fisher also considers factors such as the global gross domestic product and global inflation. This global focus, particularly the global yield curve information, is another example of how Fisher takes advantage of knowing something that most other investors don't know. (Be aware that Fisher doesn't base his approach on just one thing that he can fathom but others can't—"Never assume you have found the one silver bullet," he writes.)

The presidential cycle, global yield curve, and other atypical factors Fisher uses today to guide his investment approach are quite interesting, but, to Fisher, they're not carved in stone. "The advantages I showed you will all fade away one day" as they become known and priced into the market, he writes. That's why it's critical, he says, to continue to try to fathom what other find unfathomable. "Winning at investing requires constant innovation and constant testing," he says. Put another way, you have to be willing to go against the Wall Street grain to win in the stock market. That same rebelliousness that led Fisher to focus on the PSR years ago is still there; it's just in a different form today—and it could be in a different form tomorrow, next month, or next year, depending on what happens in the investing world.

The Fisher Strategy: Step by Step

About the Ken Fisher Strategy

The Track Record:	From 1995 to 2007, Fisher's Global Total Return fund at Fisher Investments produced net annual returns of 13.0 percent, beating both the S&P 500 (11.3 percent) and the MSCI World Benchmark (9.1 percent). In addition, Fisher's picks as a *Forbes* columnist averaged an 11.7 percent annualized return from 1996 through 2005, beating the S&P 500 Price Index return of 6.8 percent during that period.
Risk:	Using Fisher's original methodology entails a moderate amount of risk because a key component of his approach, the price-sales ratio, goes in and out of favor over time.
Time Horizon:	Expect to hold for a long time but not indefinitely—typically 5 to 10 years.
Effort:	Relatively low.

With all of Fisher's talk of evolving and adjusting, the obvious question is this: Why does our *Super Stocks*-based strategy continue to work? One big reason may be because, while the PSR is at the heart of the strategy, it is by no means the only part of it. As we reviewed earlier, Fisher's Super Stocks approach also examined several other financial criteria, such as debt-equity ratios, free cash per share, profit margins, EPS growth rates, and even price-research ratios for medical and tech firms. By looking at all of these areas, the approach ensures that the companies it targets are strong from a number of viewpoints, and over the long term those are the types of stocks that will net you nice gains.

Now, let's take a look at just what the Fisher-based strategy entails so that you can use it to beat the market. We've broken our examination of this methodology into two parts: The first several criteria are used to determine if a stock merits initial interest from our model; the subsequent criteria are then used to determine whether a stock is truly a super stock.

Leading Off

In order to get initial interest from our Fisher-based model, a stock must meet the following criteria.

Price-Sales Ratio While most investors focus on the price-earnings ratio as a way to find undervalued stocks, Fisher found that the P/E could be misleading because a variety of factors—accounting practices, one-time expenses, and so on—can impact earnings in any given year. Sales, however, give a more accurate picture of the strength (or weakness) of a company's underlying business, according to Fisher. The prospective company should thus have a low PSR. What "low" entailed was different for Fisher depending on the type of stock. The following are the PSR values he recommended in his book; they are the same values we use in our Fisher-based model to determine if a stock gets initial interest.

Noncyclical and Technology Stocks

- **PSR is 0.75 or below.** Fisher said to aggressively seek noncyclical companies with PSRs of 0.75 or less. These are tremendous values.
- **PSR is above 0.75 and less than or equal to 1.5.** Fisher said these firms are good values.
- **PSR is above 1.5 and less than or equal to 3.** If the PSR is in this range, Fisher said not to buy. If you own the stock already, however, continue to hold it.

- **PSR is above 3**. Fisher said never to buy a stock when it reaches a PSR this high. If you own it, sell, unless you are willing to take on additional risk; it all depends on your aversion or willingness to assume additional risk. If you are willing to take on more risk, consider holding the stock until the PSR reaches 6.

Cyclical Stocks

- **PSR is 0.4 or below**. Fisher said to aggressively seek cyclical companies with PSRs equal to or less than 0.4. These are tremendous values.
- **PSR is greater than 0.4 and less than or equal to 0.8**. Stocks within this range are considered good values for cyclical industries.
- **PSR is above 0.8**. Fisher said these stocks are poor values and should not be purchased. If you own any, consider selling them.

Price-Sales Ratio (PSR) for Noncyclical and Technology Stocks

1. ≤ 0.75   Pass—Best case
2. > 0.75 and ≤1.50   Pass
3. > 1.5 and ≤ 3.0   Pass—OK
4. > 3   Fail

Price-Sales Ratio (PSR) for Cyclicals

1. ≤ 0.4   Pass—Best case
2. > 0.4 and ≤ 0.8   Pass
3. > 0.8   Fail

Total Debt–Equity Ratio According to Fisher, less debt equals less risk. The model we base on his writings requires firms to have debt-equity (D/E) ratios no greater than 40 percent. (Since financial companies inherently carry a lot of debt because of the nature of their businesses, they are not required to pass this criterion of the Fisher-based model.)

Total Debt–Equity Ratio (D/E)

1. ≤ 40%   Pass
2. >40%   Fail

Price-Research Ratio According to this approach, companies in the technology and medical sectors should be looked at differently from other companies because of their need for research. For companies in these industries, Fisher liked to look at the *price-research ratio* (PRR), which measures how the market values a company's research and development. If the company is neither a technology nor medical company, do not put much emphasis on this particular variable.

To determine the PRR, divide a company's market cap (that is, its per-share price multiplied by its number of shares outstanding) by the amount it's spent on research and development over the past 12 months. To Fisher, technology and medical companies with PRRs below 5 were rare and should be purchased. Usually, these companies are snapped up by larger companies because they are very undervalued.

Companies with PRRs between 5 and 10 are also bargains and should be purchased, according to this method, while those with PRRs between 10 and 15 are borderline. Companies with PRRs greater than 15 should never be purchased because they either spend too little on R&D or are extremely overvalued.

Price-Research Ratio (PRR)

1. < 5   Pass—Best case
2. ≥ 5 and ≤ 10   Pass
3. >10 and ≤15   Pass—OK
4. >15   Fail

Super Stock Criteria

If a stock gets initial interest by doing well on the tests listed above, it must then pass four additional criteria to be considered a super stock.

Price-Sales Ratio for Super Stocks To be a super stock, Fisher required an even lower PSR than the criterion listed above. He wanted noncyclical companies to have PSRs of 0.75 or lower; for cyclical firms, he wanted PSRs of 0.4 or lower. A stock must pass the appropriate one of those standards to get strong interest from our Fisher-based model.

Price-Sales Ratio (PSR) for Noncyclical and Technology Super Stocks

1. ≤ 0.75   Pass
2. >0.75   Fail

Price–Sales Ratio (PSR) for Cyclical Super Stocks

1. ≤ 0.4   Pass
2. > 0.4   Fail

Inflation-Adjusted EPS Growth For it to be a super stock, Fisher liked a company to have an inflation-adjusted long-term EPS growth rate greater than 15 percent. A stock has to meet that standard to get strong interest from our Fisher-based model.

Inflation–Adjusted EPS Growth

1. > 15%   Pass
2. ≤ 15%   Fail

Free Cash Flow per Share To be a super stock, a company also needs positive free cash flow. A firm should have enough cash available to sustain three years of negative free cash flow. This is based on the premise that companies that run out of cash will soon be out of business. To get strong interest from the Fisher-based model, a stock must thus have a positive free cash flow per share.

Free Cash Flow per Share

1. > 0   Pass
2. ≤ 0   Fail

Three-Year Average Net Profit Margin Fisher believed stocks should be valued not on such things as earnings, which are results of other things, but instead on root causes that led to those results. Profit margins, like sales, are a cause, and Fisher said a firm should produce annual net profit margins of at least 5 percent over the past three years to be a super stock. That's the standard a stock has to meet to get strong interest from our Fisher-based strategy.

Three–Year Average Net Profit Margin

1. ≥ 5%   Pass
2. < 5%   Fail

 **Click It!**

At this book's companion website, www.guruinvestorbook.com, you can view three stocks every day that pass our Fisher-based Price/Sales Investor model. The free site also provides links to our analysis of just why a stock makes the grade.

The Fisher-Based Model Performance

Since we started tracking our eight original guru strategies in July 2003, our Fisher-based model has been our best performer. Our 10-stock Fisher-based portfolio has gained 157.4 percent over its first five years, more than seven times the S&P 500s 21.4 percent gain over that period. It got off to a fast start, nearly tripling the S&P's gains in both the partial year of 2003 and the full year 2004. After a slight setback in 2005, when it dropped 2.7 percent, the portfolio stormed back in 2006, gaining 40 percent versus the S&P's 13.6 percent, and then jumping more than 19 percent in 2007, when the S&P gained just 3.5 percent. The outperformance continued in the first half of 2008, with the Fisher-based portfolio down just 3.7 percent while the S&P dropped more than 17 percent.

The 20-stock Fisher-based portfolio has been the second best performer in its class, gaining 127.5 percent since its July 2003 inception. Interestingly, this larger portfolio has beaten the market handily every year. (In 2005, when its 10-stock cousin dipped, the 20-stock model gained 12.5 percent, more than quadrupling the S&P's gain.) Its worst year was 2007, when it rose 6.7 percent. That still nearly doubled the S&P's 3.5 percent gain. The portfolio was down through the first part of 2008, but its 7.8 percent loss was less than half of the S&P's 17.3 percent loss.

The Fisher model is in the middle of the pack when it comes to volatility. The betas for the 10- and 20-stock portfolios are 1.23 and 1.19 percent, respectively.

In addition to posting the biggest gains, the Fisher-based model has been one of our most accurate stock-pickers. About 60.6 percent of the 10-stock model's picks have made money, while just over 60.5 percent of the 20-stock portfolio's picks have gained ground. Its picks tend to come from a wide swath of industries and sectors, ranging from retailers to energy firms to industrials to financials, and beyond. The Fisher-based model isn't afraid to hold on to a stock and let it run. Some of its best picks have been Schnitzer Steel, which more than doubled while in the 10-stock portfolio from July 2006 to October 2007, and Caremark Rx, which gained 81.2 percent during an 18-month period from late 2004 to early 2006. (Interestingly, after it sold Schnitzer in October 2007, the stock dropped more than 10 percent the next month; then, the Fisher model snatched it up again, and since it has gained more than 22 percent.) It will hold stocks for shorter periods and take the profits, however; Global Power Equipment gained more than 55 percent in just two months in early 2004 before it was sold, for example. (See Table 8.1.)

Table 8.1 Model Portfolio Risk and Return Statistics

	10-Stock	20-Stock	S&P 500
Annualized Return	20.8%	17.8%	4.0%
Total Return	157.4%	127.5%	21.4%
Best Full Year	40.0% in 2006	32.0% in 2006	13.6% in 2006
Worst Full Year	−2.7% in 2005	6.7% in 2007	3.0% in 2005
Beta	1.23	1.19	1.0
Accuracy	60.6%	60.5%	N/A

Note: Returns statistics are from July 15, 2003 to July 15, 2008. See Appendix A for additional return disclosure and explanation.
Source: Guru Model Portfolio Tool, Validea.com

Fisher's Key Investing Criteria

- Look for a low price-sales ratio.
- Look for low-debt firms, unless the company is a financial firm.
- Look at the price-research ratio if the company is a medical or technology firm.
- If the company passes all of these criteria, the Fisher model has some interest. It then continues testing to see if the company is a super stock.

IS THE COMPANY A SUPER STOCK?

- Price-sales ratio should be 0.75 or less for noncyclicals or 0.4 or less for cyclicals.
- Inflation-adjusted EPS growth rate should be greater than 15 percent.
- Free cash flow per share should be positive.
- Three-year average net profit margin should be 5 percent or greater.
- If the company passes all of the super stock criteria, this method has a significant interest in the stock. The most important variable here is the price-sales ratio.

Chapter 9

Martin Zweig

The Conservative Growth Investor

Nothing can stop the man with the right mental attitude from achieving his goal; nothing on earth can help the man with the wrong mental attitude.
—THOMAS JEFFERSON

Earlier, we touched on Benjamin Graham's belief that far more often than not great investors are made—not born. Well, Martin Zweig may not have been born a great investor, but it took him less time than perhaps any other guru we follow to start making himself into one.

Thanks to a birthday gift from his uncle of six shares of General Motors stock, Zweig was just 13 years old when he began following the stock market. He started tracking GM and some other stocks, and before long, he was hooked. By the time he was in high school, Zweig writes in his book, *Winning on Wall Street,* he had made up his mind: He was going to become a millionaire, and he would do so by investing in stocks.

Millions of people have made a similar decision over the years. But unlike the vast majority of them, Zweig followed through. He began paying more and more attention to the market. Soon he was wowing his high school teachers with his knowledge of stocks. By the time he was in college, Zweig was buying and selling stocks, and as a graduate student he performed groundbreaking research in the field of stock analysis. It wasn't long before he'd reached the goal he'd set for himself in high school. In fact, you might say he obliterated it, becoming not only a millionaire, but also the owner of what *Forbes* reported was the most expensive apartment in New York City and the eighth most expensive home in the world—a $70 million penthouse that sits atop Manhattan's chic Pierre Hotel.

Given how fixated he was on beating the market at such an early age, it almost seems Zweig was destined to become one of the world's best investors. "Ever since I can remember," he wrote in *Winning on Wall Street,* "I have had an almost overwhelming desire to learn all I could about the stock market and to play it successfully. Perhaps my urge was not too different from that attributed to the mountain climber who must assault the mountain just because it's there…. [F]rom an early age I wanted to surmount the summit of the stock market, so to speak. It was a challenge I couldn't resist."

Zweig's intense desire and ambition may have been a gift of birth, but his stock market success—his stock recommendation newsletter was ranked number one based on risk-adjusted returns by *Hulbert Financial Digest* during the 15 years Hulbert monitored it—wasn't simply due to natural ability. His development into a great investor was marked by years of study and hard work, and the ability to adhere to a strict, thorough investment strategy. In this chapter, we show you how, with some hard work and discipline of your own, you can make his strategy work for you.

Who Is Martin Zweig?

Before we dig deeper into his strategy, however, let's take a closer look at Marty Zweig, who, in addition to being one of the wealthiest men on Wall Street, is also one of the more colorful gurus we follow (see the sidebar).

Not so Modest

While some of those we've already discussed—Benjamin Graham, Warren Buffett, John Neff—maintained fairly modest lifestyles given their huge net worths, Zweig doesn't seem to mind spending his money. After all, isn't the point of making it to use it? In addition to his top-of-the-line penthouse, Zweig also has a hankering for collecting some very interesting—and very expensive—toys. An article in the *Wall Street Journal* (March 29, 1999) reported that Zweig is a major collector of Hollywood, sports, and rock 'n' roll memorabilia. He's got Buddy Holly's guitar, the gun from *Dirty Harry*, the motorcycle from *Easy Rider*, and Michael Jordan's jersey from his rookie season with the Chicago Bulls. He even owns the "sperm" costume from Woody Allen's film *Everything You Always Wanted to Know About Sex*.

Zweig also reportedly once bought a $52,000 pool table, and his office "might as well be a day-care center for affluent adults," according to two stories that ran in *Financial World* several years ago (and which is now available on www.streetstories.com). According to that piece, inside Zweig's office you could find a huge traffic light, fully lit up on the windowsill; a five-foot toothbrush given to Zweig by some friends who were amused by his constant brushing and flossing during a road show; a gumball machine that still charges a penny ("if you're nice, Zweig supplies the change," the article stated); and a 1950s jukebox that frequently blared during late nights. Zweig's collecting interests span the historic (several old stock certificates, including one signed by Commodore Vanderbilt) as well as the nostalgic (two old-fashioned gas pumps that are almost identical to those he'd seen at the nearby Mobil station while growing up in Cleveland, for example.)

Zweig, born in 1942, has a fun side, but he also has worked hard— very hard—to be able to enjoy some lavish amenities, and it started with his education. First, he graduated with a degree in economics from the prestigious Wharton School of Finance at the University of Pennsylvania—the only school he applied to, he wrote, because it was the "best undergraduate business school in the country." After graduating from Wharton, where he took "every stock market course offered," Zweig then received an MBA from the University of Miami, and a couple years later he got a Ph.D. in finance from Michigan State University, specializing in the stock market.

In addition to racking up degrees, Zweig was also gained recognition for his insightful research. While writing his dissertation at Michigan State, he discovered the "put/calls" ratio, a now-popular indicator that compares how many people are buying options to how many people are calling options as a way to predict market tops and bottoms. This discovery marked the beginning of Zweig's broader investigation of how to use a variety of market and economic indicators to forecast overall market movements, something he became well known for—and quite good at. (We discuss his market timing methods in greater depth later in the chapter.)

After finishing his education, Zweig held a couple different jobs, teaching finance at the City University of New York, working as a consultant for the group that would later become the Chicago Board Options Exchange, briefly teaching new brokers at E.F. Hutton about the options business, and then working at a small brokerage firm where an old friend had asked him to be a consultant. But it was a nonwork endeavor that really opened the door to success for him. In 1970, a year after finishing his Ph.D., Zweig wrote a letter to *Barron's* critiquing a recommendation made by what Zweig called a "second-rate brokerage firm" to sell AT&T's stock. *Barron's* liked the piece and published it, and Zweig proved to be right. He explains in his book that it turned out both the market and AT&T were at their bottoms, making for a great buying opportunity. (He added that the brokerage firm that recommended selling the stock went out of business a few months later.) Zweig wrote a few more pieces for *Barron's*, making several more successful market predictions.

Around the same time, the brokerage firm where Zweig was working as a consultant asked him to start writing a newsletter for clients, using his *Barron's* writings as a launching pad. But shortly after he started writing the newsletter, which was geared towards institutions, the firm went under, with one of the partners accused of embezzling a couple million dollars.

It was bad timing, to be sure, but Zweig's work for *Barron's* ended up coming in quite handy in the aftermath of the firm's demise. Wanting to continue his newsletter, Zweig started contacting readers who had written him in response to his *Barron's* pieces, asking them if they would be interested in receiving a stock newsletter from him. He got about 40 subscribers over the next few months and his newsletter—the *Zweig Forecast*—was born.

While Zweig's newsletter was taking off, he also kept on teaching, another of his passions, working as an associate professor at Iona College for seven years. The *Zweig Forecast,* meanwhile, continued to gain steam, and eventually became one of the most highly regarded newsletters in the country, ranking number one for risk-adjusted returns during the 15 years that *Hulbert Financial Digest* monitored it. It produced an impressive 15.9 percent annualized return during that time.

In addition to his newsletter, Zweig also delved into money management. He introduced his first mutual fund, the Zweig Fund, in 1986, the year *Winning on Wall Street* was published. His second fund, the Zweig Total Return Fund, was introduced in 1988. Zweig sold some of his mutual funds in late 1998 to Phoenix Investment Partners. Today, he serves as president of Zweig Consulting, and as the asset allocation strategist for the Zweig Fund and the Zweig Total Return Fund, both of which are closed-end funds still operated under Phoenix (which is now a publicly traded firm called the Phoenix Companies). According to *Stockpickr.com,* Zweig is also the founder of Zweig Dimenna Partners, a multibillion-dollar New York-based hedge fund. The company's international fund was ranked fifteenth on *Barron's* list of The World's 75 Best Hedge Funds in April 2008, with a three-year annualized return of 37.4 percent. The fund also returned a whopping 79.1 percent in 2007, despite the stock market's many struggles during the year.

The Conservative Growth Strategy: Earnings, Earnings, and More Earnings

As we've seen, Zweig has a penchant for some lavish purchases, and the growth stock strategy he lays out in *Winning on Wall Street* can sometimes pick some flashy stocks that will give you big-time, home-run gains. But don't be fooled into thinking that Zweig's approach puts style over substance. His stock selection methodology is quite rigorous, and because of that the companies he invests in are strong on a number of levels—particularly in terms of their ability to keep producing strong earnings. In fact, 10 of the 13 criteria in our Zweig-based model involve earnings. Zweig's belief in looking thoroughly at earnings from a number of different perspectives is a big part of why we view him as a "conservative" growth investor.

Zweig's earnings-driven mindset starts with the price-earnings ratio, a variable that many of the gurus we've discussed used. Zweig's take on the P/E was different from any of them, however, because he set an absolute minimum on this variable, declining to invest in firms that had P/Es less than five. The reason: He thought that companies with P/Es lower than that were probably weak and couldn't command investors' dollars.

As a growth investor, Zweig was willing to buy stocks with fairly high P/Es, but there was such a thing as too high a P/E for him. He wouldn't buy a stock if its P/E was more than three times the market average—or if it was more than 43, regardless of what the market's P/E was.

While the P/E criterion is a critical part of the approach Zweig details in *Winning on Wall Street,* it is just the tip of the earnings iceberg. He also looked at earnings trends for the short term, wanting to see positive earnings per share in the current quarter and positive earnings growth in the current quarter (compared to the same quarter the previous year; Zweig always compared quarterly earnings to the earnings from the year-ago quarter—not the previous quarter—to eliminate seasonal variations). He also looked at earnings over the long term, requiring long-term EPS growth rates to be at least 15 percent, and preferably 30 percent or more. And, he wanted to know that a company had been persistent in increasing its earnings, so he looked for firms that had increased their EPS in each year of the past half-decade.

There's yet another, very critical, part of Zweig's EPS focus. He didn't just want a company's earnings to be increasing; he wanted the rate of their increase to be accelerating, so that he wasn't getting in after the growth was slowing down. Earnings growth for the current quarter (again compared to the same quarter a year earlier) thus had to be greater than both the long-term growth rate, and the average growth rate for the past three quarters. (A stock's EPS growth rate for the current quarter could be less than the average growth rate of the past three quarters, however, if it was at least 30 percent, since that still indicates impressive growth.)

Stock Hunting

In *Winning on Wall Street,* Zweig says there are two different broad ways to go about picking stocks: what he terms the "shotgun" approach and the "rifle" approach.

The shotgun method involves compiling publicly available data on a large number of stocks and then screening that data by your investment criteria to see which stocks pass muster—the approach we use. The rifle method, on the other hand, involves carefully analyzing a small number of stocks inside and out, looking not only at fundamentals but also at accounting practices, management changes, tax law changes, or a myriad of other economic factors.

For most investors, Zweig writes, the time-consuming rifle method isn't suitable. "Frankly," he adds, "I'm not even that comfortable with it myself. I prefer the shotgun system, where I can systematically study thousands of companies."

We agree that the shotgun approach is a much better choice for most investors. In addition to being much less time consuming, one of the great things about this kind of stick-to-the-numbers approach is that, statistically, certain sets of fundamental criteria have proven to produce a certain percentage of winners over the long term. Zweig, for example, wrote that his systematic approach had a built-in error rate of about three-eighths. "That is, out of eight stocks that I pick, three, or 38 percent, will underperform the market," he said. That means 62 percent will outperform the market (this is referred to as a stock's accuracy), which Zweig writes is "not a bad batting average at all. I doubt that the rifle approach would do any better."

Of course, if a strategy has a 62 percent accuracy rate, that's no guarantee that 6 of every 10 stocks you pick with it will always be winners—sometimes more will win, sometimes less will win. What Zweig found, however, and what we've found, is that by building a portfolio with an adequate number of stocks and sticking to a good strategy for the long term, you put the odds in your favor that you'll approximate that strategy's historical accuracy rate. Yes, by using a screening system that focuses solely on the numbers, you're acknowledging that you're going to take some swings and misses when nonfundamental factors cause a stock to falter—but good luck finding an investor who won't take some swings and misses using the rifle approach. And while it may feel like you're giving up some control over your investment decisions because you're not investigating every little detail about a firm, it's really just the opposite; instead of making decisions based on what your emotional brain tells you, you'll essentially be making decisions based on years and years of cold, hard, data. That's a far more reliable way to manage your money—if you're willing to stick to it for the long haul.

If Sales Aren't Driving, Don't Get in the Car

Zweig's earnings thoroughness extends beyond the amount of earnings a company was posting, and into the ways it was generating those profits. A key part of his philosophy is that, for earnings growth to continue over the long haul, it must be driven by sales growth. Cost-cutting measures or other nonsales boosts to earnings can only last so long before a company needs to increase its sales to keep increasing profits, he believes. Zweig doesn't say exactly what percentage of earnings should be sales-driven, so we were forced to make an interpretation in our model. We require that sales growth be at least 85 percent of earnings growth.

Given that Zweig wanted earnings to be accelerating and driven by sales, it's not surprising that he also wanted sales growth to be accelerating. He liked the most recent quarter's sales growth (compared to the same quarter a year ago) to be greater than the previous quarter's sales growth (again, compared to the same quarter a year earlier).

There's another part of Zweig's method that is related to earnings, though it might not seem to be: the debt-equity ratio. Debt, Zweig says, can make earnings results misleading. A lot of debt means a company has significant fixed interest payments, and if business slows, those payments can whittle away profits. Zweig makes a very smart point here: that debt levels vary by industry. The model we base on his approach thus makes sure that a company's debt-equity ratio is less than its industry average. This debt criterion is another example of why we consider Zweig to be a "conservative growth" investor.

There's one more area Zweig looked at when examining a stock, and this one has nothing to do with earnings. He believes that those who work for a company know the business best. If a lot of them are selling their shares (and nobody is buying), it could mean trouble. Conversely, if a lot of them are buying and no one is selling, it could bode well. This method thus looks for companies at which at least three insiders are buying shares, and where no insiders are selling.

All About the Indicators

While Zweig has an extensive fundamental-based method for picking individual stocks, it's important to know that his approach also gives great weight to a number of economic and technical indicators. Prominent among these are interest rates, with "Don't fight the Fed," being one of the key points he makes in his book. When Zweig sees the Fed starting to tighten the money supply and raise interest rates, that's an indicator a bear market is likely around the next bend. Sentiment indicators also turn negative before a bear market, at least as he defines negative. "The longer-term sentiment indicators tend to get pretty negative before the top or around the top—lots of secondaries and stock offerings, lots of public buying, lots of speculation," he says. "The market may be overvalued or it may not be. It helps if it is. It's not enough just to have a lot of speculation to stop a market."

Based on his reading of various indicators, Zweig will adjust how invested he is in the market. Here's a sampling of a few of the key indicators he discusses in his book:

- **The Discount Rate**. An increase in either the discount rate or reserve requirements is bearish, Zweig says, while decreases are bullish. Rising interest rates are generally negative for stock prices, whereas falling interest rates generally help stock prices. Zweig says the discount rate is a lagging interest rate indicator with some psychological importance. When the Fed changes the discount rate, it's because it has already moved in the same direction with the federal funds rate. The discount rate helps confirm the Fed's current policy.

- **Installment Debt**. Another Zweig favorite. If installment debt rises rapidly, consumers are borrowing a lot, which, in turn, can put upward pressure on interest rates. And, he says, in an economic upturn this signifies we're in the latter stages of the upturn, which is negative for stocks. A downturn in the installment debt rate is positive, because that's seen as indicating less pressure on interest rates resulting from less borrowing. This usually happens when the economy is soft and perhaps bottoming out.

  Writes Zweig: "A buy signal is given when the year-to-year change in installment debt has been falling and drops to under 9 percent. A sell signal comes when the year-to-year change has been rising and hits 9 percent or more. That's it."

- **The Prime Rate**. The prime rate is the rate banks charge their best customers, such as major corporations. The rates banks charge on other types of loans are based on this prime rate. Zweig advised buying if there's an initial cut in the prime rate when the prime's peak was less than 8 percent (meaning it never topped 8 percent because of the cut). If the prime's peak reaches 8 percent or higher, for a buy signal you need either two cuts in the prime or a full 1 percent cut. Any initial hike in the prime if the prime's low is 8 percent or above is a sell signal. If the prime's low is less than 8 percent, you get a sell signal with the second of two hikes or a full 1 percent jump in the rate.

Zweig used the above three indicators—the prime rate, the Fed's discount rate and reserve requirements, and installment debt—to develop what he called his *Monetary Model*. He also had another model that measured market momentum based on the Value Line Geometric Index, which he used to stay in sync with the trend of the stock market. A favorite Zweig motto is: "The trend is your friend." This overall market trend may shift only a few times a year.

Every so often, Zweig's rule of "Don't fight the Fed" is in conflict with "Don't fight the tape (i.e., the trend is your friend)." We wondered how this conflict should be resolved. The answer was found in his June 1992 newsletter, which stated, "The tape takes precedence over the Fed." Zweig then comes to a grand finale with his Super Model, which combines the monetary model and momentum indicator.

Zweig puts a lot of emphasis on his indicator models. In fact, in *Winning on Wall Street,* he writes, "Big money is made in the stock market by being on the right side of the major moves. I don't believe in swimming against the tide. It's rare for me to recommend stock purchases when my market-timing models are bearish, or a short sale when the reverse is true. . . . The idea is to get in harmony with the market. It's suicidal to fight trends." (One key note here is that while he focuses on getting in sync with the broader market, Zweig cautions against trying to predict exact market tops or bottoms, "which no one can consistently do anyhow.")

While we maintain that market timing is a path that most investors should avoid, Zweig at least supports his timing strategy with a plethora of data and research. He doesn't simply jump into or out of the market because of hunches or guesswork; he has a detailed system that is supported by historical data. That being said, following Zweig's indicators would take an immense amount of time and energy—something most investors don't have. Because of that—and because of our belief that fundamental-based, fully invested strategies are the best way for most investors to succeed—our Zweig-based computer model sticks to the stock-specific parts of Zweig's method. (And, as you'll soon see, doing so has worked extremely well.)

A couple final notes on Zweig's broader strategy involve overall investor mindset. "You've got to have a system or method that you're comfortable with," he once told *Stocks & Commodities*. "I could never be a fully invested manager. Warren Buffett's done it for years and has made more money than anybody. But I could never do it. . . . You have to have a system...and once you have it, stick to what you can do. Don't try to be something you're not."

Zweig also makes a key point about expectations. Many people think great investors always, or almost always, pick winners, but as Zweig notes, expecting to be right all the time, or almost all the time, in the stock market is simply unrealistic. "I always find the market fascinating and filled with surprises. Perhaps that's because no one on this planet will ever know all there is to know about the market—and no one can expect to be right all of the time or even most of the time," he wrote. "You can, however, be right more than you are wrong. If you are right 60 percent of the time, ride your profits, and rein in your losses, you'll find that when you're right you're very right, and when you're wrong you're only moderately wrong. In the long run, a 60 percent success rate translates into huge gains, a 50 percent rate into solid gains, and even a 40 percent rate can beat the market." That's something to remember, regardless of whether you follow Zweig's strategy or a different proven method.

Zweig's Strategy: Step by Step

About the Martin Zweig Strategy

The Track Record:	During the 15 years that it was monitored, Zweig's stock recommendation newsletter returned an average of 15.9 percent per year, during which time it was ranked number one based on risk-adjusted returns by *Hulbert Financial Digest*.
Risk:	Moderate or a little below moderate. While Zweig was a growth investor, he used an extensive, multi-faceted approach to analyzing earnings to make sure a company was likely to continue its growth, and he also used value-type variables like the price-earnings and debt-equity ratios to limit risk.
Time Horizon:	Medium to long term.
Effort:	Fairly low.

With more than a dozen variables, Zweig's approach is one of the more detailed methods we use. Many of these criteria focus on Zweig's main concern—a company's earnings. But there are other areas he examined as well, ranging from debt to insider transactions. Let's take a look at just how the model we base on his writings works.

Note: If you want to buy growth stocks and hold on for a few years, Zweig provides a strategy. In effect, he's an alternative to Peter Lynch for growth stocks. One important difference between them: Zweig is more selective. If you use our website, www.validea.com, to screen for stocks approved by each guru, you'll find relatively few pass our Zweig model but many pass our Lynch approach.

Earnings: Their Cost and Source

While Zweig was very concerned with a company's earnings and growth, he didn't look at those factors in a vacuum. He wanted to make sure he wasn't paying too much for the earnings a company was generating, and he also wanted to make sure the firm's earnings growth was sales-driven and sustainable. Here are the criteria he used to make sure a stock fit that bill:

P/E Ratio The P/E ratio of a company must be at least 5. Zweig wants companies that are able to command a multiple of at least 5 to eliminate weak companies. This is an important distinction of Zweig's. No other strategy we discuss sets an absolute minimum on the P/E ratio. Zweig does because he finds, in a practical sense, a very low P/E ratio indicates a weak company. But the P/E should also never be more than three times the market's current P/E; any higher and the stock is considered much too risky. And in absolute terms, never buy a stock whose P/E ratio is greater than 43, no matter what the market P/E ratio is.

Price-Earnings Ratio

1. ≥ 5 AND ≤ 43 AND ≤ 3 × (Market P/E)	Pass
2. > (3 × Market P/E)	Fail
3. < 5 or > 43	Fail

Revenue Growth in Relation to EPS Growth Revenue growth must not be substantially less than earnings growth. Zweig's reasoning: For earnings to continue to grow over time, they must be supported by a comparable or better sales growth rate. Cost cutting or other nonsales measures cannot sustain earnings growth in the long term. Our interpretation of "substantially less" is less than 85 percent of the growth rate of sales, although we also feel this can be relaxed somewhat when sales are growing at more than 30 percent. Ideally, these growth rates would be compared over a three-year period.

Revenue Growth in Relation to EPS Growth

1. Revenue growth ≥ 85% of EPS growth   Pass
2. Revenue growth ≥ 30% per year   Pass
3. Revenue growth < 85% of EPS growth   Fail
   and < 30% per year

Sales Growth According to Zweig, another important issue regarding sales growth is that the rate of quarterly sales growth must be rising. To evaluate this, look at the change from the quarter one year ago (Q5) to the most recently reported quarter (Q1). Then look at the quarter previous to the quarter one year ago (Q6) and compare it with the previous quarter of the current year (Q2). Once you've done that, compare the two. The percentage change in sales growth from Q5 to Q1 must be greater than the percentage sales growth that occurred between Q6 and Q2. In other words, sales growth is accelerating. Notice that Zweig doesn't compare acceleration between sequential quarters here. He always compares a quarter to the same quarter a year earlier to eliminate seasonality, so that's what we do in our model.

Sales Growth

1. Growth from Q5 to Q1 ≥ Growth   Pass
   from Q6 to Q2
2. Growth from Q5 to Q1 < Growth   Fail
   from Q6 to Q2

Earnings Stability

Zweig examines the earnings numbers of a company from various angles. Three of these angles are stability in the trend of earnings, earnings persistence, and earnings acceleration.

Trend of Earnings Zweig wanted to make sure that a company's earnings had been strong recently, and were trending upward. The following three tests, all of which are based on Zweig's writings, are used to determine whether a company possesses those qualities.

1. **Current quarterly earnings**. According to the Zweig-based model, the first of the criteria is that the current EPS be positive.

Current Quarterly Earnings

   1. Q1 EPS > 0   Pass
   2. Q1 EPS ≤ 0   Fail

2. **Quarterly earnings one year ago**. Next, the EPS for the quarter one year ago (Q5) also must have been positive.

Quarterly Earnings One Year Ago

   1. Q5 EPS > 0   Pass
   2. Q5 EPS ≤ 0   Fail

3. **Positive earnings growth for current quarter.** Lastly, in measuring earnings stability Zweig stated that the growth rate of the current quarter's earnings (Q1) compared to the same quarter a year ago (Q5) must also be positive.

Positive Earnings Growth in Current Quarter

   1. Growth from Q5 to Q1 > 0   Pass
   2. Growth from Q5 to Q1 ≤ 0   Fail

Earnings Persistence In addition to having strong recent earnings, Zweig wanted a company to have shown steady growth over the longer term. The following three tests, all of which are based on his writings, are included in our Zweig-based model to help ensure that that is the case:

1. **Annual earnings persistence**. According to Zweig, companies must show persistent yearly earnings growth. To fulfill this requirement, a company's earnings must have increased each year for past five-year period. This is annual EPS growth before extraordinary items for the previous five years. In our Zweig model, we'll allow one year of flat earnings if all the other years are increasing.

Annual Earnings Persistence

1. $Y1 > Y2 > Y3 > Y4 > Y5$ (one year of flat   Pass
   earnings is allowed)
2. All other combinations   Fail

2. **Earnings growth for past several quarters:** To make sure a company has posted consistent earnings over the past two years, the Zweig model compares the earnings growth rate of the past four quarters with the long-term EPS growth rate. Earnings growth in each of the past four quarters should be at least half of the long-term EPS growth rate. A stock should not be considered if it posted one or more quarters of skimpy earnings, which we interpret as less than half of the historical growth rate.

Earnings Growth in Past Several Quarters

1. Growth Q8 to Q4, Q7 to Q3, Q6 to Q2, and   Pass
   Q5 to Q1 $\geq$ 50% of historical growth
2. All other combinations   Fail

3. **Long-term EPS growth**. One final earnings test is required: the long-term earnings growth rate must be at least 15 percent per year, with anything over 30 percent exceptional.

Long-Term EPS Growth

1. EPS growth $\geq$ 15%   Pass
2. EPS growth $\geq$ 30%   Pass—Best case
3. EPS growth < 15%   Fail

Earnings Acceleration Finally, Zweig didn't just want a company's earnings to be increasing; he wanted the rate of their growth to be increasing—that is, he wanted earnings growth to be accelerating. The following two tests, which are again based on his writings, are how our Zweig-based model determines whether a stock possesses this quality.

1. **EPS growth for current quarter compared with prior three quarters**. One way Zweig determined whether earnings were accelerating was by looking at the percentage growth rate of the current quarter's earnings compared with the same quarter one year ago. If this is greater than the growth rate of the prior three quarters' earnings (averaged together) compared with the same three quarters one year ago, then the stock passes the test, as its earnings growth is accelerating. Otherwise, the company fails this criterion, with one exception. The exception: If the growth rate in earnings between the current quarter and the same quarter one year ago is greater than 30 percent, then the stock passes, since that is still a very high growth rate.

   EPS Growth in Current Quarter Compared with Previous Three Quarters

   1. Percentage growth Q5 to Q1 ≥ Average   Pass—Best case
      percentage growth from Q8 to Q4, Q7 to
      Q3, and Q6 to Q2
   2. Growth Q5 to Q1 ≥ 30%   Pass
   3. All others   Fail

2. **EPS growth for current quarter compared with historical growth**. In our Zweig-based model, the EPS growth rate for the current quarter must be greater than the historical growth rate. That is, growth from Q5 to Q1 exceeds the historical rate, another sign that earnings are growing more rapidly.

   EPS Growth Rate in Current Quarter Compared with Historical Growth

   1. EPS growth from Q5 to Q1 > Historical growth rate   Pass
   2. EPS growth from Q5 to Q1 ≤ Historical growth rate   Fail

Solid Financing, Optimistic Employees

That concludes the earnings-based portion of the Zweig model. But there are a couple more areas besides earnings that he also examined:

Total Debt-Equity Ratio According to Zweig, nonfinancial companies must not have a high level of debt (financial firms are exempt from this test because they often must carry large amounts of debt due to the nature of their businesses.) A high level of total debt resulting from high interest expenses can have a very negative effect on earnings if business turns even moderately down. If a company does have a high level, an investor may want to avoid the stock altogether. Zweig notices that the total debt-equity ratio (D/E) varies considerably by industry and, unlike other gurus, compares a company's D/E with its industry average, not to an absolute number, to determine if a company has a high level of debt.

Total Debt-Equity (D/E)

1. D/E < Industry average   Pass
2. D/E ≥ Industry average   Fail

Insider Transactions In our Zweig-based model, insider transactions add to a stock's attractiveness if the number of insider buy transactions is three or more during a three-month period, while insider sell transactions are zero.

Three or more insider sell transactions within three months and zero insider buy transactions are a sell signal that decreases a stock's attractiveness. If there is a dearth of buy transactions while insiders are selling, Zweig, unlike Peter Lynch, considers it to be undesirable no matter what the reasons for the sells. In contrast to this, Lynch believes that insider selling happens often for acceptable reasons, and therefore no importance can be attached to it. Both believe that insider buying is a very good sign.

Insider Transactions

1. Insider sell transactions = 0 AND Buy   Pass
   transactions ≥ 3
2. Insider buy transactions = 0 AND Sell   Fail—worst case (counts as
   transactions ≥ 3   failing two criteria)
3. All other combinations   Fail

 **Click It!**

To find current examples of stocks that pass our Zweig-based Conservative Growth Investor method, log on to www.guruinvestorbook .com. Every day, the free site will feature three stocks that get approval from our Zweig approach, with links to detailed analysis of why those stocks score so well.

The Zweig–Based Model Performance

Our Zweig-based approach was one of our original eight Guru Strategies, and since we started tracking it in July 2003, it's been one of our best—and most consistent—performers. Our 10-stock Zweig-based portfolio has gained 114.0 percent since its inception (more than five times the S&P 500's 21.4 percent return), and it is one of just two of the original models that outperformed the market every year from 2003 to 2007 (with 2003 being a partial year). Its best year was 2004, when it gained an impressive 54.8 percent—more than six times the S&P's 9 percent gain that year. Its worst year was 2007, and that was still pretty good; the portfolio gained 5.2 percent, comfortably beating the S&P's 3.5 percent return.

The stocks at the very top of the Zweig model's list in particular seem to have done extremely well, because our larger 20-stock Zweig portfolio has returned a decent amount less than the 10-stock version. Still, the 20-stock portfolio has increased 90.2 percent since its inception, which more than quadruples the S&P's 21.4 percent gain during that time.

Since it's one of our more growth-focused strategies, it's not surprising that the Zweig-based model is a little more volatile than some of our other approaches. The beta for the 10-stock portfolio is 1.24, while the 20-stock version's beta is 1.23. Still, considering the returns the model has generated, that increased volatility seems a small price to pay.

The Zweig model will find value in a number of different areas. For instance, financials and energy companies have been in particular high on its list in recent years. As you might expect with a growth strategy, the Zweig portfolio tends not to hold on to stocks for a long time. Usually it will hold a stock for a few months, though it is certainly not averse to longer periods if the stock continues to be a prospect for more growth. (See Table 9.1.)

Table 9.1 Model Portfolio Risk and Return Statistics

	10–Stock	20–Stock	S&P 500
Annualized Return	16.4%	13.7%	4.0%
Total Return	114.0%	90.2%	21.4%
Best Full Year	54.8% in 2004	41.5% in 2004	13.6% in 2006
Worst Full Year	5.2% in 2007	1.1% in 2007	3.0% in 2005
Beta	1.24	1.23	1.0
Accuracy	57.1%	55.5%	N/A

Note: Returns statistics are from July 15, 2003 to July 15, 2008. See Appendix A for additional return disclosure and explanation.
Source: Guru Model Portfolio Tool, Validea.com

Zweig's Key Investing Criteria

- Look for a reasonable P/E ratio—not too high and not too low.
- Make sure revenue is growing comparably to the 3-year EPS growth rate.
- Look for rising sales growth over the past year.
- Look for positive earnings growth in the current quarter.
- Look for earnings growth in the past several quarters to be at least half of the long-term growth rate.
- Compare EPS growth in the current quarter with the prior three quarters; avoid slowing growth.
- Compare EPS growth in the current quarter with historical growth.
- Look for earnings persistence over the past five years.
- Look for the long-term EPS growth rate to be at least 15 percent.
- Look for no debt or a low debt-equity ratio compared to a stock's industry.
- Look for insider buying and no insider selling.
- Look at the economy, especially the actions of the Federal Reserve Bank; be more risk averse while the Fed is increasing rates.

Part Four

THE PURE QUANTS

T here's safety in numbers," the old saying goes—a phrase to which James O'Shaughnessy, Joel Greenblatt, and Joseph Piotroski give new meaning. These three gurus stuck strictly to the numbers (i.e., a stock's fundamentals) when investing, casting aside such subjective measures as analysts' reports, economic trends, and their own personal feelings about a company's products or services. In doing so, they eliminated emotion from the stock-picking equation, allowing cold, hard facts to guide their decisions—a much safer course of action than most emotional investors take. You won't find hunches, guesswork, or speculation here; what you will find is steadfast devotion to quantitative systems that have proven to be incredibly successful over the long haul—if you're willing to stick with them. They're not the most glamorous strategies, and these aren't the most glamorous gurus. But results trump glamour every time when it comes to the stock market, and the results produced by these three strategies have been matched by few others throughout history.

Chapter 10

James O'Shaughnessy

The Quintessential Quant

The essence of mathematics is not to make simple things complicated, but to make complicated things simple.
—STANLEY GUDDER, MATHEMATICIAN AND AUTHOR

Thanks to the wonders of modern technology, today's average investor can now go to a multitude of websites to run stock screens that once could only be done by big investment firms. You can set targets for earnings, debt, return on equity, profit margins, and a host of other fundamental criteria and, with the click of a mouse button, find out which of the thousands of stocks in the market meet your standards.

One thing that most of these screens won't tell you, however, is how the strategy you're using has fared over time. Sure, looking for stocks with a P/E/growth ratio less than 1.0, profit margins of at least 5 percent, and a debt-equity ratio less than 10 percent sounds great, but has focusing on stocks that met these criteria really resulted in market-beating returns over the long haul?

With all of the different possible permutations, there's no real way of knowing the track record of every screen you perform, of course. But if anyone has come close to such screening omniscience, it's James O'Shaughnessy. In his 1996 book *What Works on Wall Street,* O'Shaughnessy detailed what may be the most in-depth quantitative stock market study in history, one in which he used Standard & Poor's high-powered Compustat computer database to back-test the perform-ance of dozens of stock-picking approaches over more than four dec-ades, from the early 1950s to the mid-1990s. Large market caps, small market caps, high or low price-earnings ratios, strong or weak cash flows—O'Shaughnessy studied how these and a myriad of other fac-tors (and combinations of factors) affected stock performance for most of the post–World War II era. According to his book, his study marked the first time Compustat's full historical data was released to an outside researcher.

In addition to finding out how certain strategies had performed in terms of returns over the long term, O'Shaughnessy's study also allowed him to find out how risky or volatile each strategy he exam-ined was. After looking at all sorts of different approaches, he was thus able to find the one that produced the best risk-adjusted returns—what he called his "United Cornerstone" strategy.

The United Cornerstone approach, which we used to establish our O'Shaughnessy-based model, is actually a combination of two separate models that O'Shaughnessy tested, one growth-focused and one value-focused. His growth method—"Cornerstone Growth"—produced bet-ter returns than his "Cornerstone Value" approach, and was a little more risky. The Cornerstone Value strategy, meanwhile, produced returns that were a bit lower, but with less volatility. Together, they formed an exceptional one-two punch, averaging a compound return of 17.1 per-cent from 1954 through 1996, easily beating the S&P 500s 11.5 percent compound return during that time while maintaining relatively low levels of risk. That 5.6 percent spread is enormous when compounded over 42 years: If you'd invested $10,000 using the United Cornerstone approach on the first day of the period covered by O'Shaughnessy's study, you'd have had almost $7.6 million by the end of 1996—*more than $6.6 million more* than you'd have ended up with if you'd invested $10,000 in the S&P for the same period. That seems powerful evidence that stock prices do not—as efficient market believers suggest—move in a "random walk," but instead, as O'Shaughnessy writes, with a "purposeful stride."

Who Is James O'Shaughnessy?

Born and raised in Saint Paul, Minnesota, O'Shaughnessy studied international economics and business diplomacy at the School of Foreign Service of Georgetown University, and has a degree in economics from the University of Minnesota. Today, he is the Chairman, Chief Executive Officer, and Chief Investment Officer of O'Shaughnessy Asset Management (OSAM), a Connecticut-based firm that serves institutional investors and high-net-worth clients of financial advisors. As of March 2008, the company managed more than $9 billion in assets using 15 quantitative strategies based on O'Shaughnessy's research (The different strategies each target a different type of stocks, such as small-cap value, midcap growth, or international.) Operated under Bear Stearns Asset Management for its first 11 years, OSAM became independent from Bear on April 1, 2008. Before founding OSAM, O'Shaughnessy served as Director of Systematic Equity at Bear Stearns Asset Management, and was a Senior Managing Director of the firm. He now lives in Connecticut and is married with three children.

In addition to his asset management firm, O'Shaughnessy also manages several Canadian mutual funds that invest in U.S. stocks. While his exhaustive study covered several decades of stock market returns, the track records of some of these funds give even more credibility to his investing approach. As of mid-April 2008, his RBC O'Shaughnessy U.S. Growth fund had a 10-year average return of 6.4 percent, four times its benchmark (the Russell 2000 TR CAD), according to Morningstar. Another, the RBC O'Shaughnessy U.S. Value fund, has a 10-year return of 4.5 percent, while its benchmark, the S&P 500 TR CAD, had returned just 0.2 percent per year, according to Morningstar.

As his innovative research shows, O'Shaughnessy appears to have a creative side. He has written three other books in addition to *What Works on Wall Street—Invest Like the Best, How to Retire Rich,* and *Predicting the Markets of Tomorrow.* (He's also updated *What Works on Wall Street,* most recently in 2005.) During the Internet boom several years ago, he also created an intriguing Web business, Netfolio .com, that allowed investors to essentially create their own personalized mutual funds. Netfolio ceased operations, however, when the tech bubble burst.

The results of that venture notwithstanding, O'Shaughnessy will always have at least one significant place in investing innovation history: He holds the distinction of being the first person given a patent on an investment strategy, having been granted United States Patent number 5,978,778, *Automated Strategies for Investment Management,* on November 2, 1999.

United Cornerstone Investing: Discipline, First and Foremost

While O'Shaughnessy's approach is purely quantitative, some of his most critical lessons are less about specific criteria and numbers than they are about the general mindset an investor must have. Perhaps more than anything else, O'Shaughnessy has repeatedly stressed the notion that, if you want to beat the market, you need to pick a strategy and stick with it—*no matter what.* In *What Works on Wall Street,* he writes that in order to beat the market, it is crucial that you stay disciplined: "[C]onsistently, patiently, and slavishly stick with a strategy, even when it's performing poorly relative to other methods."

Like several of the other gurus we've examined, O'Shaughnessy believed that emotions were perhaps the greatest enemy of the investor because feelings like fear, anxiety, and excitement can cause an investor to ditch his long-term plan for hot strategies or hot stocks that turn out to be financial mirages. "We are a bundle of inconsistencies," he continues, "and while that may make us interesting, it plays havoc with our ability to invest our money successfully. . . . Disciplined implementation of active strategies is the key to performance."

A decade later, his thoughts about sticking with strategies haven't changed. When his firm split from Bear Stearns, O'Shaughnessy's quantitative strategies were some of the things he took with him. In the October 2007 article, "Bear Stearns Manager Leaving with Strategy Intact," Reuters' Lilla Zuill quoted O'Shaughnessy as saying: "What always works on Wall Street is strict adherence to underlying strategies that have proven themselves under a variety of market environments."

Allocation Matters

To O'Shaughnessy, discipline is critical not only in the way you pick individual stocks (and we'll look in detail at his stock-picking strategies in just a bit), but also in the way you choose the general categories of stocks you focus on. In an April 2008 article titled "The Silent Storm" on O'Shaughnessy Asset Management's web site (available at www .osam.com/commentary.php), O'Shaughnessy used his forte—back-testing—to show how a systematic, disciplined approach to asset allocation would have produced solid results even in the first decade of this century—which, he noted, was the second-worst (through February 2008) for large stocks since 1900 and the worst for large growth stocks since the 1930s.

First, O'Shaughnessy looked at what he called a "typical generic 401(k) allocation"—that is, 50 percent large-cap "core" stocks, using the S&P 500 as a proxy; 40 percent large-cap growth stocks, using the Russell 1000 Growth index as proxy and 10 percent small-cap stocks, using the Ibbotson small stocks as proxy. Starting with $100,000 in January 2000 and rebalancing annually, this portfolio would have lost 2.9 percent per year, with the initial investment declining to $78,614 after inflation.

Then, O'Shaughnessy looked at how two of the allocation scenarios he previously recommended in his book *Predicting the Markets of Tomorrow* would have fared. The first, his "conservative" recommendation, involved 60 percent large-cap value stocks, with the Russell 1000 Value index as proxy; 25 percent small-cap stocks, with Ibbotson small stocks as proxy; and 15 percent large-cap growth stocks, with the Russell 1000 Growth index as proxy. Over the same time period, this portfolio would have gained 2.32 percent per year, making the initial $100,000 investment grow to $120,600 after inflation.

Finally, O'Shaughnessy looked at an optimal asset allocation break-down he had previously recommended in *Predicting the Markets of Tomorrow,* which involved 50 percent large-cap value stocks, with the Russell 1000 Value as proxy; 35 percent small-cap stocks, with Ibbotson small stocks as proxy; and 15 percent large-cap growth stocks, with the Russell 1000 as proxy. Using the same January 2000—February 2008 timeframe, this portfolio would have grown 2.69 percent per year, O'Shaughnessy said, leaving the investor with $124,230 after inflation—pretty impressive considering that the period was overall a bad one for stocks. In the "The Silent Storm" article mentioned previously, O'Shaughnessy writes:

> If an investor diligently followed a simple asset allocation plan over the last eight years, he would have earned a reasonable return during one of the worst markets for equities in 110 years! If he simply took an hour on the first of every year to rebalance his portfolio back to its target allocation, he would manage to sidestep a market meltdown of epic proportions. Sounds simple and sensible, yet many investors have a nearly impossible time following this simple advice. We live in the full-blooded world of the here and now—headlines scream warnings at us; experts deliver endless advice on what is hot *right now* and we feel overwhelmed and either do nothing or take rash action at the worst possible time.

The answer to how to avoid such problems is obvious to O'Shaughnessy:

> I passionately believe that investors who manage to short-circuit their underlying emotions by following a simple equity asset allocation plan with consistent discipline will vastly out-perform those who are unable to do so, whatever the overall market environment. By letting the data of 108 years inform us—rather than listening to what a talking head is saying right now on the TV or internet—we can see the simple truth that using simple, straightforward and time-tested investment

strategies leads to the best overall results in virtually all market environments.

We agree that investors should pick a proven strategy that is right for them and stick to it; that's one of the basic principles on which Validea was founded. In fact, it can be argued that the decision to follow a strategy—any strategy—is more important than the decision about what specific strategy to pick. Even a mediocre strategy that an investor sticks with through a whole market cycle, especially including the grim years when the media is writing articles making a persuasive case that the strategy is dead, can be more profitable than the investing done by someone without any strategy at all.

Buy and Hold—But Not Forever

Another key to O'Shaughnessy's overall investing philosophy is that he is a firm believer in the buy-and-hold approach. "It's irrefutable," he said in a 2000 interview with Chris Farrell of *Right on the Money!*, which aired on PBS television in early 2001. "The more you trade, the less well you do. Have a strategy and then let that strategy work."

Unlike other buy-and-hold strategists such as Warren Buffett, however, O'Shaughnessy doesn't generally hold stocks for years and years. He usually holds for a year and then rebalances his portfolios. By doing so, he makes sure he's not holding stocks that no longer meet his criteria. While he usually rebalances annually, he will rebalance some portfolios more frequently. OSAM's website details eight of the 15 strategies the company uses, and of those eight, five are rebalanced annually, one is rebalanced every six months, and two are rebalanced quarterly.

At Validea, we rebalance our portfolios over multiple timeframes depending on the particular portfolio. Generally, we've found that a monthly rebalancing has produced superior performance, though there are certain portfolios that work better with other time frames. (We'll discuss our rebalancing process and why it is very important in greater detail a bit later.) Again here, however, we believe you can make a good case that deciding to pick a rebalancing period—be it monthly, quarterly, semiannually, or annually—and sticking to it is more important than the decision about which specific period to use.

Simplicity—and a Surprise

Another key part of O'Shaughnessy's approach: Keep it simple. After studying dozens of different strategies and several decades of stock market results, you might expect him to have emerged from his study with some highly complex, esoteric formulas for how to produce the best returns. Instead, it was just the opposite.

Investing, O'Shaughnessy writes in *What Works on Wall Street,* is one example of the validity of Occam's razor—the logical principle holding that the simplest theory is most often the best one. The two components of the United Cornerstone approach he developed after his intensive review were thus remarkably simple—his Cornerstone Value approach has only five fairly straightforward criteria, and his Cornerstone Growth model has just four.

Each of these strategies starts with a simple market-cap screen. The Cornerstone Value model looks for bigger stocks—those with market caps over $1 billion—because they produce the solid and stable earnings O'Shaughnessy looked for in value plays. The Cornerstone Growth approach, meanwhile, allows for smaller stocks. It likes stocks to have caps of at least $150 million, however, to screen out those that are too illiquid.

When using the Cornerstone Value approach, O'Shaughnessy targeted "market leaders"—large, well-known firms with sales well above those of the average company—because he found that these firms' stocks are considerably less volatile than the broader market. He believed that all investors—even the youngest of the bunch—should hold some value stocks.

To target these large, prominent value stocks, O'Shaughnessy didn't just use the market cap requirement. He also liked it when these firms had a number of shares outstanding greater than the market mean, and when their trailing 12-month sales were at least 1.5 times the market mean.

Size and market position weren't enough to make a value stock attractive for O'Shaughnessy, however. Another key factor that was a great predictor of a stock's future, he found, was cash flow, with higher cash flows being better. The value model we base on his writings thus calls for companies to have cash flows per share greater than the market average.

Among large market-leaders, another criterion was even more important than cash flow per share to O'Shaughnessy: dividend yield. While high yields weren't nearly as important when examining smaller stocks (in fact, smaller companies with higher dividends actually under-performed the market in his study), O'Shaughnessy found that high dividend yields were an excellent predictor of success for large, well-known stocks. Large market-leaders with high dividends tended to out-perform during bull markets, and didn't fall as far as other stocks during bear markets. The Cornerstone Value model takes all of the stocks that pass the four aforementioned criteria (market cap, shares outstanding, sales, and cash flow) and ranks them according to dividend yield; the 50 stocks with the highest dividend yields gain final approval.

Interestingly, O'Shaughnessy found that all of the successful strat-egies he studied—even growth approaches—included at least one value-based criterion. And the value component of his Cornerstone Growth strategy—the price-sales ratio—was particularly important to O'Shaughnessy—and particularly surprising to many Wall Streeters. As part of his extensive study of stock market returns, O'Shaughnessy found that the P/S ratio was the single best indication of a stock's value, and predictor of its future. This was something of a shock to Wall Street, which has long relied on the price-earnings ratio as the essential means to evaluate a stock's value.

While low price-sales ratios—those below 1.5—were a big part of O'Shaughnessy's growth stock method, they were by no means the only factor he considered. To avoid outright dogs, the strategy also looks at a company's last five years of earnings, requiring that its earnings per share have increased each year since the first year of that period.

In addition, O'Shaughnessy also found that a company that was a winner tended to continue winning, while losers tended to continue losing. That's why he is a fan of using relative strength, which measures how a company has performed, pricewise, compared to all other stocks over the past 12 months.

O'Shaughnessy used this criterion similarly to the way he used dividend yield in his value approach. He took all the companies that passed all three of the aforementioned growth model tests (market cap, EPS persistence, and price-sales ratio) and ranked them according to relative strength. Those in the top 50 of that list made the growth stock grade.

A key part of why the growth stock model works so well, according to O'Shaughnessy, is the combination of high relative strengths and low P/S ratios. By targeting stocks with high relative strengths, you're looking for companies that the market is embracing. But by also making sure that a firm has a low P/S ratio—which is actually a value rather than growth characteristic—you're ensuring that you're not getting in too late on these popular stocks, after they've become too expensive. "This strategy will never buy a Netscape or Genentech or Polaroid at 165 times earnings," O'Shaughnessy wrote, referring to some of history's well-known momentum-driven, overpriced stocks. "It forces you to buy stocks just when the market realizes the companies have been overlooked."

One more note on O'Shaughnessy general strategy: The adage that higher risk equals higher rewards doesn't always hold true for him. He found that many of the worst performing strategies were often riskier than the best performers. Focusing on risky strategies with the assumption that you'll eventually be rewarded with high returns is thus not a good idea according to his research.

Ever Improving

The United Cornerstone strategy O'Shaughnessy laid out when his book was first published produced exceptional back-tested results, but O'Shaughnessy didn't stop there. In subsequent editions of *What Works on Wall Street,* he has updated the strategy in a way that has produced even better returns.

Other Big Winners—and Big Losers

While O'Shaughnessy found that the United Cornerstone strategy was the best of all the approaches he studied, he also found a number of other high-performing strategies.

Besides his three "cornerstone" approaches, the three other top performers as measured by Sharpe ratio (a statistic that measures risk-adjusted returns) were those that focused on stocks with:

- Price-sales ratio below 1.0 and high relative strength (Sharpe ratio: 61).
- Earnings yield (earnings per share divided by price, the opposite of the P/E ratio) greater than 5 and high relative strength (Sharpe ratio: 61).
- Price-book ratio less than 1.0 and high relative strength (Sharpe ratio: 60).

(For comparison purposes, the United Cornerstone, Cornerstone Value, and Cornerstone Growth strategies had Sharpe Ratios of 66, 62, and 61, respectively.)

The three worst performers, meanwhile, focused on:

- Stocks with high price-sales ratios (Sharpe ratio: 8).
- 90-day T-bills (Sharpe ratio: 0).
- Bringing up the rear, stocks with low one-year relative strengths (Sharpe ratio: −1).

The high relative strength criterion among the three "honorable mention" strategies and in the United Cornerstone and Cornerstone Growth strategies, as well as the low relative strength focus of the worst performer, all illustrate one of O'Shaughnessy's major tenets: Winners keep winning, and losers keep losing.

Of course, you can pick winners from stocks that have been losers in the past—we've seen how investors like David Dreman made a killing doing just that. But remember, if those investors bought a plummeting stock, they made sure it passed a number of fundamental tests. The low-relative strength strategy that O'Shaughnessy found to be the worst performer had just that one variable, meaning it picked stocks *solely on the basis that they've been performing poorly.* The message: Picking a stock because it's beaten down despite having solid financials is one thing; picking a stock simply because it's beaten down is another thing—and a dangerous one at that.

For the Cornerstone Value portion of the approach, O'Shaughnessy added in a "shareholder yield" variable. He determines shareholder yield by adding a stock's dividend yield to its share buy-back activity. (By buying back its own shares, according to O'Shaughnessy, a company decreases its number of outstanding shares, which shores up the price of the remaining shares.) To figure out the buyback activity, he simply determines the percentage difference between the number of shares a firm had at the beginning of the prior year and at the end of the prior year. If a stock had 1 million outstanding shares at the start of the prior year and 900,000 at the end of it, for example, he says its buy-back percentage would be 10 percent. That would be added to its dividend yield to determine shareholder yield.

For the Cornerstone Growth strategy, meanwhile, O'Shaughnessy added in both three-month and six-month relative strength criteria. He said that using the one-year relative strength variable by itself posed a problem: A stock could have a great one-year price appreciation and, therefore, a high relative strength; but during certain parts of the year its price could have been dropping significantly. "This seemed inconsistent with the strategy of looking for cheap stocks on the mend, so we added shorter-term price momentum screens as well," he writes. Doing so helped ensure that the strategy was focusing on stocks whose prices were on the rise at a given point in time.

O'Shaughnessy's Strategy: Step by Step

About the James O'Shaughnessy Strategy

The Track Record: Looking at a time period from year-end 1954 through year-end 1996, O'Shaughnessy's Cornerstone Growth strategy produced back-tested compound returns of 18.52 percent per year, while his Cornerstone Value model posted a 15.06 percent annual compound return, both far surpassing the S&P 500's 11.51 percent return during that time. His combined growth-value approach, meanwhile, produced a 17.1 percent return, and had the best risk-adjusted returns of all of the strategies he tested. (Later modified versions of the United Cornerstone approach yielded back-tested results of 20.17 percent per year from the end of 1963 through 2003.)

Risk:	Moderate: Be aware that O'Shaughnessy's growth stock strategy tends to be significantly more volatile than his value strategy. The growth model produced better returns in his study than his value model did, however.
Time Horizon:	To get the full benefit of O'Shaughnessy's approach, you need to use his strategy for a number of years, through a full cycle of the market. But he usually rebalances his portfolio once a year, so in that respect his time horizon for holding individual stocks is usually one year.
Effort:	Lots of paperwork, but not much research.

Because our O'Shaughnessy-based strategy had performed very well, we did not update our model after O'Shaughnessy's revised edition of *What Works on Wall Street* came out. We believed it best to continue using a strategy that had proven to be quite successful for us, rather than experimenting with a modified approach. And as you'll see below, we've continued to get strong results by using the original strategy. Here's how you can implement this double-barreled growth-value approach.

Note: To get the statistical properties O'Shaughnessy's studies were based on, you need to invest in a sizable number of stocks—25 to 50. This approach may thus be better suited for those looking to invest larger sums of money.

Part I: The Cornerstone Growth Strategy

We'll start with O'Shaughnessy's growth methodology. Like Martin Zweig, whom we discussed in Chapter 9, O'Shaughnessy wanted to get good growth stocks, but he didn't want to pay too much for them. These are the four steps he used to accomplish that.

Market Cap The first requirement of the Cornerstone Growth Strategy is that the company have a market capitalization of at least $150 million. This requirement screens out companies too illiquid for most investors but still provides enough leeway to include small growth companies.

Market Cap
    1. Market cap ≥ $150 million   Pass
    2. Market cap < $150 million   Fail

EPS Persistence The Cornerstone Growth methodology requires looking for companies that show persistent earnings growth without regard to magnitude. To fulfill this requirement, a company's earnings per share before extraordinary items must increase each year for the most recent five-year period. In our O'Shaughnessy-based model, we look at the current EPS before extraordinary items.

EPS Persistence
    1. EPS Y1 > EPS Y2 > EPS Y3 > EPS Y4 > EPS Y5   Pass
    2. All other combinations   Fail

Price-Sales Ratio O'Shaughnessy targeted stocks with price-sales ratios below 1.5, so that's the value we use in our model. This value criterion, coupled with the growth criterion, identifies growth stocks that are still cheap to buy.

Price-Sales Ratio (PSR)
    1. PSR < 1.5   Pass
    2. PSR ≥ 1.5   Fail

Relative Strength This final criterion for the Cornerstone Growth Strategy requires the relative strength (RS) of the company to be among the top 50 of the stocks that pass the previous three criteria. O'Shaughnessy believed the combination of the price/sales ratio criterion and the relative strength criterion was critical. The relative strength test gives you the opportunity to buy the growth stocks you are searching for just as the market is embracing them, while the low PSR requirement helps ensure that you're not getting in too late on these popular stocks, after they've become too expensive.

    In our O'Shaughnessy-based growth model, the relative strength criterion figures into the overall method as follows:

- If the stock passes this criterion and the other three criteria, it passes overall.
- If the stock fails this criterion, it would fail the methodology, even if it passed the other three criteria.

Relative Strength Ranking

1. In top 50 of the stocks passing first three criteria   Pass
2. Not in top 50   Fail

Note: Since the initial publication of *What Works on Wall Street*, O'Shaughnessy has updated his Cornerstone Growth strategy by adding in two more criteria: three-month relative strength and six-month relative strength. Looking for stocks that score well in those areas helps avoid stocks that may have a high one-year relative strength, but are currently performing poorly. We have chosen not to incorporate these three- and six-month relative strength criteria in our model, however. We feel it best to stick with our model and its excellent track record, rather than adding in two new criteria without knowing for sure how they might impact our model.

Part II: The Cornerstone Value Strategy

Now, on to the other prong of O'Shaughnessy's approach. When looking for value plays, he targeted large companies with nice cash flows that paid solid dividends.

Market Cap The Cornerstone Value strategy requires looking for large, well-known companies whose market caps are greater than $1 billion. O'Shaughnessy found that these stocks exhibited solid and stable earnings.

The Cornerstone Value Strategy does not include utility stocks because these stocks would dominate the list of eligible companies because of their typically high yields.

Market Cap

1. Market cap > $1 billion   Pass
2. Market cap ≤ $1 billion   Fail

Cash Flow per Share O'Shaughnessy seeks companies whose cash flow per share exceeds the average cash flow per share for the market. Companies with strong cash flows are typically the value-oriented investments that this strategy looks for. To pass our O'Shaughnessy-based model, a stock must thus have a cash flow per share greater than the market average.

Cash Flow per Share
1. Cash flow/Share > Market average cash flow/Share   Pass
2. Cash flow/Share ≤ Market average cash flow/Share   Fail

Shares Outstanding O'Shaughnessy seeks companies whose number of outstanding shares exceeds the market average, another way he targets large firms when looking for value plays. These are the better known and heavily traded companies. Our model thus requires a company to have more shares outstanding than the market average.

Shares Outstanding
1. Shares outstanding > Market average shares outstanding   Pass
2. Shares outstanding ≤ Market average shares outstanding   Fail

Trailing 12-Month Sales Another way O'Shaughnessy targets large value stocks is by looking for firms with high trailing 12-month (TTM) sales. In our O'Shaughnessy-based model, a company's trailing 12-month sales is required to be 1.5 times greater than the mean trailing 12-month sales of all stocks in the market.

Trailing 12-Month Sales
1. Sales (TTM) > [Market average sales (TTM)] × 1.5   Pass
2. Sales (TTM) ≤ [Market average sales (TTM)] × 1.5   Fail

Dividends The final step in the Cornerstone Value strategy is to select the 50 companies from the group of market leaders (those passing the previous four criteria) that have the highest dividend yield. If the company is among the 50 companies with the highest dividend yield, then the stock passes this final test. This criterion reflects O'Shaughnessy's finding that high dividend payouts were a good predictor of success when it came to large value stocks.

In our O'Shaughnessy-based value model, the dividend criterion figures into the overall method as follows:

- If the stock passes this criterion and the other four criteria, it passes overall.
- If the stock fails this criterion, it would fail the methodology, even if it passed the other four criteria.

Dividend Yield Ranking

1. In top 50 passing the previous four criteria   Pass
2. Not in top 50   Fail

Note: Since the initial publication of *What Works on Wall Street,* O'Shaughnessy has added another criterion to his Cornerstone Value strategy: shareholder yield. He defines this as the sum of a stock's dividend yield and its share buy-back yield. The buy-back yield is determined by calculating the percentage difference between the number of outstanding shares a company had at the start of the prior year and the end of the prior year. Similar to our handling of O'Shaughnessy's new growth model criteria, we have chosen not to incorporate this shareholder yield test in our O'Shaughnessy value model. We feel it best to stick with our strategy and its excellent track record, rather than adding in a new criterion without knowing for sure how it might impact our model.

 Click It!

If the Cornerstone Growth and/or Cornerstone Value approaches appeal to you and you're looking for some O'Shaughnessy-type stocks, visit www.guruinvestorbook.com. The free site lists three picks that pass our O'Shaughnessy model every day, a good way to get ideas when building your portfolio.

The O'Shaughnessy-Based Model Performance

Like O'Shaughnessy's United Cornerstone approach, our O'Shaughnessy-based strategy is also a combination of two separate models, one based on O'Shaughnessy's Cornerstone Growth strategy and the other on his Cornerstone Value strategy. Overall, this 10-stock portfolio (using the blended strategy) has produced a 90.2 percent return since its inception in July 2003, more than four times the S&P 500's 21.4 percent gain. The 20-stock portfolio has been even better, returning 96.1 percent since inception. In addition, because O'Shaughnessy found that his models worked best with a sizeable number of stocks, we also track a 50-stock O'Shaughnessy-based portfolio. That's outperformed the 10- and 20-stock versions, returning 109.1 percent since its inception compared to the S&P's 21.4 percent. All three of these portfolios have a rather small amount of volatility, with each having a beta between 1.10 and 1.11.

We've also tracked the separate performances of our O'Shaughnessy-based value and growth models, though we didn't begin doing so separately until about eight months after we began tracking the blended portfolios' overall results. Since February 27, 2004, both models have easily outpaced the market, with the value model really excelling. Its 10-stock portfolio has returned 41.1 percent since its inception, more than six times the S&P's 6.0 percent gain in that time; the 10-stock growth model has gained 31.7 percent, more than five times the S&P. The value model has been significantly less volatile—its beta is just 1.01 compared to the growth model's 1.22—and significantly more accurate—61.0 percent of its picks have gained ground compared to the growth model's 46.4 percent accuracy (using the 10-stock portfolios).

The O'Shaughnessy Value model 20-stock portfolio has gained 33.1 percent compared to that 6.0 percent gain for the S&P since its February 27, 2004 inception. The 50-stock portfolio, meanwhile, has more than doubled the S&P since we started tracking it more than two years ago.

The O'Shaughnessy-based Growth model, meanwhile, shows better performance as the portfolios get bigger. The 20-stock and 50-stock versions, both of which we have tracked since February, 27, 2004, have

gained 39.3 percent and 53.3 percent, respectively since their inceptions, compared to the S&P's meager 6.0 percent return.

Both the growth and value models will select a variety of stocks,
ranging from financials to energy companies to retailers to industrials. One interesting note is that, even though the growth model's $150
million market cap minimum allows it to pick up some small, fast-
growing firms, it will also find good growth prospects in huge companies. In April 2008, for example, the 10-stock growth portfolio held
both Exxon Mobil, which had a cap of more than $500 billion, and
Chevron, which had a cap of almost $200 billion. (See Table 10.1.)

Table 10.1   Model Portfolio Risk and Return Statistics

	10-Stock	20-Stock	S&P 500
Annualized Return	13.7%	14.4%	4.0%
Total Return	90.2%	96.1%	21.4%
Best Full Year	24.0% in 2006	27.9% in 2005	13.6% in 2006
Worst Full Year	−3.9% in 2007	−2.7% in 2007	3.0% in 2005
Beta	1.11	1.10	1.0
Accuracy	52.7%	54.8%	N/A

Note: Returns statistics are from July 15, 2003 to July 15, 2008. See Appendix A for additional return
disclosure and explanation.
Source: Guru Model Portfolio Tool, Validea.com.

O'Shaughnessy's Key Investing Criteria

GROWTH STOCKS
- Look at the market cap to make sure the stock is liquid
  enough.
- Look for EPS persistence.
- Look for a low price-sales (P/S) ratio.
- From the stocks that pass all of the first three criteria, pick
  the 50 with the highest relative strengths.

In order for O'Shaughnessy to have any interest at all, the
stock has to pass all of these criteria. With this methodology, it

is an all-or-none approach. There is no "some" level of interest, only "strong" interest or no interest.

VALUE STOCKS

- Make sure the firm's market cap is large enough.
- Look at cash flow per share.
- Look at shares outstanding.
- Look at trailing 12-month sales.
- From the stocks that pass all of the first four tests, pick the 50 with the highest dividend yield.

In order for O'Shaughnessy to have any interest at all, the stock again has to pass all of these criteria.

Chapter 11

Joel Greenblatt

The Man with the Magic Formula

Simplicity is the ultimate sophistication.

—LEONARDO DA VINCI

A s you've seen over the past eight chapters, one of the keys to beating the market over the long haul is having a strategy that looks at a stock from multiple perspectives. Sure, Peter Lynch had the P/E/G ratio, James O'Shaughnessy and Kenneth Fisher the price-sales ratio, and John Neff the P/E ratio. But they all complemented those measuring sticks with other variables that assessed a stock's financial strength. Whether it's the relatively simple four-variable O'Shaughnessy growth model or the more in-depth, 13-variable David Dreman approach, these strategies examine a stock from more than one angle. For all of our research, we've yet to come across an exceptional long-term strategy that uses just one variable; it seems that not even Jack Bauer or Governor Schwarzenegger could take down the market with just one bullet.

But guess what: You can do it with two.

In his 2005 bestseller *The Little Book That Beats The Market,* hedge fund manager Joel Greenblatt laid out a stunningly simple way to beat the market using two—and only two—fundamental variables. The "Magic Formula," as he called it, looks only at the return a company generates on its capital, and at the firm's earnings yield (which is similar, but not identical to, the inverse of its price-earnings ratio).

Sound too good to be true? It's not. Using this strategy, Greenblatt produced back-tested average returns of 30.8 percent per year from 1988 through 2004, about two-and-a-half times the S&P 500's 12.4 percent average annual return during that time. And since we started tracking our Magic Formula–based strategy in December 2005, it, too, has outpaced the market by a decent margin. (We'll look in-depth at our results later in this chapter.)

Greenblatt's book was something of a sensation, both in the investing world and beyond. With an extremely casual, conversational manner, this "little" book is a quick, easy, 176-page read that breaks stock market machinations down into concepts even an 11-year-old can understand. In fact, Greenblatt was originally inspired to write the book as a way to teach his five children how to make money for themselves, writing that the *Little Book* is "a great gift—truly one that would keep giving." Using several simple analogies, Greenblatt explains stock market principles. One of these he often returns to involves Jason, a classmate of Greenblatt's youngest son, who makes a bundle selling gum to fellow sixth-graders. Greenblatt uses Jason's simple "business" as a jumping off point to explain issues like supply, demand, taxation, and rates of return.

This people-friendly approach reflects two of Greenblatt's main contentions: First, "if you really want to 'beat the market,' most professionals and academics can't help you"; and, second, "that leaves only one real alternative: You must *do it yourself.*"

But while Greenblatt's explanations, and the details of his magic formula, are simplistic, don't assume that his approach is easy to follow. Remember those psychological barriers to investing success that we examined in Chapterc 1? This is one strategy in which they'll definitely rear their ugly heads, as you'll soon see.

What Greenblatt's approach does show, however, is that while beating the market might be *hard,* it doesn't have to be *complicated.* "It won't even take much work—just minutes every few months," Greenblatt writes of using his magic formula. The logistics aren't the hard part here. "[T]he hard part," he says, "is making sure that you understand *why* the magic formula makes sense. The hard part is continuing to *believe* that the magic formula *still* makes sense even when friends, experts, the news media, and [the market] indicate otherwise."

So why does the magic formula work? In part, it works because its two variables—*return on total capital* and *earnings yield*—combine to target solid companies that are selling at reasonable prices. According to Greenblatt, another big reason that the strategy works—and will continue to work even if everyone knows about it—is that, ironically, it doesn't work sometimes.

Confused? Don't worry. We explain just what that means in the strategy section of this chapter. But first, let's take a closer look at the Wall Street magician who came up with this simple market-beating formula.

Who Is Joel Greenblatt?

Born in 1957, Greenblatt is one of our younger gurus. Nonetheless, he's quite accomplished. A graduate of the University of Pennsylvania's Wharton School (he got his B.S. from Wharton in 1979 and his M.B.A. just a year later from the prestigious business school), Greenblatt is the founder and managing partner of Gotham Capital, a New York City–based hedge fund. From its inception in 1985 through the time his book was published, the firm averaged a remarkable 40 percent annualized return. According to *Real Estate Portfolio* magazine, which interviewed Greenblatt in the summer of 2006, Gotham returned all of its outside capital in 1995 and continued to manage only its partners' money.

Greenblatt and his partners also created Gotham Asset Management in 2002, which, according to the magazine, manages some assets itself but also chooses other money managers, in a fund of funds approach. Greenblatt formerly served as Chairman of the Board of Alliant Techsystems, an aerospace and defense company.

The *Little Book* wasn't Greenblatt's first investment writing endeavor. (In 1997, *You Can Be a Stock Market Genius* was published.) He has also spent more than a decade teaching investing classes as an adjunct professor at Columbia University, and he cofounded the Value Investors Club, a website on which members post various value investing ideas for others to see.

Greenblatt Rocks the Educational World, Too

Greenblatt's interests and contributions extend well beyond the investing world. In the final chapter of *The Little Book*, he writes that one of the things he always tells his students is that the skills he'll teach them have limited value. "It's not that they won't have the potential to make a lot of money from what they learn," he writes. "It's that there are probably higher and better uses for their time and intellect. . . . In exchange for teaching them, I always ask my students to find some way to give back."

Indeed, Greenblatt practices what he preaches, and one of the primary ways is through his interest in education. According to Robert Kolker's February 2006 *New York Magazine* article "How Is a Hedge Fund Like a School?," Greenblatt in 2002 became involved with a struggling elementary school in the New York City borough of Queens. P.S. 65Q had been created to serve a growing population of very poor South American and South Asian immigrants. In an effort to bring all of its 500-plus students up to reading standards, he donated a couple million dollars to the school. The results were stunning. "Thanks to Joel Greenblatt's friendly takeover," Kolker writes, "P.S. 65Q is a turnaround story worthy of a Harvard B-school case study. Perhaps no school in New York City has ever bounded so swiftly from abject failure to unqualified success." From 2001 to 2005, the percentage of fourth-graders passing the state's standardized reading test rose from 36 to 71, Kolker wrote, adding that P.S. 65Q won awards for its improvement.

Greenblatt didn't just want to help one school, however. He sought to "create an effective and affordable public-school prototype that could be franchised citywide—and fast." "I'm an investor," said Greenblatt. "I spend my time trying to figure out whether a business model works or not. I wanted to find a model that worked and roll it out."

It appears Greenblatt has gotten his wish. The Harlem Success Academy Charter School, of which Greenblatt is chairman, opened in 2006. According to the school's website, it was the first of forty academically rigorous charter schools to be founded by the Success Charter Network. Perhaps Greenblatt has found another magic formula, this one focused on helping turn struggling schools into strong performers.

Magic Formula Investing: It (Only) Takes Two

While anything labeled "magic" has a supernatural air to it, the truth of the matter is that Greenblatt's "magic" investing formula is not smoke and mirrors. In fact, it's actually just simple, sound investment advice. The core principle behind it, Greenblatt says, is that *"buying good companies at bargain prices makes sense."* We wholeheartedly agree.

The first variable in Greenblatt's two-criteria approach, *return on capital* (ROC), addresses the first half of that core principle—"buying good companies." Essentially, ROC is a way to see how much money a company is making by using its assets. In that regard, it is similar to the return on assets figure that Warren Buffett uses and Peter Lynch uses on financial firms. What Greenblatt found was that companies with high returns on capital likely had a special advantage over their competition. He writes that the advantage could be a good brand name, such as Coke, which lets a firm charge more than its competitors. Or it could be a strong competitive position such as the one possessed by eBay, which has more buyers and sellers than any other auction website, making it hard for competitors to offer the same benefits.

While return on assets is determined by dividing a company's net earnings by its total assets, Greenblatt's return on capital differs from that figure in a couple ways. Here, Greenblatt is concerned primarily with a company's underlying business—he wants to see how well that business is doing. Rather than using a company's reported earnings, as is done when calculating ROA, he thus uses *earnings before interest and taxes* (EBIT), so that debt payments and taxes don't obscure how well the firm's actual operating business is doing.

Another difference is that Greenblatt doesn't divide the earnings portion of the equation by total assets, as is done when calculating ROA. Instead, he divides it by "tangible capital employed," which is equal to net working capital plus net fixed assets. He explains:

> The idea here was to figure out how much capital is actually needed to conduct the company's business. Net working capital was used because a company has to fund its receivables and inventory (excess cash not needed to conduct the business was excluded from this calculation) but does not have to lay out money for its payables, as these are effectively an interest-free loan (short-term interest-bearing debt was excluded from current liabilities for this calculation). The depreciated net cost of these fixed assets was then added to the net working capital requirements already calculated to arrive at an estimate for tangible capital employed.

Remember, the bottom line here is that Greenblatt wants to see how much money a company needs to run its day-to-day business, and how well it is using that investment in the business to generate earnings.

The second piece of Greenblatt's magic formula is earnings yield, which essentially shows "how much a business earns relative to the purchase price of the business." Typically, earnings yield is calculated by dividing a company's trailing 12-month earnings per share by its current price per share—the earnings-price (E/P) ratio, which is essentially the inverse of the P/E ratio. Greenblatt also makes some slight adjustments here.

First, he again uses EBIT rather than earnings. Second, he divides EBIT not by price but by "enterprise value," which includes not only the price of the company's shares, but also the amount of debt it uses to generate earnings. Greenblatt is really measuring how much of a return, or yield, you could expect to get if you were to buy the whole business—including all of its debt. Looking at a simple E/P ratio can be misleading, he says, because it doesn't take that debt into account.

And that's it—the two-step magic formula, with both of the variables being weighted equally. In his study, Greenblatt ranked the 3,500 largest stocks in each of those categories. Those with the lowest combined ranking were at the top of his "buy" list. For example, if a stock is ranked number 80 on return on capital and 50 on earnings yield, its combined ranking would be 130. That would be better than a stock that ranked 200th on return on capital and 10th on earnings yield, for a combined ranking of 210.

The Magic Formula, Streamlined

On the website we've created for this book, www.guruinvestor-book.com, we calculate return on capital and earnings yield in basically the same way that Greenblatt does. If you're using a different screening site, however, many don't have return on capital or earnings yield criteria—at least not in the way that Greenblatt defines them. Don't worry, though; Greenblatt says that by using return on assets (in place of return on capital) and the E/P ratio (in place of his earnings yield criterion), you can best approximate the magic formula.

If you're going to use this even simpler method, Greenblatt says to first screen for stocks with ROAs of at least 25 percent. Then, from those stocks, check for those with the lowest P/E ratios (since the P/E is the inverse of the E/P, this essentially means you're screening for high E/P stocks). If a stock has a very low P/E—5 or lower—Greenblatt says that may indicate that the previous year or the data being used "are unusual in some way," however, so you may want to ignore such companies. You also might ignore firms that have announced earnings in the last week, he says, to minimize the chance that you are using untimely or incorrect data.

One more thing. There are a few types of firms that Greenblatt excluded from his magic formula research: utilities, financials, foreign firms (which usually have the letters ADR—American Depository Receipt—next to their name on stock listings), and "companies where we could not be certain that the information in the database was timely or complete." In the *Real Estate Portfolio* article referenced earlier, he said of utilities and financials: "There's nothing wrong with those companies, it's just that they're financed in a different way. Their capital structure is much more leveraged than the typical company." (That's not the type of company Greenblatt is targeting.) We thus exclude financials, utilities, and foreign stocks from our Greenblatt-based model.

You Gotta Believe

So that's how Greenblatt's strategy works. Now, on to an even more important issue: why it works.

Earlier, we noted that a big part of why the magic formula works over the long term is that it doesn't work all the time. In fact, according to Greenblatt, the strategy underperformed the market, on average, in five of every twelve months during his study, which covered 17 years. It also failed to beat the market in about one of every four years, and did poorly for more than two years in a row in one out of every six periods tested. There were even times when it underperformed for three years in a row.

That might sound disconcerting, but to Greenblatt it's great news. First off, he's not looking at month-to-month returns, or even one-year or two-year returns. His goal is to make money over the long term—at least three to five years—so down months or even down years don't worry him. He knows that, over the long term, the formula beats the market, so he sticks with it.

Most people don't, however—and that's a good thing. In fact, that's what allows him, and those who stick to the formula, to make money over the long term. "If the magic formula worked all the time, everyone would probably use it," he explains. "If everyone used it, it would probably stop working. So many people would be buying the shares of the bargain-prices stocks selected by the magic formula that the prices of those shares would be pushed higher almost immediately. In other words, if everyone used the formula, the bargains would disappear and the magic formula would be ruined!"

To Greenblatt, these down years are thus not a disappointment or an annoyance, but instead a necessity. Most people (and this goes back to those psychological barriers to investment success that we detailed in Chapter 1) won't stick with the magic formula for the long haul because they get too anxious or afraid when they see that their portfolio is losing ground for a couple months or a year, so they bail. And that allows those relatively few investors who truly believe in the magic formula to be able to get those good stocks on the cheap. Greenblatt says that even professional fund managers will bail on a strategy that has some down times because they are under great pressure to produce results every quarter or even month. If they don't, their clients will leave them, or they could even lose their jobs, so they end up doing what everyone else does—they buy "the most popular companies, usually the ones whose prospects look most promising over the next few quarters or the next year or two." And, as we've seen throughout this book, those super-popular stocks are often overhyped and overpriced.

While Greenblatt focuses on the fact that the magic formula works in part because it doesn't work all the time, that notion is by no means limited to his strategy. None of the strategies in this book—and no successful long-term strategies you'll come across—work all the time. But if you stick with them when others who can't handle the short-term underperformance head for the door, you'll reap some excellent rewards in the long run. That point is an essential one, whether you're following Greenblatt's formula or any of the other strategies we detail in this book.

Portfolio Management

If you do choose to use his magic formula, Greenblatt has a couple tips about optimal portfolio management. First, while he recommends having a portfolio of about 20 or 30 stocks, he says that to reproduce the results from his study, you should slowly build up your holdings—not buy 20 or 30 stocks all at once. Specifically, he recommends that you buy five to seven magic-formula-chosen stocks every two or three months, each time investing 20 to 33 percent of the money you plan to invest overall in your first year.

Second, while Greenblatt's research was based on holding stocks for one-year periods, he notes that you can adjust this slightly to help limit taxes. For taxable accounts, Greenblatt says that you should sell winning picks a few days after holding them for a year, and sell losing picks a few days before one year is up. By doing this, all of your gains will be considered long-term capital gains, which are subject to lower tax rates (a maximum of 15 percent, at the time this book was published) than short-term gains are subject to. Your losses, on the other hand, will be considered short-term losses, meaning you can deduct them from other income that could have been taxed at rates as high as 35 percent.

Greenblatt's Strategy: Step by Step

About the Joel Greenblatt Strategy

The Track Record: From 1988 through 2004, Greenblatt's simple "Magic Formula" averaged annual back-tested gains of 30.8 percent per year, more than doubling the S&P 500's 12.4 percent gain during that time. The strategy beat the S&P in 14 of those 17 years.

Risk: Moderate. The fact that Greenblatt uses only two variables in his strategy makes this approach susceptible to shorter-term underperformance when those variables go out of favor. Still, the formula has worked for decades—and has continued to work even after Greenblatt published it.

Time Horizon: Greenblatt's research is based on holding periods of one year. Be aware, however, that he says you should commit to continuing the process for three to five years—regardless of results—to make it likely that the Magic Formula will net you market-beating gains, since it doesn't beat the market every year.

Effort: Minimal. With only two variables to deal with, this approach is quite straightforward.

Now, on to how we implement Greenblatt's one-two punch. While the two-variable model is a relatively simple approach, be sure to note how Greenblatt and we calculate the two variables, since the methods are a bit different than usual. Toward the end of both criteria, we've also listed the alternate, more traditional variables Greenblatt suggested using as a way to best approximate the results of the Magic Formula. But keep in mind that, while it makes sense that the alternate approach would produce similar results, Greenblatt did not provide any testing data to confirm that, and we haven't tracked a strategy based on the alternate model.

Market Capitalization For his study, Greenblatt focused on the 3,500 largest U.S. companies. He didn't include utilities, financial stocks, foreign stocks, or companies whose financial information he couldn't be sure was timely or complete.

Market Capitalization

1. Among largest 3,500 U.S. companies   Pass
2. Not among largest 3,500 U.S. companies   Fail
3. Company is foreign, or is a utility or financial stock   Fail

Return on Capital Greenblatt determines ROC by dividing pretax operating earnings (earnings before interest and taxes, or EBIT) by tangible capital employed (net working capital plus net fixed assets), which is the same calculation we use in our Greenblatt-based model.

Greenblatt writes that he uses EBIT instead of reported earnings because different firms operate with different levels of debt and tax rates. Using EBIT allows for a comparison of different companies' operating earnings without distortions of differing tax rates and debt levels.

In addition, by using tangible capital employed instead of total assets or equity, you can better determine how much money is actually needed to conduct the firm's business. This criterion thus allows you to compare actual earnings from operations (EBIT) to the cost of the assets used to produce those earnings. Like Greenblatt, our model uses the earnings from the previous year—not projected future earnings.

Once Greenblatt has the return on capital for the 3,500 stocks that pass the market cap test, he ranks them, with number 1 being the company with the highest ROC and number 3,500 being the stock with the lowest ROC. We do the same.

Note: Greenblatt says that in the absence of these data points, you can simply use the more common return-on-assets rate in place of return on capital.

Determine Return on Capital
(Earnings before interest and taxes)/(Net working capital + Net fixed assets)

Determine Earnings Yield To find earnings yield as Greenblatt measures it, we divide earnings before interest and taxes (EBIT) by "enterprise value." He figures enterprise value by adding the market value of a stock's equity (including preferred equity) and its net interest-bearing debt. The more commonly used method for determining earnings yield—the earnings-price ratio, doesn't take into account the debt financing a company uses to help generate operating earnings.

Greenblatt uses last year's earnings—not future projections—in determining earnings yield, so we do the same. The higher the earnings yield, the better, because that means the company is earning more relative to its business' purchase price.

As with return on capital, our Greenblatt-based model ranks each of the stocks that pass the market cap test by earnings yield, with number 1 being the company with the highest earnings yield and number 3,500 being the stock with the lowest earnings yield.

Note: In the absence of these data points, Greenblatt says to look for stocks with the lowest P/E ratios—which is the same as those with high E/P ratios.

Determine Earnings Yield
(Earnings before interest and taxes)/(Enterprise value)

Combine the Rankings Greenblatt takes each of the stocks that pass the market cap test and combines their rankings from the return on capital and earnings yield criteria. We do the same. The lower the combined numerical ranking, the better.

Combine the Rankings Test (Using 20-stock portfolio)
1. (Return on capital rank) + (Earnings yield rank) ➔   Pass
   among 20 lowest of eligible stocks
2. (Return on capital rank) + (Earnings yield rank) ➔   Fail
   NOT among lowest 20 of eligible stocks

 **Click It!**

At this book's companion website, www.guruinvestorbook.com, you can view three stocks every day that pass our Greenblatt-based Magic Formula Investor model. The free site also provides links to our analysis of just why a stock makes the grade.

The Greenblatt-Based Model Performance

We began tracking our Greenblatt-based model in December 2005. Since then, a 10-stock portfolio of stocks scoring highest using the model has returned 10.2 percent, while the S&P 500 has declined 4.0 percent during that period. Our 20-stock Greenblatt-based portfolio, meanwhile, has been almost as good, returning 9.6 percent over the same time frame. The 10-stock portfolio has been a consistent market-beater, outpacing the S&P in 2006, 2007, and the partial 2008 year. The 20-stock version, on the other hand, lagged the market slightly in 2006 and 2007, but came close to holding its ground in the first half of 2008 while the S&P faltered, putting its overall returns well ahead of the index. Remember, Greenblatt says the formula doesn't work every year; it's a long-term strategy.

The Greenblatt method rates fairly low on the volatility scale compared to our other models. The 10-stock portfolio has a beta of 1.08, and the 20-stock a beta of 1.11. One interesting note: While both portfolios have made nice gains and outperformed the market, the 10-stock version has gained money on just 48 percent of its picks, while its 20-stock cousin has picked winners just 48.6 percent of the time, both on the lower side compared to many of our other models. What does that mean? It means the winners tend to win by more than the losers lose.

We exclude financials, utilities, and foreign companies from our Greenblatt-based model, just as Greenblatt did in his study. Still, the portfolios hold a pretty wide assortment of stocks. As of May 2008, for example, the 10-stock portfolio held an egg-producing company (Cal-Maine Foods), a petroleum refiner (Holly Corporation), a real estate operations industry company (Jones Lang LaSalle), and an office furniture manufacturer (Knoll)—quite an eclectic bunch. (See Table 11.1.)

Table 11.1   Model Portfolio Risk and Return Statistics

	10-Stock	20-Stock	S&P 500
Annualized Return	3.8%	3.6%	−1.5%
Total Return	10.2%	9.6%	−4.0%
Best Full Year	14.4% in 2006	13.4% in 2006	13.6% in 2006
Worst Full Year	9.1% in 2007	2.5% in 2007	3.5% in 2007
Beta	1.08	1.11	1.0
Accuracy	48%	48.6%	N/A

Note: Returns statistics are from December 2, 2005 to July 15, 2008. See Appendix A for additional
return disclosure and explanation.
Source: Guru Model Portfolio Tool, Validea.com.

Greenblatt's Key Investing Criteria

- Use the 3,500 largest U.S. stocks; do not include financials and utilities.
- Rank stocks according to Return on Capital, with highest being number 1.
- Rank stocks according to Earnings Yield, with highest being number 1.
- Add the two rankings together, and pick the stocks with the lowest numerical combined ranking. (If a stock is ranked number 80 on return on capital and 50 on earnings yield, its combined ranking would be 130, for example. That would be better than a stock that ranked 90th on return on capital and 65th on earnings yield, for a combined ranking of 155.)

Chapter 12

Joseph Piotroski

The Undiscovered Academic

The talent of success is nothing more than doing what you can do well, and doing well whatever you do without thought of fame. If it comes at all it will come because it is deserved, not because it is sought after.
—Henry Wadsworth Longfellow

S ay the words "great stock market strategist" to most people and the image that probably pops into their heads is some variation of Gordon Gekko, Michael Douglas's slick, egomaniacal, Armani-wearing, greed-is-good-preaching character in the movie *Wall Street*. They'll likely envision a smooth-talking wheeler-dealer, someone with more cash than he knows what to do with and a penchant for taking big risks—and hitting big with them.

But as we've seen in some of the previous chapters, stock market gurus come in all shapes and sizes, and there may be no better example of that than Joseph Piotroski. He isn't a cagey Wall Street big-shot; in fact, he's not even a professional investor. Piotroski is an academic and a good ol', numbers-crunching accountant. During the work week, you won't find him in the press making headlines or in the board room making billion-dollar deals; instead, you'll find him in the classroom, teaching accounting courses at Stanford University, whose website states that Piotroski's research focuses on "financial reporting issues." Talk about a far cry from Gordon Gekko.

While Piotroski may be the least-known of all the investing strategists we follow, his contributions to the field of stock market analysis make him absolutely worthy of guru status. In 2000, while teaching at the University of Chicago, he authored a highly regarded academic paper on stock investing that turned quite a few heads on Wall Street. His research focused on companies that had high book-market ratios— the type of unpopular stocks whose book values (equal to their total assets minus their total liabilities) were high compared to the value investors ascribed to them (their market capitalization—share price multiplied by their number of shares).

Using a series of balance sheet, accounting-based measures, Piotroski developed a methodology to identify high book-market companies that were likely to become big winners. His explanation of this method isn't as fun a read as Lynch's or Dreman's books; his paper is filled with math and accounting terms like "cross-sectional regression," and tables whose headings say things like "Decomposition of ΔROA: Changes in Asset Turnover and Gross Margins." But here's the thing: The strategy works, and it works big time. Piotroski's research found that buying high book-market firms that passed his tests and shorting those that didn't would have produced a 23 percent average annual return from 1976 through 1996—more than double the S&P 500's gain during that time. And, as you'll soon see, our Piotroski-based method is evidence that the strategy still works today.

Who Is Joseph Piotroski?

Because Piotroski is not nearly as well known as the Warren Buffetts, Peter Lynches, and David Dremans of the world, it is somewhat difficult to answer the question: Who is Joseph Piotroski? After all, he isn't interviewed much, if at all, and you won't find him giving investment advice on CNBC or CNN, so there's little to go on in terms of his personality and demeanor. So, just as Piotroski does with his investment strategy, we'll have to stick to the cold, hard facts.

Piotroski has spent much of his adult life in the Midwest. According to his biographies on the Stanford University and University of Chicago websites, he received a bachelor's degree in accounting from the University of Illinois in 1989, and later worked as a tax consultant for Coopers and Lybrand, a Chicago firm. He continued his academic career at Indiana University, earning an M.B.A. in finance in 1994, before moving on to yet another Big Ten school, the University of Michigan, where he earned a Ph.D. in accounting in 1999. That same year, he joined the faculty at the University of Chicago's Graduate School of Business.

Piotroski didn't wait long to make an impact on the academic world, with his groundbreaking paper published just a year after he started teaching. "Value Investing: The Use of Historical Financial Statement Information to Separate Winners from Losers" was featured in the *Journal of Accounting Research* in 2000, and it wasn't long before the high book-market strategy Piotroski set forth in it made a splash in the investing world. His findings were even reported in major financial publications like *SmartMoney*.

Piotroski's research didn't stop there. He wrote several other intriguing academic papers, including a 2004 piece he coauthored for the *Journal of Accounting Research* entitled "What Determines Corporate Transparency?," in which he examined the issue of how new Securities & Exchange Commission (SEC) disclosure regulations affected stocks. Another paper he coauthored, "Insider Trading Restrictions and Analysts' Incentives to Follow Firms," was published in the *Journal of Finance* in 2005.

In one of the rare interviews we could find, Piotroski told *Chicago GSB Magazine* in its winter 2002 issue that he was pleased with the success of his high book-market research: "This is the type of analysis I like to do," he said in *An Accountant Looks at the Market,* written by Patricia Briske and Allison Benedikt. "It's the approach I teach my students. And I think I'm a value investor at heart."

Briske and Benedikt write that Piotroski found it rewarding to see his students apply his work. "I now have a lot of former students who have internships or full-time jobs, and they're running screens that are similar to mine," he was quoted as saying. "I think that's great because they're taking my research to the real world to see what happens."

Piotroski left the University of Chicago in June 2007, moving on to Stanford, where he took an associate professor of accounting position in the Graduate School of Business.

The High Book-Market Strategy: A Critical Distinction

Piotroski wasn't the first to study high book-market stocks, but his research was key in that it went a step further than previous studies, many of which stopped after simply identifying high book-market firms (which in and of itself can yield decent results). What Piotroski realized was that, quite often, such companies have high book-market (B/M) ratios for an unappealing reason: They are in financial distress, and investors wisely stay away from them. High book-market strategies that had previously worked relied on getting big gains from a few winning high book-market companies, Piotroski said, which overcame the poor performance of many of those other high book-market firms that were going downhill.

To Piotroski, the key to improving returns was finding a way to avoid those slugs and focus on the solid high book-market companies that were being unfairly overlooked for one reason or another. These firms can be great investment opportunities, because their stock prices will likely jump once Wall Street realizes it's been shunning a winner. (This is similar to the way other gurus we've discussed targeted overlooked stocks using different value ratios, and then applied a battery of financial tests to stocks to make sure they weren't being overlooked for good reason; John Neff's price-earnings-focused method comes to mind.)

In his study, Piotroski considered high book-market firms to be those whose B/M ratio values were in the top 20 percent of the market (which at the time of writing this book were stocks with a B/M ratio of at least 1.08; this corresponds to a price-book value below 0.93). That's the easy part. The harder part is, of course, distinguishing between high book-market firms with good prospects and those with weak prospects. To do so, Piotroski used a series of balance sheet-related criteria—not surprising considering his background in accounting. By focusing on high book-market stocks that also passed these financial tests, he found that an investor that had been indiscriminately focusing on high book-market stocks could increase his returns by at least 7.5 percent annually.

The balance sheet tests Piotroski used to separate strong high book-market stocks from the rest measured three main areas:

1. **Profitability**. Piotroski looked for companies that had the ability to generate funds internally. "Given the poor historical earnings performance of value firms," he wrote, "any firm currently generating positive cash flow or profits is demonstrating a capacity to generate funds through operating activities." That's a good sign.

2. **Financial leverage/liquidity**. This category deals with changes in capital structure and the company's ability to meet future debt service obligations. Piotroski found that most high book-market companies were "financially constrained." So, he wrote, "I assume that any increase in leverage, a deterioration of liquidity, or the use of external financing is a bad signal about financial risk."

3. **Operating efficiency**. These variables measure how a company is using what it has to make money and grow its business. Are its profit margins increasing? Is productivity rising so that the firm is making more money using the same assets?

Within these categories, many of these specific nine tests Piotroski used were fairly simple, such as return on assets (which Warren Buffett and Peter Lynch also used) and cash flow from operations, both of which measure profitability and both of which Piotroski required to be positive.

A little more complicated was his comparison of cash from operations to net income, with the former hopefully being greater than the latter. Past research "shows that earnings driven by positive accrual adjustments (i.e., profits are greater than cash flow from operations) is a bad signal about future profitability and returns," he wrote. "This relationship may be particularly important among value firms, where the incentive to manage earnings through positive accruals (e.g., to prevent covenant violations) is strong." Essentially, this criterion makes sure that a company that made money last year did so because people were buying its products or services, not because it reaped a one-time windfall due to a lawsuit, write-off, or some other nonoperating—and thus potentially one-time—occurrence.

Looking for Improvement

Several of Piotroski's other financial criteria don't necessarily look for fundamental excellence, but instead for improvement. This makes a lot of sense; a company whose return on assets had declined from 10 percent to 1 percent and whose cash flow from operations had dwindled from $10 million to $10,000 would pass the above ROA and cash flow tests, for example, but it certainly wouldn't be the type of strong performer Piotroski was targeting. Looking at how a company's fundamentals had been changing allowed him to not only get an idea of the firm's financial position, but also of whether that position was improving or declining.

One area in which Piotroski looked at changing financials was return on assets: He wanted a firm's ROA to be greater in its most recent fiscal year than it was the year before; essentially, he wanted to see that the company was getting more profitable. Among the other "change" criteria he examined were the long-term debt-asset ratio, which he wanted to be declining; the current ratio (current assets/ current liabilities), which he wanted to be increasing; gross margin, which should be rising; and asset turnover, which measures productivity by comparing how much sales a company is making in relation to the amount of assets it owns. (That should be increasing.)

One more interesting "change" area Piotroski examined was the number of shares outstanding a company had. Firms issue new stock when they are trying to raise capital, which Piotroski viewed as a sign that they can't generate enough cash internally to fund their business. He thus didn't like to see a company's number of shares outstanding increase from one year to the next.

(To look at each of these variables in more detail, see the "Step by Step" section that follows.)

Think Small

A couple more interesting parts of Piotroski's research involved stock size and risk levels. In addition to finding that high book-market stocks that passed his financial tests did better than those that didn't, he also found that smaller high book-market firms were more likely to produce high returns than their larger counterparts. The reason: Small stocks are more likely to fly under the radar of analysts and investors, so you are more likely to uncover winners using fundamental analysis of these smaller, less-followed stocks. The bigger strong stocks don't usually slip through the cracks.

In addition, while previous high book-market studies had hypothesized that high book-market stocks' outperformance was related to financial distress, Piotroski found otherwise. The high book-market firms that were in the best financial health were in fact the most likely to generate the strongest returns, he found. In a sense, the less risky the stock, the better the returns.

Great Minds Think Alike

If Piotroski's approach sounds a little familiar, it may be because it has some general similarities to the contrarian approach of David Dreman, which we reviewed in Chapter 5. Both Piotroski and Dreman started with stocks that were beaten up or overlooked. They then applied a series of fundamental tests to those stocks to separate the probable winners from the losers, and both used book value as a key part of their methodologies. (If you'll recall, one of Dreman's contrarian indicators was the price-book ratio, which is simply the inverse of the book-market ratio that Piotroski used; Dreman looked for firms with P/B ratios in the market's bottom 20 percent, while Piotroski looked for firms with B/M ratios in the market's top 20 percent, which is essentially the same thing.)

There's another key similarity between these two gurus: Piotroski's research seems to lend statistical credence to

Dreman's thoughts about "surprises" driving the market. Piotroski found that investors underreact to historical information, and thus have trouble predicting a firm's future performance (i.e., its future earnings). Earnings announcements—one of the market "surprises" Dreman referenced—thus have a big impact on stocks, giving a sort of wake-up call as to where a firm's earnings really stand. The proof: Piotroski found that one-sixth of the annual return difference between high book-market stocks that did well on his fundamental tests and those that did poorly occurred over just 12 days—the four three-day periods surrounding quarterly earnings announcements.

Piotroski's Strategy: Step by Step

About the Joseph Piotroski Strategy

The Track Record:	Piotroski's study found that buying high book-market stocks that passed his fundamental tests and shorting those that didn't would have produced a 23 percent annual return from 1976 through 1996, more than double the S&P 500's annual gain.
Risk:	Low. Piotroski focused on companies that had high book-market ratios, meaning that their stocks were already cheap compared to the intrinsic values of their businesses. In addition, he used an array of financial tests to make sure that these firms weren't being justifiably undervalued because they were financially weak.
Time Horizon:	One to two years. Those are the holding periods Piotroski examined in his study.
Effort:	Moderate. This method tests a stock's strength using 10 different fundamental tests, more than many of our other guru strategies.

Just like several of the other strategies we've discussed—the John Neff price-earnings and Kenneth Fisher price-sales approaches come to mind—Piotroski's method starts with a valuation metric: the book-market ratio.

After using that ratio to significantly pare down the number of potential investments, Piotroski—like Neff and Fisher—applied a variety of fundamental tests to the remaining stocks to determine the strengths of their underlying businesses. In Piotroski's case, he wasn't just looking for strong balance sheets; he also wanted those balance sheets to be improving. Here's how the model we base on his writings works.

Book-Market Ratio The first step in the Piotroski-based approach is, of course, to find high book-market ratio stocks—those whose market values don't accurately reflect the underlying value of their businesses. In his study, Piotroski focused on the stocks whose B/M ratios were in the top 20 percent of the market. If a stock's B/M ratio meets that guideline, it passes this first test on our Piotroski-based model.

If a stock doesn't pass this test, it fails the Piotroski method, regardless of how well it does on the remaining criteria.

Book-Market (B/M) Ratio
1. In top 20 percent of market   Pass
2. Not in top 20 percent of market   Fail

Return on Assets After finding high B/M ratio stocks, Piotroski applied a number of fundamental tests to them to find the most financially promising companies. One measure he used was return on assets, which shows how profitable a company is. He wanted a firm's ROA to be positive, so we require a company to have a positive ROA for the most recent year to pass this test, indicating that it is in fact profitable.

Return on Assets (ROA)
1. ROA > 0   Pass
2. ROA ≤ 0   Fail

Change in Return on Assets For many of the variables Piotroski used (such as return on assets), he looked not only at the stock's raw score, but also at whether its score on that variable had been improving recently. Return on assets is one of those areas. This makes sure that a troubled firm whose return on assets is dwindling but still positive (and thereby passing the previous test) isn't bought. To pass this test on our Piotroski-based model, a stock's ROA in the most recent year must be greater than it was the previous year.

Change in Return on Assets
1. ROA most recent year > ROA previous year   Pass
2. ROA most recent year ≤ ROA previous year   Fail

Cash Flow from Operations Piotroski looked for firms that were overlooked but had strong underlying businesses. One way he measured the strength of their businesses was by looking at whether their operations were generating a profit. If a company has a positive cash flow from operations, it thus passes this test in our Piotroski-based model.

Cash Flow from Operations (CF)
1. CF > 0   Pass
2. CF ≤ 0   Fail

Cash Flow from Operations Compared to Net Income Piotroski wrote that past research "shows that earnings driven by positive accrual adjustments (i.e., profits are greater than cash flow from operations) is a bad signal about future profitability and returns. This relationship may be particularly important among value firms, where the incentive to manage earnings through positive accruals (e.g., to prevent covenant violations) is strong."

This criterion makes sure that the money a firm made in the most current fiscal year wasn't simply due to a one-time event, but instead due to its operations. Piotroski wanted the cash generated through operations to be greater than the firm's net income, so a stock must meet that standard in the most current fiscal year to pass this part of our Piotroski model.

Cash Flow from Operations Compared to Net Income
1. Cash Flow from Operations > Net income   Pass
2. Cash Flow from Operations ≤ Net income   Fail

Change in Long-Term Debt–Assets Ratio Piotroski said that by raising external capital (and taking on debt is a nonoperations way to raise capital), a financially distressed firm is signaling its inability to internally generate the funds it needs. Increasing long-term debt is also likely to put additional constraints on the firm's financial flexibility, he wrote. This model thus looks for companies whose long-term debt-assets ratios are lower in the most recent year than they were in the previous year.

Change in Long-Term Debt-Assets Ratio (LTD/A)
1. LTD/A for most recent year < LTD/A previous year   Pass
2. LTD/A for most recent year ≥ LTD/A previous year   Fail

Change in Current Ratio The company's current ratio (the ratio of its current assets to its current liabilities) should be increasing. Piotroski assumed that an improvement in liquidity, as shown through an increasing current ratio, was a good signal about a firm's ability to handle its current debts. To pass this criterion in our model, a company's current ratio for the most recent year must be greater than it was the previous year.

Change in Current Ratio (CR)
1. CR most recent year > CR previous year   Pass
2. CR most recent year ≤ CR previous year   Fail

Change in Shares Outstanding As with taking on debt, selling new shares of stock is a nonoperations way to raise capital, which Piotroski saw as a sign that a company's operations weren't strong enough to raise money internally. In our model, the number of outstanding shares of stock a company had in the most recent fiscal year thus shouldn't be greater than the number of shares outstanding it had in the previous year.

Change in Shares Outstanding (SO)
1. Number of SO in most recent year ≤ Number of SO in   Pass
   previous year
2. Number of SO in most recent year > Number of SO in   Fail
   previous year

Change in Gross Margin It's a good sign when a company is expanding its margin because on average it is making more on each product it sells. "An improvement in margin," Piotroski writes, "signifies a potential improvement in factor costs, a reduction in inventory costs, or a rise in the price of the firm's product." All of those are good things for a company's bottom line. If gross margin in the most recent year is greater than it was the previous year, a stock passes this test on our Piotroski model.

Change in Gross Margin

1. Gross margin most recent year > Gross margin previous year   Pass
2. Gross margin most recent year ≤ Gross margin previous year   Fail

Change in Asset Turnover Asset turnover basically measures how much sales a company is making in relation to the amount of assets it owns. "An improvement in asset turnover signifies greater productivity from the asset base," writes Piotroski. "Such an improvement can arise from more efficient operations (fewer assets generating the same levels of sales) or an increase in sales (which could also signify improved market conditions for the firm's products)." To pass this final test on our Piotroski-based model, a stock's asset turnover for the most recent year must be greater than it was the previous year.

Change in Asset Turnover

1. Asset turnover most recent year > Asset turnover previous year   Pass
2. Asset turnover most recent year ≤ Asset turnover previous year   Fail

---

Click It!

To find current examples of stocks that pass the Piotroski-based high book-market investor approach, log on to www.guruinvestorbook.com. Every day, the free site features three stocks that get approval from our Piotroski method, with links to detailed analysis of why those stocks score so well.

The Piotroski-Based Model Performance

The Piotroski strategy was among the second major wave of models we started tracking back on February 27, 2004. In the four-plus years since then, it has been a strong performer, with our 10-stock Piotroski-based portfolio returning 33.2 percent since its inception, more than five times the S&P 500's 6.0 percent gain during that time. The portfolio started with a bang, gaining almost 40 percent in the partial year of 2004, seven times the S&P's 5.7 percent gain for the partial year. The model beat the market in each of the next two years before struggling in 2007. Like many of our other value-centric models, the 2007 performance was due in large part to the unusually momentum-driven market that year, something we do not expect to continue.

The 20-stock Piotroski-based portfolio, meanwhile, has also done quite well, gaining 22.6 percent compared to that 6.0 percent S&P gain. It's year-by-year performance has generally been similar, with the portfolio having a big partial-year 2004, outperforming years in 2005 and 2006, and a bit of a stumble in 2007.

Both portfolios have been in the middle of the pack on the volatility scale, with the 10-stock version's beta being 1.19 and the 20-stock's being 1.21. The model has been very accurate in its picks, with the 10-stock portfolio making money on 59.0 percent of its picks and the 20-stock portfolio having the second-highest accuracy among its 20-stock peers (61.6 percent).

The Piotroski-based model picks a variety of stocks, and seems to have a particular hankering for industrial and technology firms. The tech firms it targets, however, aren't likely to be those that most investors have heard of—you won't find Microsoft, Google, or IBM getting approval from this method because those are the types of very visible stocks that the market usually doesn't overlook. In fact, while it will pick some well-known firms (energy giant BHP Billiton and La-Z-Boy were among its holdings in April 2008), the average investor probably won't have heard of more than a couple stocks in our Piotroski portfolio at any given time. And if they have heard of them, they probably don't have the most exciting businesses. This again makes sense considering that firms with high book-market ratios and strong fundamentals are, by definition, flying under Wall Street's radar.

As we noted earlier, Piotroski found that his strategy worked better with the stocks of smaller companies, and our model seems to bear that out. As of late April 2008, it had strong interest in just one stock that had a market cap higher than $700 million. This trend isn't because

246   THE PURE QUANTS

Table 12.1 Model Portfolio Risk and Return Statistics

	10-Stock	20-Stock	S&P 500
Annualized Return	6.8%	4.7%	1.3%
Total Return	33.2%	22.6%	6.0%
Best Full Year	17.9% in 2006	23.7% in 2006	13.6% in 2006
Worst Full Year	−4.9% in 2007	−6.9% in 2007	3.0% in 2005
Beta	1.19	1.21	1.0
Accuracy	59.0%	61.6%	N/A

Note: Returns statistics are from February 27, 2004 to July 15, 2008. See Appendix A for additional return disclosure and explanation.
Source: Guru Model Portfolio Tool, Validea.com.

we include a market cap restriction in the model; instead, it's because, as Piotroski noted, stocks that pass his method are being overlooked by Wall Street, and larger stocks are less likely to elude the Street's attention. (See Table 12.1.)

Piotroski's Key Investing Criteria

- Firm must have high book-market ratio; if not, it fails this method even if it passes all other tests.
- Return on assets should be positive and increasing.
- Cash flow from operations should be positive and greater than net income.
- Long-term debt-assets ratio should be decreasing.
- Current ratio should be increasing.
- Number of shares outstanding should not be increasing.
- Gross margin should be increasing.
- Asset turnover should be increasing.

Part Five

FROM THEORY TO PRACTICE

Having a great stock-picking strategy is a key part of succeeding in the market—but it's not the only key. There are a number of other challenges and questions that confront investors: Just how many stocks should you buy? How long should you hold them for? Should you use one strategy to pick stocks, or several? And what about the tax implications of your buying and selling decisions? Understanding such issues is essential if you want to build your wealth over the long term. In the next three chapters, we examine each of those questions and several others, showing you the guru-inspired path to a comprehensive, practical stock investing strategy.

Chapter 13

Putting It Together

The Principles of Guru Investing

The whole is more than the sum of its parts.

—ARISTOTLE

S o there you have it. Ten chapters, ten different, easy-to-follow strategies proven to beat the market over the long haul. We're done, right?

Not so fast. Our journey to better returns isn't over yet; in fact, in a way it's only just begun. While each of the strategies we've discussed is a good choice if you want to grow your portfolio over the long term, they really are better viewed as individual tools that work best when you know how to use them together. Remember earlier when we compared these strategies, collectively, to a souped-up Porsche with a standard transmission? Well, now that you've got the car, it's time to learn just how it works—and how to drive stick.

In this chapter, we'll essentially teach you just that—that is, why Guru Investing works, and how you can use these guru-based models to maximize your returns and limit risk. After years of using our models, we've learned a good deal about how to manage a portfolio that uses these strategies. We've also learned much about investing mindset—that is, how to fend off those pesky psychological barriers to investing success that we examined in Chapter 1. So hop into the driver's seat; it's time to learn to drive.

Six Guiding Guru Investing Principles

Principle 1: Combining Strategies to Minimize Risk and Maximize Returns

Over the long haul, there is no better—or safer, when you consider inflation—investment class than stocks. But as we've seen, in the short term, Mr. Market (as the great Benjamin Graham called the stock market) can be extremely fickle. Sometimes he likes growth stocks; sometimes he likes value. Often he likes stocks with low price-sales ratios; other times, he thumbs his nose at them. There's no single strategy that will please him all of the time—and if you try to predict his whims by jumping from strategy to strategy, as we've seen, you'll far more often than not end up buying high and selling low. The conundrum is thus how to even out those rough patches while sticking to your guns.

One of the best ways to do this, we've found, is to use a strategy that blends together different guru-based models that have a lower degree of correlation. What do we mean by "a lower degree of correlation"? It's simple, really. It means combining strategies that perform differently in the same kind of market conditions. The simplest example would be growth stocks and value stocks. When growth stocks are in favor, value stocks tend to be out of favor; when growth stocks are out of favor, value stocks tend to be in favor. If you use a two-pronged approach that includes a growth-focused strategy and a value-focused strategy, you'll see less volatility in your portfolio. Your highs might not be quite as high—but, more importantly, your lows won't be as low during down times.

Why is it particularly important to smooth out those down times? The biggest reason is that downside volatility isn't just unpleasant—it also costs you money. Let's see why.

Consider a $10,000 portfolio (you could use any amount) that gains 25 percent one year, loses 30 percent the next, and gains 14 percent in the third. On the surface, it would seem like your average annual gain was 3 percent, because that's what you get when you average 25, 30, and 14 and divide by 3 years. But let's look at what you actually would "gain."

The first year, your 25 percent gain on that $10,000 investment grows your portfolio to $12,500. The second year, you lose 30 percent on that new amount, dropping the $12,500 down to $8,750. Then, you gain 14 percent on that $8,750 in the third year. That leaves you with $9,975 after three years—$25 *less* than what you started with.

What happened to the 3 percent per year gain we were expecting? In a sense, it got washed away in the 30 percent drop in that second year, which significantly knocked down your capital. The 30 percent decline was 30 percent of $12,500 ($3,750); by comparison, the 14 percent gain the next year was 14 percent of just $8,750 (what you were left with after that bad second year). Because of that lower starting point, your 14 percent gain in the third year didn't get you back about half of the 30 percent you lost in year two, as you might expect; it instead recouped just $1,225—less than a third of what you lost in the second year.

The bottom line here is that in the stock market, your gains are *compounded*; that is, after your first year, you start earning money not on your initial investment, but on whatever you had at the end of the previous year—be it more or less than your initial investment. A bad down year thus doesn't just mean you lose a bunch of money one year; it's also limiting the potential money you can make *next* year, because any percentage gain will now be made on a lower base.

On the other hand, compound interest works for you if you're gaining ground, since you are generating returns off your principal *and* your gains from the previous year(s). The more you can smooth out the valleys and keep your portfolio growing in a steady upward trend, the better, even if it means you're smoothing out some of the peaks in big "up" years.

There's another less tangible reason to limit your downside vol-atility: You'll feel less of an urge to ditch your approach when times get tough. Ideally, the data we've presented showing that sticking to a strategy is imperative has been so moving that you won't need this reassurance. But when investment dollars start disappearing in chunks, emotions can get so intense that even the best investors can lose their cool and jump ship. Anything that helps keep you stay the course and stick to your long-term strategy is thus a help, and combining strategies to limit losses during down times does just that.

If this type of blending sounds familiar, it's because you've seen it before. James O'Shaughnessy used such an approach in developing his United Cornerstone strategy, which we covered in Chapter 10. O'Shaughnessy's United Cornerstone approach didn't produce the best absolute returns in his study of more than four decades of stock mar-ket data; that distinction belonged to an approach in which he targeted stocks with price-sales ratios less than 1.0 and high relative strengths. But O'Shaughnessy settled on the United Cornerstone approach because it had the best *risk-adjusted* returns, as demonstrated by its Sharpe ratio—a risk-adjusted return measure developed by Nobel-laureate William Sharpe.

The Sharpe ratio takes into account not only returns, but also standard deviation. (If mathematical terms such as *standard deviation* make your head hurt, don't worry; it's basically just a measure of how volatile a strategy or a portfolio is). Notes O'Shaughnessy in *What Works on Wall Street,* "Generally, investors prefer a portfolio earning 15 percent a year with a standard deviation of 20 percent to one earning 16 per-cent a year with a standard deviation of 30 percent. A 1 percent abso-lute advantage doesn't compensate for the terror of the wild ride." The best combination of lower-risk, higher-return strategies, O'Shaughnessy found, was the blended United Cornerstone approach.

Our own findings support O'Shaughnessy's research. A "Total Blend" portfolio of stocks that used all 10 of the strategies detailed in this book—weighting each one equally—would have produced a better Sharpe ratio than any of the individual strategies from July 2003 through April 2008. That is, it would have had a better combi-nation of high returns and low risk than any of our individual mod-els. Its annualized return of 19.89 percent was better than all but three of our individual models, and it posted those returns while having a lower standard deviation than all of the individual models except the Greenblatt approach (and it trailed that by only 0.08 percentage points).

Premium Blend Using blended strategies in a single portfolio isn't just a way to smooth out returns. Done properly, it can also *improve* returns over the long haul. While the "Total Blend" approach we examined in the previous section puts the top picks of different individual strategies into a single, large portfolio, another type of blending involves looking for stocks with the most *combined interest* from different strategies. Most of our models examine a series of different variables when analyzing a stock, which means that using just one of these strategies ensures you're getting a stock that is financially strong on a number of different levels. But when you focus on stocks with *multiguru approval,* you're getting stocks that have really been put through the ringer.

A good case in point is the Validea Hot List portfolio that we track on our website. The Hot List looks for stocks that get the most combined interest from our strategies. It also gives greater weight to the strategies with the most historical success, meaning that the stocks it picks are fundamentally strong on a number of levels and get interest from strategies that have been very successful over the long term.

The results show what a multiguru blending approach can do. After five years of tracking, the Hot List had a higher annualized return than all but two of our guru-based models (our Kenneth Fisher- and Benjamin Graham–based approaches). From its July 15, 2003 inception through July 15, 2008, the portfolio gained 123.4 percent, more than five times the S&P 500's 21.4 percent gain during that time. What's more, the Hot List posted those impressive gains while having a standard deviation (remember, that's a measure of volatility) not much greater than most of our individual strategies. On a risk-adjusted basis (i.e., based on its Sharpe ratio), the only strategy that beat the Hot List by any significant amount was our Fisher model.

While an individual guru model may outperform the Hot List in a given period (as the Fisher model has done in recent years), we believe that over the longer term a blended approach will achieve the best results, because it limits downside risk when an individual strategy is going through a down period.

How does using a blended approach keep volatility in check and still beat out so many individual strategies in terms of absolute returns? A big part of it has to do with the thoroughness of our diverse group of individual models. For example, you can usually find a handful of stocks in the market that pass both our Peter Lynch-based fast-grower approach and our James O'Shaughnessy-based value model. These stocks must be growing earnings at a clip of at least 20 percent over a five-year span and have manageable debt to pass the Lynch fast-grower test, but they also must have the size and strong dividend yield and cash flow that the O'Shaughnessy value method requires. That combination of factors makes for a very, very complete stock, one that is growing earnings quickly, is conservatively financed, and is even paying a nice dividend. Over the long haul, it's hard to imagine many stocks with this kind of multiguru approval not improving.

Guru Investing Principle 1: Combine Strategies

- Because of compounding, downside volatility isn't just uncomfortable—it actually costs you money.
- If you're looking to smooth out returns, pick stocks using Guru Strategies with lower degrees of correlation (those that perform differently in the same type of market conditions). Example: Have half your portfolio include stocks passing the James O'Shaughnessy growth strategy, and the other half stocks passing the David Dreman contrarian model.
- To maximize returns, look for stocks that get approval from the highest number of gurus, giving more weight to those models with the best historical track records.

Principle 2: Stick to the Numbers—or the Market Will Stick It to You

Blending strategies can smooth returns and take some of the emotion out of your portfolio management—but not all of it. You can do more blending than a Bahamian bartender and you'll still have to deal with the urge to buy and sell based on emotional reactions. As we discussed earlier, investors often sell good stocks of good companies that are having short-term problems because they can't see the forest for the trees; they let fear get the best of them, and mistakenly think short-term hiccups will be long-term problems for a company or an industry when the long-term data indicates otherwise. In addition, when buying, people have the urge to jump on hot, trendy stocks that turn out to be overpriced and overhyped.

A key to limiting the impact emotions have on your buying and selling decisions is following a quantitative investing strategy, like the guru-based methods we've examined. If you do that, a big part of the task of removing emotion from your portfolio management is already done. That's because you'll be using an approach that sticks to the numbers—a stock's fundamentals. You won't buy stocks because they're getting good press, because a magazine predicts that a stock's price will double, or because a friend tells you it's a sure thing; similarly, you won't sell when a stock gets bad press, or you hear rumors that it's on the way down. Instead, you'll buy and sell when the numbers are right and only when they're right. (We'll talk more specifically about how to use the numbers to determine when to sell a little later.) No hunches, no guesswork—just strategies that have long histories of producing strong results by using cold, hard facts and figures.

Why stick solely to the numbers? After all, we're intelligent people; surely using our own insights, whether alone or in tandem with the numbers, can work better than using such an impersonal, rigid, quantitative approach, right?

Wrong. As humans, there are a lot of things we do well. Unfortunately for investors, predicting and forecasting are not among them. Think back to Chapter 1, and the study that Philip Tetlock detailed in his book *Expert Political Judgment: How Good Is It? How Can We Know?* Tetlock's research found that even so-called "experts" couldn't explain more than 20 percent of the total variability in outcomes when trying to predict future events.

Statistical models, meanwhile, aren't perfect at forecasting the future—but they're a lot better than humans. If you'll recall, Tetlock found that sophisticated algorithms could explain 47 percent of outcomes in his study—more than twice as much as "expert" human forecasters.

James O'Shaughnessy, the growth-value guru we discussed in Chapter 10, gives some excellent insights into this phenomenon in *What Works on Wall Street*. In the book, O'Shaughnessy cites additional studies that all found that human prognosticators couldn't match statistical-actuarial forecasting models. In one study, for example, an actuarial model did better in predicting whether certain high school students would be successful in college than did admissions officers at many colleges. In another, a researcher named Jack Sawyer reviewed 45 different studies that compared human and actuarial predictive ability. "In *none* [of the 45] was the clinical, intuitive method—the one favored by most people—found to be superior," O'Shaughnessy writes. "What's more, Sawyer included instances in which the human judges had more information than the model *and* were given the results of the quantitative models before being asked for a prediction. *The actuarial models still beat the human judges!*"

How can that be? It's because people are emotional creatures, and emotions lead to inconsistency in how we assess problems. Explains O'Shaughnessy: "Models beat human forecasters because they reliably and consistently apply the same criteria time after time. . . . Models never vary. They are always consistent. They are never moody, never fight with their spouse, are never hung over from a night on the town, and never get bored. They don't favor vivid, interesting stories over reams of statistical data. They never take anything personally. They don't have egos. They're not out to prove anything."

We agree. No matter how objective you might try to be, you can't completely turn off your emotions. Once you read that article about "The Next Apple," or about an analyst's report on a particular stock, it's tough to get it out of your head. Even if you're conscious of the negative impact emotions can have on your decision-making, it might not help. They still may seep into your mind unconsciously, without you even realizing it. Or, you might try so hard *not* to succumb to your emotions that you end up simply doing the exact opposite of what they're telling you—which also might not necessarily be for the best.

Even if you just try to modify a proven, quantitative strategy with your own additions, you're asking for trouble. Your modifications may work for a while, but over the long term, you have no idea how they will impact your returns. By sticking to a proven, purely quantitative buying and selling system, you neutralize your brain, and you put your faith in strategies that are supported by years and years of data—not by hunches or fleeting emotions.

Guru Investing Principle 2: Stick to the Numbers

- Many studies show that human beings' forecasting abilities cannot match those of statistical or actuarial models, because human emotions cloud decision-making.
- Using proven, quantitative strategies allows you to make buy and sell decisions solely on the numbers—a stock's fundamentals—helping to remove emotion from the process.
- Tinkering with a proven quantitative strategy may work today, tomorrow, or a few months from now. But you have no idea what the repercussions will be over the long term. It's best to stick firmly to strategies that are backed up by long, proven track records.

Principle 3: Stay Disciplined over the Long Haul

In addition to having a disciplined, fundamentals-based approach that tells you which particular stocks to buy or sell, discipline is also a crucial part of investment success in another way: You have to be willing to stick with your approach for the long term, even if your strategy— or the entire market, for that matter—is going through a nasty down period. In other words, while the quantitative strategies we've outlined in this book stick to the numbers, the real trick is making sure that *you stick* to the strategies for the long haul.

The reason you need to stick to your strategy harkens back again to Chapter 1, when we examined the nature of the way that the stock market makes its gains. Remember, most of its gains come on a limited number of days—and no one knows when they're going to come. In addition, when the market turns up, it turns up very quickly, something Peter Lynch has pointed out. If you jump out of the market during a downturn or a bear market waiting for the upswing, you'll likely miss out on those big initial rebound days.

It's a similar situation when it comes to individual strategies. Your strategy might identify an undervalued stock, but it can take months, or even years, for the rest of the market to catch on. The stock may even drop after you buy it, and make you wonder whether you've made the right choice. Why hold on to the stock while you're waiting for it to make its move? Why not wait until it starts to move upward, and then jump on? The reason is that if you wait to buy it until you see sure signs of upward movement, you'll likely have missed out on some big initial bounce-back gains that you can't get back.

Of course, this doesn't mean that sticking to your strategy will always yield winners over the long haul. There will be times when you buy an undervalued stock, and, for whatever reason, it just doesn't rise. That's the incredibly complex, unpredictable world of the stock market. If you stick to a proven strategy that has a track record of success, however, you put the odds in your favor that you'll have more gainers than you will losers. And over the long run, that should lead to some very nice gains for your portfolio.

Just how crucial is it to do whatever you can to stay disciplined and stick to your strategy for the long term, even when the temptation to bail is highest? It may just be the single most important factor in whether you succeed or fail—and that's not an exaggeration. In an April 2008 interview with the investing website *Advisor Perspectives* (www.advisorperspectives.com), Mark Hulbert, whose well respected *Hulbert Financial Digest* ranks the performance of investment newsletters, was asked if there was a common denominator among the newsletters that have offered consistently reliable guidance over his 30-year tenure. Here's what Hulbert had to say:

> It turns out the most compelling common denominator is the top newsletters consistently follow a discipline. A disciplined adherence to a strategy works, as long as it is a decent strategy. A lot of times, the newsletters at the bottom jump ship as soon as their strategy is out of favor, and end up selling low and buying high. They are always being whipsawed in and out of the market.

Hulbert said this was a "profound observation" about investing. "It is not the strategy itself that makes the difference," he said. "It is the discipline, especially when one is out of sync with the market. For every strategy, be it growth or value, large or small cap, there is a newsletter that has done well and one that has done poorly." (We agree that the decision to stick to a strategy may be more important than what specific strategy you pick. But we also think that there are certain strategies, like those developed by the gurus we've discussed, that offer better long-term returns than others.)

In a column written for the American Association of Individual Investors (AAII) in February 2008, Hulbert offered some advice for how investors can help themselves stay disciplined: by cutting down how often they look at their portfolios. "According to behavioral finance researchers, constantly looking at how your portfolio is performing is not a benign act," he wrote. "It leads you to focus more of your attention on the short term than you would otherwise, leading you in turn to miss the veritable forest for the trees."

In that column, Hulbert cited a study performed by University of Chicago Professor Richard Thaler—"The Effect of Myopia and Loss Aversion." In that 1997 study, Thaler (along with fellow researchers Amos Tversky, Daniel Kahneman, and Alan Schwartz) had a group of undergraduate students simulate investment decisions, and told them that they would be paid (between $5 and $30) depending on their actual investment success or failure. As part of the study, different students were allowed to check their portfolios at differing time intervals. What Thaler found was that those who were allowed to look at their portfolios the most did the worst, because they tended to put less money into stocks and more into bonds, which are traditionally thought of as "safer" investments even though stocks clearly outperform them over the long term. "The subjects with the most data did the worst in terms of money earned," the study results stated, "since those with the most frequent data invested the least in stocks (and thus earned the least)."

This makes perfect sense: *Since the market will inevitably gyrate up and down in the short-term, those looking frequently at their portfolios will see a lot of anxiety-provoking stops and starts; those who don't look as frequently will see the longer-term trend, which, when it comes to the stock market, is historically positive, and feel more comfortable putting more money into stocks.* By stepping back from your portfolio, you're more likely to stay disciplined and keep your money in the market—and over the long term, there's no better place for it to be.

There's definitely a level of trust involved here. You have to trust the research that shows market timing is a dangerous game. You have to trust the data that shows that over the long term, the stock market is far and away the best investment vehicle there is if you stick with it—particularly when you factor in inflation concerns. You have to trust those investors who have had great success in beating the market in the past. And in the end, you have to accept you're going to have to deal with those uncomfortable fluctuations if you want to make money in the market over the long haul. Those ups and downs are the reason why you get paid a premium for investing in stocks; without them, you wouldn't get that premium, and the excess long-term returns that the market offers compared to other investment vehicles wouldn't exist.

Expectations Are Key To help yourself see the investment forest rather than the trees, you should have the right mindset going into your market endeavors. As you're building your portfolio, tell yourself that, at some point, you're bound to experience a short-term 10 to 20 percent drop, and that you'll also endure less frequent larger drops. About six years after his retirement, Peter Lynch addressed this idea in an interview with PBS television. Lynch said that 10 percent declines in the market had occurred in more than half the years in the twentieth century; 25 percent declines—a bear market—had occurred, on average, every six years. "They're gonna happen." Lynch said. "If you're in the market, you have to know there's going to be declines. And they're going to cap and every couple of years you're going to get a 10 percent correction. That's a euphemism for losing a lot of money rapidly. . . . And a bear market is a 20–25–30 percent decline. They're gonna happen. When they're gonna start, no one knows. If you're not ready for that, you shouldn't be in the stock market. I mean stomach is the key organ here. It's not the brain. Do you have the stomach for these kinds of declines?"

Lynch was speaking about the broader market, but the same applies to your own portfolio. Think back to Joel Greenblatt. He stresses again and again that his magic formula won't beat the market every year. In fact, his testing found that the formula underperformed the market one out of every four years from 1988 through 2004. But if you had used the formula for any two-year period during that time, your chances of underperforming fell to one in six. And, over three-year periods, the formula beat the market 95 percent of the time—and it never lost money in any of the three-year periods over that 17-year span (Greenblatt says that even in its worst three-year period during that 17-year span, the formula actually gained 11 percent).

It's a similar story for just about any strategy you can imagine. All of the greats—Lynch, Buffett, Dreman, Graham—have had years when they failed to beat the market. But they stuck with their strategies, and that's what enabled them to post such great long-term returns. When it comes to our guru-based models, even our best 10-stock performer as of the time of this writing, the Kenneth Fisher strategy, hasn't been perfect. While the Fisher model nearly tripled the market in the partial year of 2003 and again in 2004, it lagged the S&P 500 in 2005. In fact, our 10-stock Fisher portfolio lost ground, falling 2.7 percent. But if you'd bailed on the strategy at that point, you'd have missed out on at least some of the 40 percent gain the portfolio had in 2006—again nearly tripling the market.

If you acknowledge at the outset that all strategies—even great ones—go through down periods, you won't be surprised when your portfolio does take a short-term hit. As with many things in life, it's the surprise that often leads to anxiety and fear. If you're ready for those down times, you'll be amazed at how much more calm you'll remain when your portfolio takes some short-term lumps.

Unfortunately, most investors don't do that. (In fact, Lynch has supposedly said that while he was at Magellan's helm, more of the fund's investors *lost* money than gained money because they would jump out of the fund when things got rough—selling low—and then jump back in when the fund was doing well—buying high.) Not being prepared for those downturns makes it all the more easy to be bowled over by emotions when times get tough. And if you give in to your emotions, you'll probably end up selling after big losses, and buying only after the market has made some big gains.

The proof is in the pudding. In the AAII column referenced earlier, Hulbert said the newsletter that his group rated as the best performer since mid-1980 (*The Prudent Speculator*) has demonstrated great faith in the market's upward trend, and been rewarded for it. The newsletter "has been the most buffeted by short-term market gyrations" of any he has monitored, he said. "And yet, none surpasses it in its willingness to either ignore or tolerate those gyrations." Hulbert said a testament to the newsletter's faith in the market's long-term benefits came after its model portfolio lost 57 percent in the crash of 1987. While others panicked, *The Prudent Speculator* kept its fully invested approach, and ended up winning big over the long haul. "Long-term investors need not lose sleep over the markets' short-term gyrations because the markets' long-term patterns will eventually assert themselves," Hulbert wrote.

Guru Investing Principle 3: Stay Disciplined Over the Long Haul

- It's essential to stick to your strategy for the long term. Even the best strategies have down periods, and it can sometimes take over a year to reap the benefits of a good method. If you try to time your use of a strategy, you'll likely miss out on some big gains.
- Expectations shape reactions; be prepared for short-term 10 to 20 percent downturns that are inevitable in the stock market—and the less frequent but also inevitable 35 to 50 percent downturns you'll occasionally experience. You can't predict when they'll happen, so you just have to roll with them if you want to reap the market's long-term benefits.
- Give the Internet a rest. Checking your portfolio every day, let alone every 10 minutes, can make you want to jump in and out of the market, which hurts your long-term performance.

Principle 4: Diversify, but You Can't Beat the Market by Owning It

In general, diversification is a good thing. Putting all your eggs in one basket—that is, putting all your money in just a couple stocks—is far too risky for most investors. Even the best companies with the strongest fundamentals can run into trouble. Maybe their star CEO leaves and is replaced by a dunce; maybe a fire destroys their largest facility; maybe the company just plain makes a big mistake, like making oversized bets on risky loans.

Whatever the case, it's clear that you need to spread your money over a reasonable number of investments. But many investors—especially professional fund managers—spread it too thin. Some mutual funds hold hundreds of stocks, spread over every industry. With that many stocks covering that broad a swath, you're bound to end up approximating the overall market's returns. And if market-approximate returns are what you're looking for, you're better off just buying an S&P 500 index fund or Vanguard Total Market Index Fund, which would have much lower fees than the average mutual fund.

So, what is a "reasonable" number of stocks to hold to limit risk without just mirroring the market? Well, in a 2003 study entitled "Stock Diversification in the U.S. Equity Market," California State University-Chico Professor H. Christine Hsu and H. Jeffrey Wei found that "the benefit of risk diversification is somewhat limited when the number of stocks in the portfolio goes beyond 50." (You should know that Hsu and Wei's study was actually taking aim at investors who didn't diversify enough, and that they said investors with a relatively high degree of risk-aversion should hold more than 50 stocks. Nonetheless, their finding about risk diversification being limited when you go over 50 stocks is quite relevant.)

Keep in mind, however, that while you don't need to hold stocks in every sector or industry, you should maintain some diversification across those categories. You don't want to have a portfolio that's 80 or 90 percent retail stocks, for example, because you'll really get hammered if the industry hits any prolonged struggles. It's best to establish your own system—for example, making a rule that a particular sector won't make up more than, say, 40 percent of your holdings—and then stick to it over the long haul.

As you've seen from the results of our model portfolios throughout this book, our own experience has found that when using a rigid fundamental-based system, portfolios of 10 or 20 stocks can be quite successful. The system isn't going to beat the market with every pick, but we know that, historically, our models have been right more than they've been wrong. By holding 10 or 20 stocks, we put those odds in our favor. While these 10- or 20-stock portfolios are somewhat more volatile than the market, they're large enough to eliminate a good deal of firm-specific risk, while small enough so that you don't have to spend too much time managing your portfolio. And the greater-than-market volatility has certainly been worth the price: Since their inceptions, most of which were four or five years ago, all of the 10-stock portfolios we track based on the strategies detailed in this book have beaten the market, and nine of the ten 20-stock portfolios have also beaten the market. In fact, in most cases these portfolios have doubled, tripled, or quadrupled the market's gains over a fairly lengthy period, lending a lot of credence to the notion of not spreading investment dollars too thin.

Guru Investing Principle 4: Diversify, but Don't Own the Market

- Diversification is good—to a point. Maintain a focused portfolio that includes enough stocks to limit stock-specific risk, but don't hold so many that you end up simply mirroring the market's returns.
- In a rigid fundamental-based investing system, portfolios as small as 10 stocks can significantly beat the market over the long haul.
- While you don't need to hold stocks in every sector or industry, set guidelines to make sure you maintain at least some diversification across those areas within your portfolio.

Principle 5: Size- and Style-Focused Systems Only Limit Investment Possibilities

Another piece to typical diversification plans involves "style-box" investing. Look at the mutual fund listings in the newspaper or online, and you'll find a plethora of funds that are focused by market cap and value-growth style. Small-cap growth, large-cap value, midcap growth—these funds choose only stocks from one specific area of the market. This can be particularly relevant for institutional investors, which are sometimes required to put a certain percentage of their funds into these traditional style-box categories.

Style-box investing can work well for institutions that manage enormous portfolios. But for individual investors, one problem is that each of these approaches can go in and out of favor fairly frequently. Large-cap value may be all the rage for six months, and then it might go in the tank.

John Mauldin gives a great example of this in his 2004 book *Bull's Eye Investing*. Mauldin shows that from 1993 to 1999, large-cap growth stocks beat large-cap value stocks, as well as small-cap growth and small-cap value stocks, returning 21.64 percent. Small-cap value was the worst performing group in that timeframe, gaining 13.9 percent.

But if you extend the period three more years, making it 1993 to 2002, small-cap value actually was by far the best performer of the four, gaining 15.23 percent. Large-cap growth came in second, more than four percentage points behind (11.08 percent).

If you limit yourself to a particular style-box category, you're thus going to have trouble gaining any ground, regardless of your stock-picking ability, when that category is out of favor. A better approach for individual investors, we believe, is to allow yourself to roam the entire universe of stocks at all times. If the majority of good values at a given time are, say, midcap growth stocks, why limit the amount of midcap growth stocks you own? If you're sticking to fundamentals, a good value is a good value, regardless of what style-box class it fits into. Some may say that splitting your investments up among the different style-box categories is diversifying your investments, a way to lower risk. In reality, all it does is limit your potential gains, and over the long term, *that's* risky.

We're not the only ones who think this way. There is a growing movement called "strategy-based investing" that also thinks there is a better approach. Strategy-based investing holds that the traditional style-box categories that focus on market capitalization and growth-value distinctions aren't really separate asset classes, so that limiting your picks to such categories doesn't just lead to underperformance—it also doesn't limit risk that much, which is supposed to be its purpose.

Research indicates that strategy-based investing does have its merits. One study, performed by Craig Callahan and C. Thomas Howard and detailed in the May 2006 issue of *Investment Advisor Magazine,* found that style-box investing costs managers about 300 basis points in returns per year. Other studies have yielded similar results.

In the end, it just plain makes sense. Fundamentals and price matter—not market cap or growth-value distinction. Go wherever the best values are in the market, and you'll be best off in the long run.

> **Guru Investing Principle 5: Don't Limit Yourself**
>
> - Studies show that "style-box" investing can limit your gains by about 300 basis points per year.
> - Using "strategy-based investing" allows you to pick the best values in the market at any given time, regardless of market cap or growth-value designations.

Principle 6: You Don't Have to Hold Stocks for the Long Term to be a Long-Term Investor

We've talked a lot about "long-term investing" in this book. But it's critical to understand that the long-term investing we speak of may not be the same as the long-term investing you've come across before. Typically, people think of long-term investing as "buy-and-hold" investing; that is, you do your research, buy a stock, and then hold on to it for a long period, usually years, no matter what.

We think there's a better way to grow your portfolio, however, particularly if you're using a fundamental-based investing system, as we and most of the gurus we've discussed do. Suppose for a minute that you are targeting stocks that have low debt, strong earnings, and good value ratios. A particular stock you're researching meets your fundamental criteria, so you buy it because you know that over time stocks with strong fundamentals tend to do well.

But what happens if, a month from now, that company's fundamentals deteriorate significantly? Perhaps it takes on a ton of new debt, or maybe it announces terrible earnings and sales results for the past year, so that it no longer meets the criteria you used to select it in the first place. Should you continue to hold it? After all, isn't that what a good "long-term investor" does—hold stocks for a long time?

Not necessarily. Remember what your reason for buying the stock was: that it met the fundamental criteria you use for your portfolio. Now that that has disappeared, why should you be obliged to hold on to it?

Many investors will, however, hold on to such a stock. Sometimes there are legitimate reasons—tax considerations are one thing that can affect a "sell" decision, as we'll see a little later. But other times, the reasons investors hold on to these stocks aren't good. Maybe it's because they know that to succeed in the market you have to think long-term, and they figure that means holding on to your stocks for a long time; maybe it's because the stock has slipped in price on the fundamental decline, and they don't want to take a loss. Whatever the case, they hold on to a stock that used to have good prospects because it had good fundamentals (and over time, good fundamentals tend to be rewarded with price gains), but which now lacks those good fundamentals and, therefore, lacks good prospects.

Holding on to a stock that no longer has strong fundamentals doesn't just hurt because that stock may not perform all that well. There's also what is called an *opportunity cost* to holding the stock. Say, for example, you hold a stock with questionable fundamentals and it gains 1 or 2 percent. That's okay, you think; the stock is still making me money, so it's not hurting me, right?

Actually, it very well may be hurting you. That's because another stock with strong fundamentals may have earned you 9 or 10 percent during that time if you'd bought it instead. While the stock you held on to gained 1 or 2 percent, you're really losing about 8 percent—the 8 percent more you could have had by taking the opportunity to ditch the fundamentally-flawed stock and buy that other, stronger stock. (Of course, this isn't always the case. But given the fact that fundamentally strong stocks tend to do best, it's likely to happen more often than not over time.)

Rather than blindly holding on to stocks for a long period of time, we believe that long-term investing is really about sticking to a strategy over the long haul. If you use a strategy that focuses on low price-sales ratios, strong relative strengths, and improving earnings (like the O'Shaughnessy growth model), and one of your holdings' fundamentals change so that it no longer meets those criteria, you shouldn't hesitate to sell it and replace it with another stock that does meet your requirements. This might mean that you'll sometimes sell stocks after holding them for brief periods—but you're still a long-term investor, because your investment decisions are driven by a long-term strategy that you stick to over the long haul.

Guru Investing Principle 6: Stick to the Strategy—Not the Stocks

- If a stock no longer meets the fundamental criteria that led you to buy it, don't feel obligated to hold on to it.
- You're a long-term investor if you stick to a strategy for the long haul—not because you blindly hold on to individual stocks for long periods.

The Key Guru Investing Principles

Now, *there* you have it. Now you have the strategies, and the six key principles to guide your use of them. You've learned how to combine strategies to limit risk or enhance returns; you've learned how to build your portfolio without watering it down or limiting your options; and you've learned how to keep those pesky emotions in check.

But we're not quite ready to give you the keys to the car yet. There's still one more guiding guru principle that we haven't explained—and it's an important one. In fact, it's so important—and so often overlooked by investment strategies— that we've decided to dedicate an entire chapter to it. Intrigued? Just turn the page, and you'll find out what this final, and crucial, piece of information is.

Chapter 14

The Missing Piece

Determining When to Sell

Flying isn't the hard part; landing in the net is.
— Mario Zacchini, one of the original
"Flying Cannonballs"

Things are looking pretty good for us right now. We've got a great car with a powerful 10-cylinder engine (the 10 market-beating investment strategies we've examined), and now we know how to drive it. In fact, we can really get this baby purring, so much so that we're leaving the market in the dust.

There's just one problem: Where are the brakes on this thing?

While a lot of strategies out there tell you how to buy stocks that will make nice gains, there are few that address the second half of the stock investing equation: when to sell—the proverbial brakes on our car.

It's amazing, really, because for many investors, deciding when to sell is a harder decision than deciding what to buy. Cabot Research, a behavioral finance consulting firm, has found that even top-performing mutual fund managers may be missing out on 100 to 200 basis points per year because of poor sell decisions, *Institutional Investor*'s Amy Feldman noted in a June 13, 2008 article entitled "Know When To Fold 'em." Seeing as how amateur investors tend to do much worse than the pros (as we learned in Chapter 1), it's likely that the average, nonprofessional investor suffers even greater losses because of poor sell decisions.

Part of the reason investors struggle with selling is that advice on the topic is somewhat lacking in the investment world. A survey performed by Cabot and the CFA Institute found that more than 70 percent of professional investors used a selling approach that was not highly disciplined or driven by research and objective criteria, Feldman noted in her piece, so it seems most of the pros aren't offering a whole lot of guidance here. But another part of why sell decisions are so hard involves an old, familiar foe: our own brains.

Just as our brains tell us to avoid unpopular stocks and jump on hot stocks when we're buying, they also cause havoc when we're trying to figure out when we should sell a stock. If you've ever put money into the market, you've almost surely found this out the hard way.

A few phenomena make selling—and sticking to a selling plan—a difficult task. For starters, there's the "fear of regret." When we make an error in judgment, we feel badly; often, we'll beat ourselves up with "woulda-coulda-shoulda" thinking, which is never pleasant. And that's certainly true when we take a loss on a stock. Hindsight is always 20/20, and we end up thinking that we could have easily avoided what turned out to be a bad move. Because of the unpleasantness of those feelings, one theory on why people sell at the wrong time is that they avoid selling stocks that have lost value, instinctively wanting to postpone those feelings of pain and regret—even if those stocks now have little prospect of rebounding.

This is similar to the concept of "myopic loss aversion" that we examined in the previous chapter. In his 1999 paper, "The End of Behavioral Finance," Professor Richard H. Thaler of the Chicago University explains that loss aversion refers "to the observed tendency for decision makers to weigh losses more heavily than gains; losses hurt roughly twice as much as gains feel good." Locking in losses thus hurts a lot—so we'll avoid selling stocks for a loss even after they no longer have good prospects to delay that hurt.

Why are losses so painful? The fact that they are a shot to our egos seems to be part of the reason. Professors Kent Daniel and Sheridan Titman state that people tend to ignore or underweight information that lowers their self-esteem in "Market Efficiency in an Irrational World," which appeared in the 1999 volume of the *Financial Analyst Journal.* "For example," they write, "investors may be reluctant to sell their losers because it requires that they admit to making a mistake, which could lead to a loss in confidence and have deleterious consequences. For similar reasons, investors may systematically overweight information that tends to support their earlier decisions and to filter out information that suggests the earlier decisions were mistakes." Essentially, we'll twist the facts to avoid admitting mistakes so that we feel better about ourselves, and our stock-picking abilities. That keeps us from feeling badly about ourselves, but it also keeps us from learning from those mistakes.

Another common mistake many investors make is holding on to winners too long. In his 2001 book *Navigate the Noise: Investing in the New Age of Media and Hype,* Richard Bernstein notes that growth fund managers often do just that "because they are encouraged to do so by all the good news regarding companies' prospects." A perfect example would seem to be the tech stock boom of the late 1990s. Many investors—professional and amateur, made a fortune as the Internet bubble grew. The problem was that the bubble kept growing, long, long after these stocks had risen above reasonable values. Still, the buzz was that the "Internet Era" had arrived, and would fundamentally change the stock market; when it came to the World Wide Web, the theory went, there were limitless possibilities—and thus limitless returns. Blinded by the hype, most of those people who had made huge sums of money ignored logic and held on to their stocks too long, only to see them come crashing down.

To try to avoid some of these problems, some people will set price targets for stocks they buy. They'll determine ahead of time that, if the stock gains, say, 30 percent, they'll sell it and take the profits. This sounds good on the surface, but really it's just another problem. All gaining stocks were not created equal; one stock may gain 30 percent and then drop, but another may gain 30 percent and then gain another

200 percent. Setting arbitrary selling targets like this can hurt just as much as they help, if not more.

Selling Smart

So with all of these challenges, how do you stave off emotion and make good, sensible "sell" decisions? The same way that you keep emotion at bay when deciding what stocks to buy: By using a disciplined system that makes sell decisions based on cold, hard fundamentals—not emotion-driven hunches, or arbitrary price targets. That's what we've done with our model portfolios, as well as with our investment management business, and we think that's a big reason why the results have been so good.

To understand how—and why—our "sell" system works, you have to go back to the basic premise behind our "buy" strategy. And that is that over the long term, investors gravitate toward stocks with strong fundamentals because those are the strongest companies, and that causes those stocks' prices to rise over time. We buy because of the fundamentals—not just because the price is high or low or rising or falling. Remember, the only way price comes into the decision to buy is in how it relates to the stock's fundamentals—that is, in the form of such variables as the price-sales ratio or price-earnings ratio.

When you're building your portfolio, then, you want to pick the stocks that have the best fundamentals—because (sorry to sound like a broken record) *over the long run, investors gravitate toward stocks with strong fundamentals because they are the strongest companies.*

Okay, great, you're saying, but that's buying stocks; we've already covered that. What does this have to do with selling stocks?

Well, it has everything to do with selling. If you're buying stocks because they have strong fundamentals, and (everyone now), over the long term, stocks with strong fundamentals tend to rise, you should hold on to a stock *as long as it continues to meet the fundamental criteria you used to select it.* Whether the stock has dropped sharply since you bought it or whether it has skyrocketed is no matter; what matters is where the stock's fundamentals stand *right now.* Price—just as with buying—matters only in terms of how it relates to the fundamentals (what the stock's P/E or P/S ratios are, for example). Many investors will sell a stock because its price has fallen and they think they need to cut their losses, or because the price has risen and they think the "smart" thing to do is to take the profits rather than risk the stock coming back down. But those are arbitrary, emotional decisions. Remember, you bought the stock because its strong fundamentals made it a good bet to gain value; if its fundamentals are still strong, why wouldn't it still be a good bet to gain more value?

If the stock's fundamentals have slipped, however, so that it no longer meets the criteria you used to buy it, it's time to sell and replace it with another stock that does meet your criteria (and one that thereby has better prospects of rising in value).

The selling assessment is thus an ongoing reevaluation of where a stock stands right now. You must continually reassess what the stock's prospects are going forward—not what they were a month ago, six months ago, or whenever you bought it.

The next question, then, is what "continually assess" means. Should you check once a day to make sure your holdings still meet your criteria? Once a week? Once a month? Once a year? Since mid-2003 we've been running model portfolios based on each of our Guru Strategies. For each model, we've constructed separate port-folios that use different rebalancing periods—monthly, quarterly or annually. The model portfolio returns reported at the end of each guru chapter are those of our 10- and 20-stock portfolios using the monthly rebalancing period. On average, this monthly rebalancing tends to produce the highest raw return; the quarterly and annual portfolios, while still ahead of the market, tend to produce less excess return over the time period for which we have results. As of May 23, 2008, the average annualized gain for the 10 guru-based strate-gies discussed in this book was 16.2 percent when the portfolios were rebalanced monthly, 15.4 percent when rebalanced quarterly, and 10.4 percent when rebalanced annually.

The prevalence of inexpensive discount brokerages has made trad-ing very cost-effective today (especially for larger portfolios) and, for many reading this, a monthly portfolio rebalancing is attractive and can be done easily and cheaply with the right online broker. Nevertheless, it's important to understand that the monthly rebalancing approach does require more a bit more work, time, and commitment—if you're

When to Rebalance?

While the 10 Guru Strategies detailed in this book have performed well when rebalanced over a variety of different time frames, a monthly rebalancing has generally provided the best results. The following are the average annualized returns of all the separate strategies, by rebalancing time frame. (Results do not include fees).

Period Length	Average Return
Monthly	16.2%
Quarterly	15.4%
Annually	10.4%

Source: Validea.com

a busy professional, a retiree who likes to travel or a stay-at-home-mom with young children a less frequent rebalancing approach might work better for you and give you a better chance at following the strategy more consistently. So the important point here, whether you use a one-month rebalancing or a different time frame that works for you, is this—*you need to re-examine your portfolio at set intervals, to assess how your holdings stand relative to the reasons you bought them. If they no longer meet the criteria you used to pick them, you should consider replacing them with new stocks that do make the grade.*

You can also use your rebalancing period to reweight your portfolio in case some of your holdings have gained or lost a bunch, and now make up a disproportionate part of your portfolio. The idea here is to keep things close to equally weighted. It doesn't have to be perfect, though; if one stock gains a little ground so that it makes up a few more percentage points of your portfolio than the other stocks, you don't need to go selling a couple shares—and getting hit with trading charges—just to even things out exactly. To keep this simple, you might want to set a reweighting target percentage. For example, anytime a holding's weight in your portfolio becomes 10 percent more or less than your target weight, you buy or sell shares of it to bring it back to that target.

By sticking to a firm rebalancing plan, you keep emotion and hype from impacting your selling decisions. You sell at regular intervals, and you sell based on fundamentals. Just as with buying stocks, there's no place for hunch-playing or knee-jerk reactions here.

There are a couple rare occasions, however, when you should sell a stock without waiting for the rebalancing date to arrive. If a firm is involved or allegedly involved in a major accounting or earnings scandal, you should sell the stock immediately, because you can no longer trust its publicly disclosed financial data. In addition, if a firm has become a serious bankruptcy risk since the last rebalancing, you should also sell its stock immediately.

Staying a Step Ahead of Uncle Sam

While a stock's fundamentals are the main part of deciding when you should sell, there's another factor that can affect your timing in a subtler way: taxes. (*Note:* If your account is nontaxable, such as a retirement account, this doesn't apply.)

When it comes to how the government taxes your stock earnings, there are two main categories: short-term gains and long-term gains. Short-term gains—those from investments you've held a year or less—are subject to your normal tax rate, which can be as much as 35 percent, depending on your income. Long-term gains—money you've made on investments you've held for more than a year—are taxed at a much lower rate for most investors, just 15 percent.

Most stock market investors fall into a tax bracket higher than 15 percent, which means that your long-term gains are taxed less than your short-term gains—sometimes considerably less. When it comes to selling stocks you've made gains on, this can thus be a big factor. When you come to a rebalancing date and find that a winning position no longer meets your fundamental criteria, consider how long you've held it. If you've held it more than a year, go right ahead and sell it. But if you've held it for less than a year, you should take into account how you'll be taxed on the gain.

The idea here is that as the tax benefit you'll get by reaching that one-year mark gets greater, you should be willing to tolerate a bit more of a decline in a holding's fundamentals. How much is up to you; there's no one "right" answer here, and there's obviously a bit of risk in holding a stock with declining fundamentals as you try to reach the one-year mark. But the important thing is that whatever guidelines you decide to use for your portfolio, you should stick to them. You don't want to start treating different stocks differently based on guesswork or hunches about where they'll be when you reach that one-year mark.

Remember, Nobody's Perfect

Another thing to keep in mind when it comes to selling stocks is that no investor—not even the greatest investors in the world—are right all the time. Remember what Martin Zweig says: "In the long run, a 60 percent success rate translates into huge gains, a 50 percent rate into solid gains, and even a 40 percent rate can beat the market."

When it comes to the stock market, no one is right all the time—or even nearly all the time. Even the great Warren Buffett makes bad investments. Just read Berkshire Hathaway's annual report, and Buffett will often speak candidly about where he's gone wrong.

Our own experience supports Zweig's contention. Of all of the portfolios we've mentioned in this book, the one with the greatest accuracy through our five years of tracking was our 10-stock David Dreman portfolio, which had made money on 62.7 percent of its picks since its inception. And by being right 62.7 percent of the time—on less than two-thirds of its picks—it had more than tripled the gains of the S&P 500 over five years. For the most part, our portfolios had accuracies between 50 and 60 percent—far from perfect—and most had still doubled, tripled, or quadrupled the market. Being aware that no one can be right all the time, or even nearly all the time, can make it easier on your ego when your selling system calls for you to take a loss on a stock.

While you'll never be right all the time, you can be right more than you're wrong, however. In the end, the key is to develop a fundamental-based selling and rebalancing plan and stick with it, *no matter what.* When your portfolio does lose ground from time to time, you'll inevitably feel the urge to sell certain stocks and go after others on a whim or a hunch to make up ground. But if you have a detailed, quantitative selling system in place, you can help keep short-term emotions from wreaking havoc with your long-term performance.

The Key Guru Selling Points

- Rebalance your portfolio at fixed intervals (i.e., every month, every quarter, every year), selling stocks that no longer meet the fundamental criteria you used buy them in the first place. Replace them with new stocks that do meet your criteria.
- Sell stocks immediately if they are involved in accounting or earnings scandals, or if they become a major bankruptcy concern. In these cases, do not wait until your next rebalancing date to sell.
- For tax reasons, it's generally best to sell winning positions after you've held them for a year and losing positions before you've held them for a year. If a stock you've made money on no longer meets your investment criteria and you've held it for close to a year, consider holding it until you pass that one-year mark to limit taxes.
- Don't be discouraged when your system calls for you to lock in losses on a stock; not even the best investors in the world are right all the time.

Conclusion

Time to Take
the Wheel

To map out a course of action and follow it to an end requires courage.
—RALPH WALDO EMERSON

Alright, it's time. You've learned about the strategies that history's greatest investors used to achieve "guru" status, and how, step by step, you can use those approaches to beat the market. You've also learned some simple but crucial principles that will allow you to make the best use of those strategies when managing your portfolio. And you've even learned how you can develop a plan for dealing with one of the greatest challenges an investor faces: deciding when to sell. So now, at last, it's time to turn the keys to the Guru Strategy car over to you.

One of the great things about this guru-powered car, you'll find, is that you can customize it however you like. Interested in deep value stocks? There are plenty of options, like the David Dreman and Benjamin Graham strategies. Want growth? Try Martin Zweig's approach, or the James O'Shaughnessy growth model. And, as you saw in Chapter 13, you can mix and match these strategies however you like in your portfolio to limit your risk and enhance your returns.

Whatever strategy or strategies you use, the most critical thing that I hope you've learned is that you need to take a good map with you on your journey and stick to it no matter what. There will be all sorts of distractions along the road to your investment goals. You'll come upon supposed shortcuts that promise to get you where you're going twice as fast. You'll see and hear from all sorts of people who are telling you that they've found a better way to go than the road you're on. Sometimes, you'll even think that your map must be wrong, and that it has you headed in the opposite direction of where you want to go.

But remember, the people who gave you directions—the gurus upon whom these strategies are based—are expert mapmakers. They know how to get where you want to go because they've been there before—unlike most of the people who will be telling you to take those shortcuts or alternate routes.

You have what you need to avoid the obstacles and bad advice along the way, and to do what it takes to beat the market. Remember, while being a good investor is hard, it doesn't have to be complicated. The greatest difficulty isn't in the details of stock-picking or portfolio management; you don't have to be a rocket scientist (or, for purposes of our guru car metaphor, a Formula One race car driver) to produce nice returns. No, the hard part will be clearing those psychological and emotional barriers we reviewed, so that you stick to your road map no matter what happens—and you now have the tools and knowledge to help you do just that.

With those tools in hand, you can go to any of a number of good stock-screening Web sites out there and find the stock-specific data—P/E ratios, earnings per share, debt-equity ratios, and so on—that you need to put these guru-based strategies to work. Just plug the data into the formulas we laid out earlier for the different Guru Strategies, going step-by-step through the method or methods of your choice to see how a particular stock stacks up.

Still, if you need some help getting started (or at any point along your journey, for that matter), don't forget that you have a source of continuing help: this book's companion website, www.guruinvestorbook.com. On the free site, you'll be able to see three stock recommendations every day from each of the ten Guru Strategies we've covered, with a link to our detailed analysis of why each stock passes a particular guru-based approach. That's 30 Guru Strategy–approved stocks a day—a great way to get your portfolio started. Think of it as an investor's AAA roadside assistance program for your journey.

Finally, if you're just not in the mood to drive yourself, we do offer a sort of "personal driver" option: our www.validea.com subscription website. The site has Guru Strategy ratings for thousand of stocks that are updated daily. It also tracks model portfolios of stocks chosen by each guru-based model, as well as some model portfolios that combine different strategies that we've reviewed.

And now, you're ready to hit the road. Take the keys, and enjoy the ride. If you stick to your roadmap, you should be quite happy with where you end up.

Appendix A

Performance of Guru-Based 10- and 20-Stock Model Portfolios

able A.1 and Table A.2 list the returns for each of the guru-based model portfolios from their respective inception dates through July 15, 2008, which represents five years of performance for the majority of the models, and includes the bear market which began in mid to late 2007. The model portfolios listed in Tables A.1 and A.2 and throughout this book are based on the authors' interpretation of the publicly disclosed investment strategies from each of the gurus, or from individuals that have studied the gurus. The model portfolio results do not reflect the actual returns generated by the gurus themselves. They are presented to give the reader insight as to how the model portfolios developed by Validea.com—which are based on the quantitative stock selection strategies of each of these gurus—have performed.

The performances of the portfolios are not back-tested results. The returns are based on model portfolios that have been running in a live, simulated environment. Further, all stocks present in the portfolios meet reasonable liquidity requirements that were developed to prevent small and illiquid stocks from affecting performance results. Most of the portfolios were started on July 15, 2003, but in a few cases portfolios were launched on later dates. The performances of both the 10- and 20-stock portfolios are based on a monthly rebalancing that is conducted on a 28-day cycle. On rebalancing dates, each stock being held in or added to the portfolio is brought back to an equal weight within the portfolio (i.e., 10 percent per stock for the 10-stock models and 5 percent per stock for the 20-stock models). Returns, which are time-weighted total returns, are calculated using the end of day pricing on each rebalancing date.

Portfolio returns do not include dividends or trading costs and past performance of the models is not necessarily indicative of future results.

All model portfolios can be accessed real-time on Validea.com (www.validea.com).

Table A.1 Guru Model Portfolio: 10 Stock

10 Stock Portfolios	Inception Date	2003	2004	2005	2006	2007	2008	Total Return	Annual Return
Benjamin Graham	7/15/2003	45.10%	21.50%	10.40%	26.00%	-8.10%	6.70%	140.40%	19.20%
John Neff	1/2/2004	N/A	21.20%	15.10%	22.30%	-1.90%	-22.00%	30.60%	6.10%
David Dreman	7/15/2003	36.20%	30.00%	18.40%	34.30%	-12.00%	-27.70%	79.20%	12.40%
Warren Buffett	12/5/2003	2.00%	37.30%	-4.60%	16.50%	-12.20%	-11.40%	21.20%	4.30%
Peter Lynch	7/15/2003	39.60%	34.70%	8.40%	23.30%	-13.50%	-20.20%	73.50%	11.60%
Kenneth Fisher	7/15/2003	30.70%	26.00%	-2.70%	40.00%	19.10%	-3.70%	157.40%	20.80%
Martin Zweig	7/15/2003	32.10%	54.80%	5.80%	17.30%	5.20%	-19.80%	114.00%	16.40%
James P. O'Shaughnessy	7/15/2003	51.60%	1.00%	22.40%	24.00%	-3.90%	-14.90%	90.20%	13.70%
Joel Greenblatt	12/2/2005	N/A	N/A	-2.80%	14.40%	9.10%	-9.20%	10.20%	3.80%
Joseph Piotroski	2/27/2004	N/A	39.90%	9.00%	17.90%	-4.90%	-22.10%	33.20%	6.80%
S&P 500	7/15/2003	11.10%	9.00%	3.00%	13.60%	3.50%	-17.30%	21.40%	4.00%

Table A.2 Guru Model Portfolio: 20 Stock

20 Stock Portfolios	Inception Date	2003	2004	2005	2006	2007	2008	Total Return	Annual Return
Benjamin Graham	7/15/2003	30.50%	34.60%	8.50%	26.40%	−1.40%	3.70%	146.30%	19.70%
John Neff	1/2/2004	N/A	11.40%	15.60%	21.60%	−10.60%	−17.70%	15.40%	3.20%
David Dreman	7/15/2003	27.20%	30.50%	21.50%	29.60%	−7.80%	−26.30%	77.50%	12.10%
Warren Buffett	12/5/2003	2.50%	27.50%	−7.70%	9.60%	−6.30%	−12.80%	7.90%	1.70%
Peter Lynch	7/15/2003	38.00%	24.80%	10.10%	20.50%	1.10%	−18.30%	88.80%	13.50%
Kenneth Fisher	7/15/2003	24.50%	25.00%	12.50%	32.00%	6.70%	−7.80%	127.50%	17.80%
Martin Zweig	7/15/2003	32.50%	41.50%	6.70%	11.00%	1.10%	−15.20%	90.20%	13.70%
James P. O'Shaughnessy	7/15/2003	40.10%	11.90%	27.90%	19.40%	−2.70%	−15.80%	96.10%	14.40%
Joel Greenblatt	12/2/2005	N/A	N/A	−2.20%	13.40%	2.50%	−3.60%	9.60%	3.60%
Joseph Piotroski	2/27/2004	N/A	31.00%	10.80%	23.70%	−6.90%	−26.70%	22.60%	4.70%
S&P 500	7/15/2003	11.10%	9.00%	3.00%	13.60%	3.50%	−17.30%	21.40%	4.00%

Appendix B

Guru Yearly Track Record Comparison (Actual or Back-Tested Returns)

T able B.1 lists the returns for each of the gurus profiled throughout this book compared to the total return of the S&P 500 over the given time frames using publicly available performance data. This performance table was added to the book to help give readers an understanding of how the strategies, portfolios, and funds managed by the gurus have performed each year in comparison to each other and in comparison to "the market."

We think it is important that readers note that every guru has had down years in absolute numbers, and sometimes even two or three down years in a row in comparison to the market. Yet they have compiled excellent track records over the long term by sticking with their strategy, and not tweaking it or abandoning it after a down year or two. You will notice that in almost all cases, their returns are robust after a one-, two-, or three-year loss. Although it can feel like an eternity when the strategy you are following is down (especially two years in a row!), one of the secrets to exceptional investing returns *over the long run* is sticking with a proven strategy even when the strategy has been out of favor for a year or more.

The performance of each guru listed in Table B.1 is calculated using different performance reporting methodologies or is based on hypothetical, back-tested results. For further explanation and references, refer to the list that follows Table B.1.

Table B.1 Guru Performance

Year	S&P 500	Benjamin Graham	John Neff	David Dreman	Warren Buffett	Peter Lynch	Martin Zweig	Ken Fisher	James O'Shaughnessy	Joel Greenblatt	Joseph Piotroski
1945	42.76%	26.89%									
1946	−11.85%	−8.16%									
1947	0.83%	12.31%									
1948	9.94%	14.57%									
1949	19.51%	20.05%									
1950	35.66%	26.91%									
1951	17.96%	16.46%									
1952	15.12%	15.55%									
1953	14.36%	1.17%									
1954	46.36%	13.65%									
1955	24.11%	20.19%									
1956	12.32%	26.53%									
1957–1963	No Guru Performance during this time										
1964	16.50%		4.30%						25.10%		
1965	12.50%		29.10%						30.80%		
1966	−10.10%		−3.30%		−10.50%				−5.10%		
1967	24.00%		31.50%		17.60%				53.50%		
1968	11.00%		21.40%		85.00%				38.50%		
1969	−8.40%		−3.80%		13.50%				−21.50%		
1970	3.90%		6.40%		−7.10%				4.30%		
1971	14.60%		7.50%		76.90%				23.90%		
1972	18.90%		10.20%		14.50%				16.80%		

(Continued)

Table B.1 (*Continued*)

Year	S&P 500	Benjamin Graham	John Neff	David Dreman	Warren Buffett	Peter Lynch	Martin Zweig	Ken Fisher	James O'Shaughnessy	Joel Greenblatt	Joseph Piotroski
1973	−14.70%		−25.00%		−10.10%				−16.70%		
1974	−26.40%		−16.80%		−43.70%				−20.70%		
1975	37.20%		54.50%		−5.00%				47.90%		
1976	23.60%		46.40%		134.20%				35.80%		57.30%
1977	−7.40%		1.00%		55.10%	12.70%			14.80%		12.10%
1978	6.40%		8.80%		10.10%	29.50%			20.80%		2.30%
1979	18.20%		22.60%		110.50%	49.80%			32.10%		36.60%
1980	32.30%		22.60%		32.80%	64.60%			41.50%		46.60%
1981	−5.00%		16.80%		31.80%	−22.60%			1.90%		25.70%
1982	21.40%		21.70%		38.40%	−1.30%			28.30%		46.30%
1983	22.40%		30.10%		69.00%	82.80%	17.40%		35.60%		32.40%
1984	6.10%		19.50%		−2.70%	−10.10%	5.90%		1.30%		−0.90%
1985	31.60%		28.00%		93.70%	34.20%	29.80%		38.80%		29.70%
1986	18.60%		20.30%		14.20%	7.70%	28.90%		19.10%		23.70%
1987	5.10%		1.20%		4.60%	−17.60%	14.00%		3.10%		4.30%
1988	16.60%		28.70%		59.30%	20.50%	3.50%		28.10%	27.10%	11.70%
1989	31.70%		15.00%		84.60%	23.90%	22.70%		3.70%	44.60%	21.80%
1990	−3.10%		15.50%		−23.10%	−9.90%	5.10%		−5.10%	1.70%	24.50%
1991	30.50%		28.60%		35.60%	27.20%	34.90%		44.10%	70.60%	62.50%
1992	7.60%		16.50%	16.70%	29.80%	−8.20%	6.10%		18.60%	32.40%	34.90%
1993	10.10%		19.40%	6.00%	38.90%		6.50%		25.30%	17.20%	13.00%
1994	1.30%		−0.10%	−2.50%	25.00%		2.80%		−0.30%	22.00%	0.50%
1995	37.60%		25.20%	42.20%	57.40%		17.90%		22.40%	34.00%	36.00%
1996	23.00%			28.80%	6.20%		11.70%	28.60%	26.70%	17.30%	29.90%

1997	33.40%	31.90%	34.90%	33.60%	40.40%
1998	28.60%	12.00%	52.20%	21.40%	25.50%
1999	21.00%	−13.20%	−19.90%	17.20%	53.00%
2000	−9.10%	41.30%	26.60%	15.60%	7.90%
2001	−11.80%	1.20%	6.50%	−10.20%	69.60%
2002	−22.10%	−18.50%	−3.80%	−5.70%	−4.00%
2003	26.70%	31.30%	15.80%	−7.30%	79.90%
2004	10.90%	13.50%	4.30%	20.50%	19.30%
2005	4.90%	7.70%	0.80%	5.30%	
2006	15.80%	17.30%	24.10%	17.70%	
2007	5.50%	−1.40%	28.70%		

Guru	Performance Explanation	Source
Benjamin Graham	Return of Graham-Newman Corp. (total return)	www.cfapubs.org/doi/abs/10.2470/rf.v1977.n1.4731.4
John Neff	Return of the Windsor Fund during Neff's tenure (VWNDX) (total net return)	*John Neff on Investing* (2001), Appendix A
David Dreman	Return of DWS Dreman High Return Fund (KD-HAX) (total net return)	DWS funds
Warren Buffett	Return of Berkshire Hathaway Class A stock (price return only; however we are not aware of any dividends). Buffett himself publicly prefers to measure his returns by the annual growth of book value of Berkshire, but to be consistent we have researched Berkshire's annual stock price performance.	Yahoo Finance/CSI (BRK-A) and CBS MarketWatch Historical Quotes/FTInteractive for BRK.A
Peter Lynch	Return of Fidelity Magellan Mutual Fund (FMAGX) (total net return)	CBS Marketwatch Historical Quotes for 1982–1992; prior to that from Fidelity Investments
Martin Zweig	Price return of the recommendations in the Zweig Performance Ratings Report investment newsletter using the Hulbert methodology	*The Hulbert Financial Digest* (1996), table of annual performance for Zweig newsletter
Ken Fisher	Return of Global Total Return Composite (total net return using fiscal year start date)	*The Only Three Questions That Count: Investing by Knowing What Others Don't* (2006), Appendix K
James O'Shaughnessy	Annual performance of the United Cornerstone Growth and Value Strategy (price return based on back-tested strategy)	*What Works on Wall Street*, rev. ed. (1998) Table 20–4

Guru	Performance Explanation	Source
Joel Greenblatt	Back-tested performance of Magic Formula strategy (price return based on back-tested strategy)	*The Little Book that Beats the Market* (2005), Table 6.1
Joseph Piotroski	Back-tested performance of high-scoring Book-to-Market Stocks (price return based on back-tested strategy). Piotroski reported yearly returns above a value weighted index, and we have added the S&P 500 total return index to his to come up with the numbers in this table.	"Value Investing: The Use of Historical Financial Statement Information to Separate Winners from Losers," Appendix 1
S&P 500 Index	Total Return	Yahoo Finance, S&P/Barra website for 1975–2004; for 1945–1956 see source for Graham; for 1964–1974 see source for Neff

References

Below are a list of references and sources that were used in writing this book. We have broken them down by chapter so that you can better use them as a guide to further read about a specific guru.

Introduction

Dalbar, Inc. "Quantitative Analysis of Investor Behavior." July 2003.

Chapter 1: Learn from the Worst

Bogle, John C. "Statement of John C. Bogle before the United States Senate Committee on Banking, Housing, and Urban Affairs," February 26, 2004. www.investorscoalition.com/hearings.html.

Colvin, Geoffrey. "Ditch The 'Experts.' " *Fortune,* 30 January 2006.

Dalbar, Inc. "Quantitative Analysis of Investor Behavior." 2007.

Deener, Bill. "On Top of the News." *San Diego Union-Tribune,* 4 April 2004.

Dreman, David. *Contrarian Investment Strategies: The Next Generation.* New York: Simon & Schuster, 1998.

Ibbotson, Roger G., and Rex A. Sinquefield. "Stocks, Bonds, Bills and Inflation," 1982. Institute of Chartered Financial Analysts, Charlottesville, Virginia. (Updated by Ibbotson Associates, "Stocks, Bonds, Bills and Inflation 2007 Yearbook," Chicago.)

Ip, Greg. "What A Recession Could Mean To You." *Wall Street Journal.* 20 January 2008.

Lynch, Peter. "Betting on the Market: Interview with Peter Lynch." *PBS Frontline.* www.pbs.org/wgbh/pages/frontline/shows/betting/pros/lynch.html.

Morningstar. "Morningstar Investor Return: Morningstar Methodology Paper," March 31, 2008. http://corporate.morningstar.com/us/documents/ MethodologyDocuments/FactSheets/InvestorReturnsMethodology.pdf.

O'Shaughnessy, James P. *What Works on Wall Street,* rev. ed. New York: McGraw-Hill, 2005.

Sahadi, Jeanne. "Coping with Dow 14,000." *CNNMoney.com*, 18 July 2007.

Sharpe, William F. "Likely Gains from Market Timing." *Financial Analysts Journal 31*, no. 2 (March–April 1975): 60–69.

Siegel, Jeremy. *Stocks for the Long Run.* New York: McGraw-Hill, 2007.

Tetlock, Philip E. *Expert Political Judgment: How Good Is It? How Can We Know?* Princeton, N.J.: Princeton University Press, 2006.

Wall, Barbara. "Newsletters: Many Should Go Directly into the Circular File." *International Herald Tribune.* 8 June 1996.

Zweig, Jason. *Your Money and Your Brain: How The Science of Neuroeconomics Can Help Make You Rich.* New York: Simon & Schuster, 2007.

Chapter 2: The Cavalry Arrives

Graham, Benjamin, Zweig, Jason, and Buffett, Warren. *The Intelligent Investor,* rev. ed. New York: HarperCollins, 2003.

Hagstrom, Robert G. *The Warren Buffett Way.* New York: John Wiley & Sons, 1994.

Lynch, Peter. "Betting on the Market: Interview with Peter Lynch." *PBS Frontline.* www.pbs.org/wgbh/pages/frontline/shows/betting/pros/lynch.html.

Lynch, Peter, and John Rothchild. *One up on Wall Street.* New York: Simon & Schuster, 1989.

Chapter 3: Benjamin Graham: The Granddaddy of the Gurus

Buffett, Warren E. "Benjamin Graham: 1894–1976." *Financial Analysts Journal 32*, no. 6 (November–December 1976): 19.

————."The Superinvestors of Graham-and-Doddsville." Speech given at Columbia Business School, May 17, 1984. www.4.gsb.columbia.edu/valueinvesting/schlossarchives/public.

Cray, Douglas W. "Benjamin Graham, Securities Expert." *New York Times,* 23 September 1976.

Graham, Benjamin, Jason Zweig, and Warren E. Buffett. *The Intelligent Investor,* rev. ed. New York: HarperCollins, 2003.

Lowe, Janet. *Benjamin Graham on Value Investing: Lessons from the Dean of Wall Street.* Chicago: Dearborn, 1994.

————. *The Rediscovered Benjamin Graham: Selected Writings of the Wall Street Legend.* New York: John Wiley & Sons, 1999.

————. *Value Investing Made Easy.* New York: McGraw-Hill, 1997.

Ross, Nikki. *Lessons from the Legends of Wall Street.* Chicago: Dearborn, 2000.

Chapter 4: John Neff: The Investor's Investor

"Barron's Roundtable." *Barron's,* 22 January 2007.

Neff, John, and S.L. Mintz. *John Neff on Investing.* New York: John Wiley & Sons, 1999.

Train, John. *Money Masters of Our Time.* New York: HarperCollins, 2000.

Chapter 5: David Dreman: The Great Contrarian

Dreman, David. *Contrarian Investment Strategies: The Next Generation.* New York: Simon & Schuster, 1998.

Dreman Value Management, LLC. "History." *Dreman.com.* www.dreman.com/about_dreman/history.html.

"Dreman's Fund Finds Value in U.S. Stocks Tainted by Litigation." *Bloomberg.com,* 10 February 2005.

Kuhn, Susan E., and John Labate. "Where to Invest Now." *Fortune,* 22 March 1993.

Chapter 6: Warren Buffett: The Greatest Guru

Bailey, Jeff, and Eric Dash. "How Does Warren Buffett Get Married? Frugally, It Turns Out." *New York Times,* 1 September 2006.

Boroson, Warren. *J.K. Lasser's Pick Stocks Like Warren Buffett.* New York: John Wiley & Sons, 2002.

Buffett, Mary, and David Clark. *Buffettology*. New York: Simon & Schuster/Fireside, 1999.

Buffett, Mary, and David Clark. *The New Buffettology*. New York: Simon & Schuster/Rawson Associates Scribner, 2002.

Buffett, Warren E. *Berkshire Hathaway Inc. 2007 Annual Report.*

Gharib, Susie. "'Meet the Buffetts'—Peter Buffett, The Youngest Buffett." *PBS Nightly Business Report,* 1 May 2008. www.pbs.org/nbr/site/onair/transcripts/080501c/.

"'Meet the Buffetts'- Susie Buffett." *PBS Nightly Business Report,* April 30, 2008. www.pbs.org/nbr/site/onair/transcripts/080430c/

Goldman, Lea. "Homes of the Billionaires." *Forbes.com,* 5 March 2008.

Hagstrom, Robert G., *The Warren Buffett Way*. New York: John Wiley & Sons, 1997.

Loomis, Carol J. "Warren Buffett Gives Away His Fortune." *Fortune Magazine,* 25 June 2006.

Lowenstein, Roger. *Buffett: The Making of an American Capitalist*. New York: Doubleday, 1995.

Zweig, Jason. "Buffett Advice: Buy Smart . . . And Low." *Money Magazine,* 5 May 2008.

Chapter 7: Peter Lynch: The Star "GARP" Manager

Lynch, Peter. "Betting on the Market: Interview with Peter Lynch." *PBS Frontline.* www.pbs.org/wgbh/pages/frontline/shows/betting/pros/lynch.html.

Lynch, Peter, and John Rothchild. *Beating the Street*. New York: Simon & Schuster/Fireside, 1994.

Lynch, Peter, and John Rothchild. *One up on Wall Street*. New York: Simon & Schuster, 1989.

Paulson, Michael. "Peter Lynch's Guide to Philanthropy." *Boston Globe,* 27 February 2005.

Chapter 8: Kenneth L. Fisher: The Price–Sales Pioneer

Fisher, Kenneth L., Jennifer Chou, and Lara Hoffmans. *The Only Three Questions That Count*. Hoboken, N.J.: John Wiley & Sons, 2007.

Humboldt State University. "About the Chair Founder, Kenneth L. Fisher. *Kenneth L. Fisher Chair in Redwood Forest Ecology*. www.humboldt.edu/~sillett/fisher.html.

Fisher Investments, *Ken Fisher: Forbes Columnist, Author, Money Manager.* www
.kennethfisher.com/.

Chapter 9: Martin Zweig: The Conservative Growth Investor

"Phoenix Buys Mutual Funds From Zweig." *New York Times,* 17 December 1998.

Stock & Commodities. "Martin Zweig of The Zweig Forecast." *Thom Hartle.*
V. 12:4 (158–164) http://traderscom.stores.yahoo.net/~v12-c04-zweig-pdf.
html.

Taub, Stephen, et al. "The Wall Street 100." *Financial World,* 11 July 1989. www
.streetstories.com/mz_fw_top100.html.

Taub, Stephen, et al. "The Wall Street 100." *Financial World,* 10 July 1990. www
.streetstories.com/mz_fw_top100.html.

Zweig, Martin. *Winning on Wall Street.* New York: Warner Books, 1986.

Chapter 10: James O'Shaughnessy: The Quintessential Quant

Farrell, Chris. "An Interview with James O'Shaughnessy." *Right on the Money!*
Twin Cities Public Television, 2001.

O'Shaughnessy, James P. "The Silent Storm." *O'Shaughnessy Asset Management,*
April 2008. www.osam.com/commentary.php.

———. *What Works on Wall Street,* rev. ed. New York: McGraw-Hill, 1998.

———. *What Works on Wall Street,* rev. ed. New York: McGraw-Hill, 2005.

O'Shaughnessy Asset Management. "Strategies." www.osam.com/strategies.php.

Zuill, Lilla. "Bear Stearns Manager Leaving with Strategy Intact." *Reuters.com,* 5
October 2007.

Chapter 11: Joel Greenblatt: The Man with the Magic Formula

Greenblatt, Joel. *The Little Book That Beats the Market.* New York: John Wiley &
Sons, 2006.

Kolker, Robert. "How Is a Hedge Fund Like a School?" *New York Magazine*. 13 February 2006.

University of Pennsylvania. "Joel Greenblatt, W'79, WG'80." www.alumni.upenn .edu/club/email/fairfieldco/index.html.

Wright, Christopher M. "Q&A with Joel Greenblatt." *Real Estate Portfolio,* July–August 2006. www.nareit.com/portfoliomag/06julaug/capital.shtml.

Chapter 12: Joseph Piotroski: The Undiscovered Academic

Briske, Patricia, and Allison Benedikt. "An Accountant Looks at the Market." *Chicago GSB,* Winter 2002. www.chicagogsb.edu/magazine/win02/features/ market1.htm.

Bushman, R., Piotroski, J. and A. Smith. "Insider Trading Restrictions and Analysts' Incentives to Follow Firms." *The Journal of Finance 60* (1) (2005): 35–66.

Bushman, R., Piotroski, J. and A. Smith. "What Determines Corporate Transparency?" *Journal of Accounting Research 42* (2) (2004): 207–252.

Piotroski, Joseph D. "Value Investing: The Use of Historical Financial Statement Information to Separate Winners from Losers." *Journal of Accounting Research 38* (2000): 1–41.

Stanford University Graduate School of Business. "Joseph D Piotroski." *Faculty Profiles.* http://gsbapps.stanford.edu/facultybios/biomain.asp?id=45860309.

University of Chicago Graduate School of Business. "Joseph D Piotroski." *Faculty Directory.* www.chicagogsb.edu/faculty/bio.aspx?&min_year=20074 &max_year=20083&person_id=701271.

Chapter 13: Putting It Together: The Principles of Guru Investing

Callahan, Craig T., and C. Thomas Howard. "Judgment Day: A New Way To Categorize and Evaluate Mutual Funds—and Their Managers." *Investment Advisor.* September 2007.

Greenblatt, Joel. *The Little Book That Beats the Market.* Hoboken, N.J.: John Wiley & Sons, 2006.

Hsu, H. Christine, and H. Jeffrey Wei. "Stock Diversification in the U.S. Equity Market." *Business Quest,* 2003. www.westga.edu/~bquest/2003/diversify.htm.

Hulbert, Mark. "The More Things Change, the More They Stay The Same." *American Association of Individual Investors—The AAII Journal,* November 2007. www.aaii.com/includes/DisplayArticle.cfm?Article_Id=3281.

Lynch, Peter. "Betting on the Market: Interview with Peter Lynch." *PBS Frontline.* www.pbs.org/wgbh/pages/frontline/shows/betting/pros/lynch.html.

Mauldin, John. *Bull's Eye Investing: Targeting Real Returns in a Smoke and Mirrors Market.* Hoboken, N.J.: John Wiley & Sons, 2004.

O'Shaughnessy, James P. *What Works on Wall Street,* rev. ed. New York: McGraw-Hill, 2005.

"Our Interview With Mark Hulbert." *Advisor Perspectives.* April 1, 2008. www.advisorperspectives.com/newsletters08/Our_Interview_with_Mark_Hulbert.html.

Tetlock, Philip E. *Expert Political Judgment: How Good Is It? How Can We Know?* Princeton, N.J.: Princeton University Press, 2006.

Thaler, Richard H., et al. "The Effect of Myopia and Loss Aversion on Risk Taking: An Experimental Test." *Quarterly Journal of Economics 112,* no. 2 (1997): 647–661.

Chapter 14: The Missing Piece: Determining When to Sell

Bernstein, Richard. *Navigate the Noise: Investing in the New Age of Media and Hype.* New York: John Wiley & Sons, 2001.

Daniel, Kent, and Sheridan Titman. "Market Efficiency in an Irrational World." *Financial Analysts Journal 55,* no. 6 (1999): 28–40.

Feldman, Amy. "Know When To Fold 'em." *Institutional Investor,* 13 June 2008.

Thaler, Richard H. "The End of Behavioral Finance." *Association for Investment Management and Research 53,* no. 2 (November–December 1999): 12–17.

Zweig, Martin. *Winning on Wall Street.* New York: Warner Books, 1986.

About the Authors

John P. Reese

John P. Reese is CEO of Validea Capital Management and Validea.com. He also advises the Omega American and International Consensus mutual funds offered in Canada. He is a graduate of Harvard Business School and the Massachusetts Institute of Technology and a columnist for *TheStreet.com* and *Forbes.com*. He holds two patents in computerized stock analysis and lectures around the country. His last book was the highly regarded *The Market Gurus*.

Jack M. Forehand, CFA

Jack M. Forehand is cofounder of Validea Capital Management and leads the development of the firm's quantitative investing system. He has an economics degree from the University of Connecticut and holds the Chartered Financial Analyst (CFA) designation.

Index